Wading In Blood

Murder in Michigan

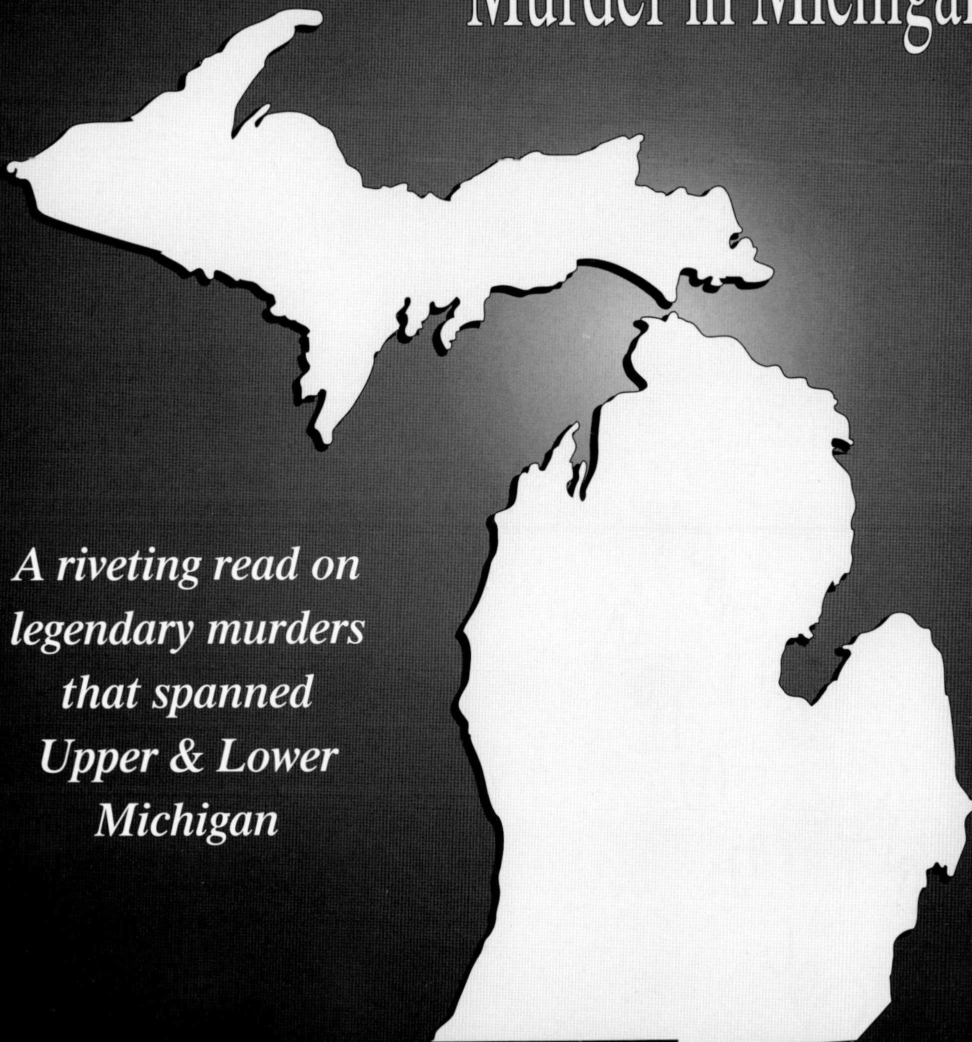

A riveting read on legendary murders that spanned Upper & Lower Michigan

~Sonny Longtine~

First edition published by:

Sunnyside Publications
1201 N. Front Street
Marquette, Michigan 49855

Printed in the United States of America

ISBN 978-0-9785808-2-7

Research, writing, photography
Sonny Longtine

Cover Design
Victoria Tourtillott

Book Layout
Victoria Tourtillott

Illustrations
Judith Greene

Photography
(See Photography Credits)

Printing
Signature Press

Sonny Longtine
Dec. 3. 2009

CONTENTS

The Upper Peninsula 1

The Lower Peninsula 177

OTHER BOOKS BY SONNY LONGTINE

Marquette: Then and Now

Michigan's Upper Peninsula: Life Legends and Landmarks

Courage Burning

INTRODUCTION

Murderers are supposed to look like murderers.

Surely they must have malicious grimaces, black smoldering eyes, and menacing expressions that harbor a heart of darkness. Charlie Manson and Attila the Hun look like murderers. We like murderers to be easily identified. But most murderers are not evil appearing; they look no different from you and I.

Early research supported this notion that murderers or criminals could easily be identified by their appearance. At the turn of the century, famed Italian criminologist Cesare Lombroso carefully described the physiology of a criminal: hard, shifty eyes, a large projecting jaw, a flattened nose, and fleshy lips were physical attributes that Lombroso said were common to criminals. His stereotypical criminal had more of a Neanderthal resemblance than that of modern man. Although his theory as to criminal physiognomy has been largely discredited, it nonetheless has a popular following.

What one looks like, however, has little to do with what's in one's heart.

Ted Bundy, John Wilkes Booth, and Lawrencia "Bambi" Bembenek hardly looked like murderers, yet juries found them guilty. Ted Bundy was dashing and articulate, yet he murdered 31 women. Handsome and charismatic Booth assassinated Abraham Lincoln, and Bambi Bembenek, vivacious and hauntingly beautiful, gunned down her lover's ex-wife.

Murder has many motivations: greed, jealously, anger, power, insanity, retribution, survival, and thrill killing all provide a basis for murder. Survival murders, (spousal abuse), are easier to understand and forgive than those committed by a sinister motivation. All murders are not equal.

Contrary to public opinion and television, not all murderers are caught. In 2006, Michigan had 713 murders and many of the perpetrators are still free.

Solving murders is often related to demographics. Of the Michigan murders, 70 percent statewide were solved while only 45 percent were solved in Detroit. Literally—"getting away with murder"—is more than a trite expression—it happens, in some places more than others. The media reflects the public's interest in murder. *Court TV*, *Law & Order*, and the *CSI* dramas on television inundate the viewers with tales of ghastly murders. Bloody cadavers dissected by pathologists on television are now a common sight.

The 1967 movie *Bonnie and Clyde,* with Faye Dunaway and Warren Beatty, depicts glamorous, blood-soaked bank bandits as chic, and popularized murder as a last resort for the oppressed. Bonnie and Clyde were seen as "bank robbing Robin Hoods" that took from rich bankers who were the real enemies of the people. Spellbound audiences watched the movie's end with sympathy, where the protagonists were slaughtered in orgy of blood and bullets. We abhor murder, but we watch it and read about it with mesmerized detachment.

We are mystified, scared, compelled, and absorbed by murder; it is both repelling and alluring. Some murderers are intriguing or mysterious and titillate human curiosity, while others are eccentric, flamboyant egotists, or neurotic compulsives.

Public interest in murder is not just a contemporary phenomenon; history is replete with a fascination for murder. The Elizabethans in the 1500s had a curious interest in pamphlets that described the crimes and trials of notorious characters, and executions were an enormous and delightful spectacle.

Perhaps most of us, whether we admit it or not, have had homicidal thoughts. "I could kill him," is a frequent utterance said by many in the fervor of the moment. But it's most often a harmless expression of frustration not acted upon. However, it does signify that even the most angelic have entertained murder, be it only for a fleeting moment.

ACKNOWLEDGEMENTS

Writing a book is a formidable task as well as solitary one, but without utilizing the specialized skills of others, this book would have never become a reality.

Victoria Tourtillott did the magnificent book layout. Her unequaled attention to detail, particularly with the photographs, enriched the books presentation. She spent hours bringing old and seemingly unredeemable photographs to life. My never-ending requests for changes she speedily completed with skill and patience. This was always appreciated.

Becky Tavernini skillfully edited the manuscript, ferreting out superfluous language and my never-ending need to editorialize. At times I wrote flourishing whimsical narrations that were excessive and distracted from the story. Becky's editing was clear: Less is more. The result is a more tightly written text that quickly flows from page to page.

Judy Green, an Arizonian, provided the artful sketches. At times she had poor-quality images to work with, but masterfully she elevated them to print quality.

As always, Jack Deo and Superior View Studio provided me with photographs that I could not have obtained elsewhere.

John Pepin, a *Mining Journal* reporter, who expertly covered the Richardson murder trial, was a tremendous help in providing me pointers on navigating a courtroom during a trial.

My friend Larry Flanders, a skilled teacher, writer, and poet, superbly proofread the manuscript. He and his wife Astrid graciously provided shelter and sustenance on several of my research jaunts across the Upper Peninsula.

The following institutions or people contributed to make this book a certainty.

Bayless Public Library
Beaver Island Historical Society

Houghton Mining Gazette
John Longyear Research Center
Leelanau Historical Society
Marquette Mining Journal
Michigan Technological University
Archives/Van Pelt Library
Midland County Historical Society
Ontonagon Historical Society
Peter White Public Library
State of Michigan; Archives of Michigan
photo collection
Wayne State University:Walter P. Reuther
Library

Angeli, Mike
Bahrman, Karen
Cashman, William
Culver, Don and Jeanie
Crimmins, Molly
Ellens, Janette
Girard/Jackson, Sue
Gregorich, Joe and Judy
Holland, Christinc
Humphrey, Jim
Johnson, George
Jorns, Bill
Klimmek, Dave
Kroken, Eileen
Lundberg, Patricia
Lauren, Sister Mary Ann
McDonald, Laverne
Numinen, Karl
Schwemin, Shirley
Stiles, Mary
Sutton, Heather

The UPPER PENINSULA

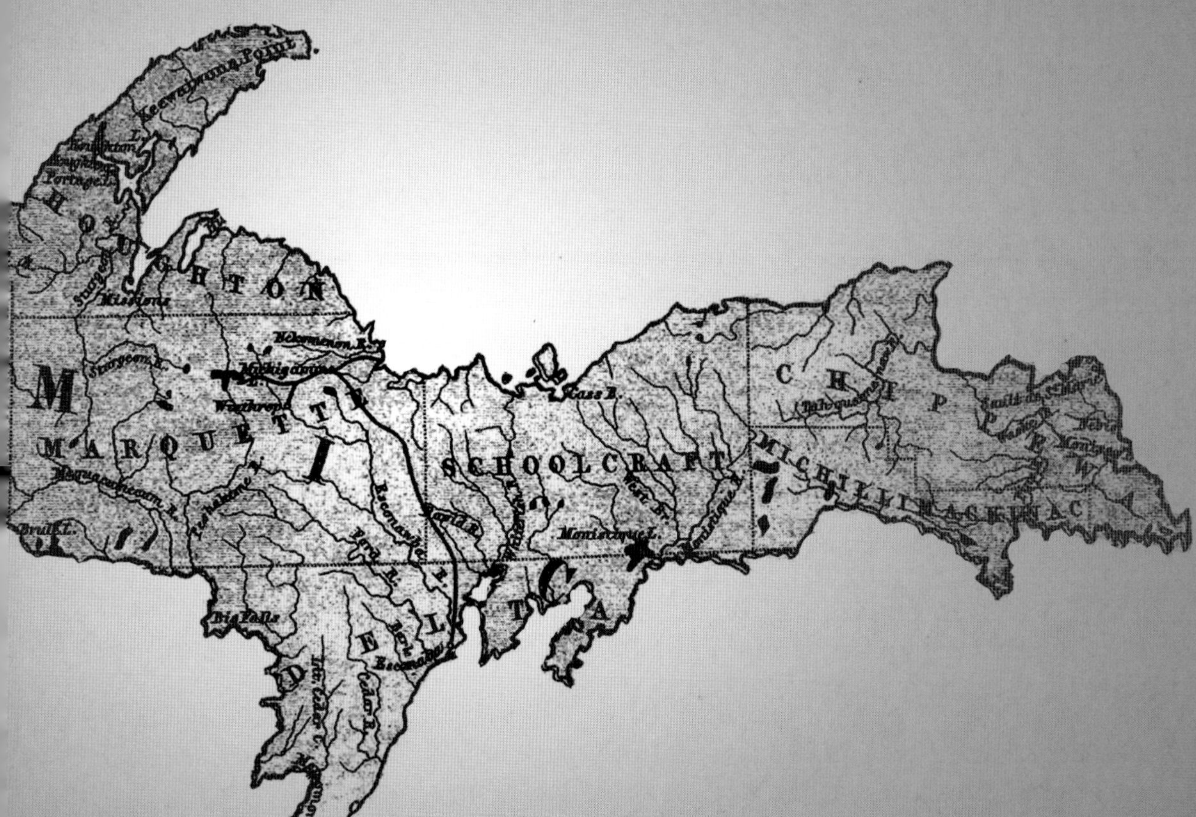

Who? KILLED JAMES SCHOOLCRAFT

James Schoolcraft, brother of famous Henry Schoolcraft, was gunned down by an unknown assailant in Sault Ste. Marie in 1846

Born white, but raised by Indians—it has a romantic ring—a white child is spirited away by neighboring Indians and then raised by a tribe who inculcate the white child with Indian skill and wisdom. The captured child becomes one with nature and is strong, courageous, and speaks with enlightenment. The hybrid stripling grows into manhood and becomes a bridge binding white and Indian cultures in mutual understanding.

This is the stuff of poetic legends that Kipling or Longfellow might have easily written about. It would make a good movie script, but it is not rooted in reality. The story of John Tanner, a white man raised by Indians, is unique, but is one that disdains the romantic notion of successfully blending two markedly different cultures.

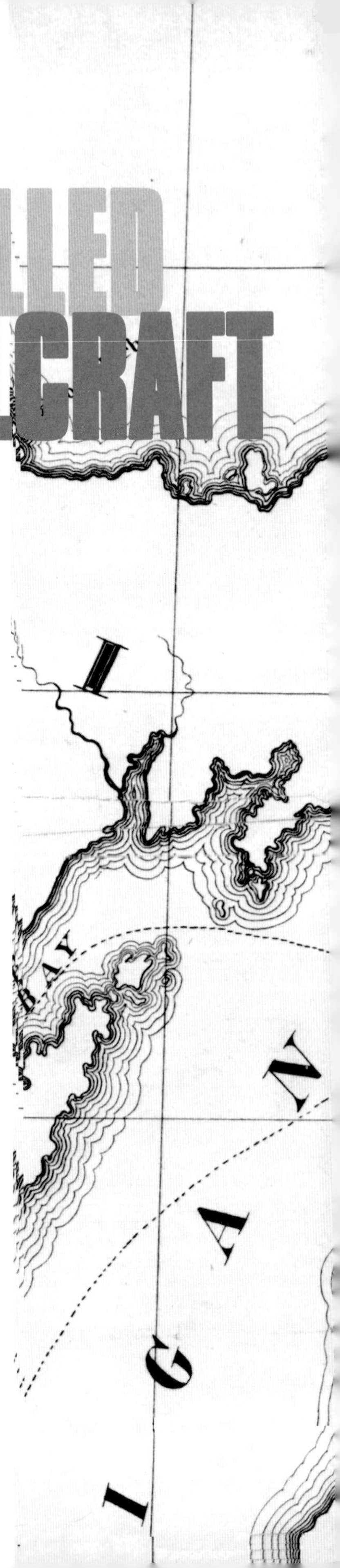

O R
TAH QUA ME NAW BAY
Copper Mines
Falls
Fort Brady
Sault de St Marie
Bruce Mines
ST. JOSEPHS ID.
NORTH CHANN
Drummonds Is
GREAT
Mackinaw
STRAITS OF MACKINAW
Bois Blanc I.
Beaver I.
L A K
SAGINAW BAY

Tanner was born in 1780 to a Virginia clergyman, Reverend John Tanner, Sr. John Senior desired to go west and moved to Kentucky, eventually settling near the mouth of the Big Miami on the Ohio River. It was a dangerous time on the frontier, and native tribes were often hostile to encroaching white men.

John Tanner Jr. was nine years old at the time his parents moved to Kentucky. They were very much aware of their unfriendly surroundings and cautioned the young Tanner not to leave the house. However, as a typical inquisitive and impulsive child, on one occasion he disobeyed his parents and ventured into the yard where he gathered walnuts. Outside he was surprised by Indians who snatched him and took him north. All that was left were a pile of nuts, which fell from his hat under the tree. Search parties looking for the kidnapped child never found him. His parents never saw him again.

Search parties looking for the kidnapped child never found him. His parents never saw him again.

The Ojibwa kidnappers headed to Detroit and then up the west coast of Lake Huron, where a Native American woman who had recently lost a child of about Tanner's age adopted him. The nomadic tribe moved Tanner from place to place in Michigan. It was not a pleasant experience for him. His adoptive mother treated him decently, but the male members of the family were pitiless. He was starved, beaten, and cruelly treated by the male members of the family. Writers examining Tanner's adult personality described him as morose, sullen, and suspicious of others; they attributed this to the harsh treatment he received when growing up.

The nomadic tribe moved Tanner from place to place in Michigan.

After years of abuse, a prominent Ottawa woman who lived near where Petoskey is now located, purchased him for ten gallons of rum. Tanner's new foster mother held the position of principal chief in the tribe; it was quite unusual for a woman to hold that position in a war-like tribe. By all accounts, his new mother treated him well. Tanner's foster father died a few years after he was adopted.

The family left Petoskey, and headed west, eventually settling in Winnipeg, Canada. By now, Tanner had grown into a young man and had taken an Indian wife named "Red-sky-of-the-morning." The union produced three children, one daughter and two sons. One son became a missionary in Canada while the other son was killed in the second battle of Bull Run. Tanner had become a skilled hunter and was offered the chieftainship of the tribe, but he turned it down.

Tanner had become a skilled hunter and was offered the chieftainship of the tribe, but he turned it down.

Tanner's marriage was unsatisfactory and he contemplated returning to the United States. His wife was equally unhappy and mulled over suicide. They eventually parted ways.

Always on the move, Tanner eventually returned to Northern Michigan and settled in Sault Ste. Marie, where General Lewis Cass hired him as an interpreter. He also acted as an interpreter for various missionary groups, and at times was employed by fur companies and Indian traders.

Apparently Tanner was not considered a good father. In 1830, the legislative council of the territory of Michigan passed legislation that authorized the territorial sheriff to remove Martha Tanner from the custody of her father, John Tanner. It was the only time territorial legislation was passed that was specifically written for a private

Fort Brady in Sault Ste. Marie and once a military Installation, is now a part of Lake Superior State's campus. An officer at the fort was implicated in James Schoolcraft's murder. Schoolcraft was gunned down near the fort.

citizen. His daughter was taken to a missionary establishment and eventually became a teacher. After having a productive life, she died on Mackinac Island.

While at the Sault, Tanner got married for the second time to a white Christian woman from Detroit. His second marriage did not fare any better than his first and lasted only a year. The Tanners lived in wretched conditions in Sault Ste. Marie until Henry Rowe Schoolcraft, a famous Indian ethnologist, and some friends rescued Mrs. Tanner from the pathetic hovel and secured passage for her on a boat back to Detroit. She was relieved to get away from her miserable existence with Tanner.

Henry Rowe Schoolcraft, ethnologist and famous brother of James Schoolcraft, detested suspected slayer John Tanner.

In 1846, the shaggy haired and unattractive Tanner was 66 years of age, and his life was about to take a turn for the worse. He was accused of killing Henry Schoolcraft's brother, James. In August of that year, it was purported that Tanner gunned down James Schoolcraft near Fort Brady in the Sault. Records indicate that Schoolcraft was walking from his residence at the Fort and down a path toward a field he had been clearing. Dense bushes fringed the path where the assassin lay in wait. Although Schoolcraft was a strong athletic man, in the prime of life, he was not a match for a one-ounce ball and three buckshot that ripped through his body. After he was hit, he apparently vaulted forward with a huge leap and exited out of his slippers, leaving them intact and together on the walkway. It was reported that Tanner had been on a rampage for several days prior to the murder and had just burned down his own house. Tanner was said to have remarked earlier, "I had yet to deal with two or three of the citizens of Sault Ste. Marie [sic]."

If Tanner murdered Schoolcraft it was never proven. After the murder Tanner disappeared and was never heard from again.

After the murder Tanner disappeared and was never heard from again.

Several stories examine why Tanner would want to kill Schoolcraft. It was speculated that he was angrier with Henry Schoolcraft than he was with James, but apparently James was an easier target. And what better revenge could there be than to murder his brother? When Henry was the Indian agent at the Sault, it is conjectured that he had rebuffed Tanner, and that the murder of his brother was Tanner's way of getting even for not only this but also for arranging transport for Tanner's second wife's escape. Tanner never forgot that. Just prior to Schoolcraft's murder, Tanner remarked with bitterness, "Nobody will live with me; here I have lived alone for years—everybody has left me—they have taken away my children, my furniture, everything I had and left me without anything...everybody is my enemy, and it's all owing to Henry Schoolcraft."

Henry believed to his dying day that Tanner had killed his brother. He said, "...this lawless vagabond waylaid and shot my brother James, having concealed himself in a cedar thicket." In a continuing bitter commentary of Tanner, Schoolcraft vehemently spewed, "He [Tanner] is now a gray-headed, hard featured, old man, whose feelings are at war with everyone on earth, white or red."

Henry believed to his dying day that Tanner had killed his brother.

Another theory concerned Tanner's daughter and the attention James Schoolcraft was paying to her. A conjecture that an army Lieutenant was the killer was also in the Sault rumor mill. Lt. Bryant P. Tilden, an army officer at Fort Brady, was said to harbor bitter feelings toward Schoolcraft over a rift they had over a woman, and that he killed Schoolcraft. The buck and ball cartridge used in the murder was military issue and gave this theory further validity. Speculation was that Tilden was aware that Tanner was in the vicinity when he shot Schoolcraft. For Tilden, this was a fortuitous occurrence and made it easy for him to cast the blame on a suspicious and unlikable Tanner. It was rumored that after killing Schoolcraft Tilden returned to Fort Brady and told his superior officers that he saw Tanner in the area of the Schoolcraft shooting.

Tanner was an easy mark for someone to blame. After all, he was known as a loose cannon, and just the day before the murder he burned down his home. Ironically, Tilden was put in charge of a party to hunt down Tanner. They never found him. Shortly after the murder Tilden was transferred to the Mexican war. Reportedly, he made a deathbed confession some years later that he had killed Schoolcraft.

Depending on whom you believe, Tanner was variously described. Some saw him as surly, uncommunicative, treacherous, and a dangerous savage; however, others extolled his virtues and saw him as noble man with generous qualities and trustworthy Indian ethics, one of which was his honest intercourse with traders.

As an adult, Tanner was a lonely man caught between two worlds, to neither of which he belonged. Though he was born white and raised as an Indian, he shunned both worlds, never feeling he belonged to either. Prior to his disappearance from the Sault he lived in a small cabin by himself and had limited contact with others.

What happened to John Tanner? No one knows for sure. One possibility is that he died in a swamp near the Sault. A handgun and a rifle found in the swamp near skeletal remains were identified as belonging to Tanner. Perhaps it was Tanner, but more than likely it will remain an unsolved mystery.

The most Indian thing about the Indians is not his moccasins or his calumet, his wampum or his stone hatchet, but traits of character and sagacity, skill, or passion.

Ralph Waldo Emerson

An Intolerable Tormentor

Quiet August Pond was repeatedly bullied by village fishermen until he could take no more

In the early 1600s, Seul Choix was a favorite place for Native Americans who sought whitefish and lake trout that teemed in the offshore waters.

A majestic white, conical tower soars 78 feet heavenward. Ornate brackets support the tower's graceful lantern crown. Billowy clouds gently buffet the tower and then lazily float on. The tower's base securely rests on a grassy field not far from Lake Michigan. The grass yields to tender winds that sweep across the small cape jutting into the lake. This is Seul Choix (pronounced Sis-Shwa, a French expression meaning "only choice") where a much-needed lighthouse was built in 1895. It is the only lighthouse on a 75-mile stretch on northern Lake Michigan between St. Ignace and Manistique. This idyllic setting draws tourists who climb the tower, walk the expansive grass, stroll the sandy beach, and enjoy the serenity of the peaceful point on warm summer days.

In the early 1600s, Seul Choix was a favorite place for Native Americans who sought whitefish and lake trout

The majestic Seul Choix (Sis-Shaw) lighthouse rests on a site that once had a small fishing village in the 1850s. The community's tranquility was shattered when Isaac Blanchard was murdered in 1860. The lighthouse was not built until 1895.

that teemed in the offshore waters. French fur traders and immigrants followed the Native American to the fishing site and established a small community on the promontory. By 1850 it was a village replete with a trading store.

But in 1859 all was not well in the restful setting. Rancor, anger, and murder now permeated the fishing hamlet.

August Pond was a quiet fisherman who lived the good life in the village with his wife and three children. The eldest child was 12 years old while the youngest was an infant. They lived in a shanty that was more shack than house; it had one door, one window, and a bark roof. The room was crowded with three people in its 256 square feet. The flimsy wood door only had an inside rope latch for security.

August Pond was a quiet fisherman who lived the good life in the village with his wife and three children.

Adjacent to Pond's house was a fish net house that he owned. Two fishermen, Daniel Whitney and Dennis Cull, occupied it. The fishermen were employed by Pond and used the net house as their sleeping quarters. Whitney and Cull ate their meals with the Ponds, and the group functioned much like an extended family. Pond was an industrious man content to quietly go his own way.

David Plant, Isaac Blanchard, and Joseph Robilliard were fisherman who also lived in the hamlet. They were the village bullies, and Plant was the most belligerent of the three. They had it in for Pond, and for one week in June 1859, they unmercifully harassed him. There wasn't any reason to harass Pond, but it was evident they immensely disliked him and humiliated him whenever they had a chance.

Fishing was the economic livelihood at Seul Choix, a diminutive community on the north shore of Lake Michigan, located just east of Manistique.

Plant, while at the residence of a Mrs. Downy, said, "I must whip Pond or there would be a fracas." Later in the week Plant, Blanchard, and Robilliard confronted Pond and threatened him. Plant told Pond "…that he did not use his neighbor's right; that they ought not to pick on men not of his size and abuse them, and if Pond wanted to fight anybody, he had better take a man of his size." Plant's threats were without any provocation by Pond. During the conversation Plant hit Pond in his face, knocked his hat off with the blow and then kicked him. Pond did not retaliate, but picked up his hat, put it on, and ran off into the woods.

During the conversation Plant hit Pond in his face, knocked his hat off with the blow and then kicked him.

Later that evening Plant, Robilliard and Blanchard broke into Pond's net-house and demanded a startled and sleeping Whitney to tell them where Pond was. Whitney told Plant that he didn't know. Plant never told Whitney why he wanted to see Pond. The vigilante trio then went to Pond's house and terrified Mrs. Pond. She knew they were up to no good and had been harassing her husband. She told the intruders that he was not there. Pond, fearing for his life, never returned home that evening but stayed at a neighbor's house.

The following day Plant and his collaborators were again on the prowl for Pond. They found him near Peter Closs's residence and made more threats. "It's a good while since you have a grudge against me; I must whip to satisfy myself," Plant hostilely told Pond. Again Pond did not respond to the bullying; he quietly went home.

"I must whip to satisfy myself," Plant hostilely told Pond.

That night, after drinking on a fishing boat, and between one and two o'clock in the morning, Plant, Robilliard, and Blanchard went to Pond's net house and began to tear the roof off. From there they went to Pond's house and banged on the door. Again, a frightened Mrs. Pond told Plant that her husband wasn't there. Plant demanded she get some sugar for his whiskey. She complied and slid him sugar through a crack in the door. Meanwhile, an intimidated and petrified August Pond was hiding under the bed and fearing for his life.

The rabble-rousing threesome then went to neighbor (and Pond's cousin) Peter Ward's house where they raised hell. Plant told Ward, "I want to see Gust Pond; he abused an Irishman, and I want to abuse him just as bad as he abused the Irishman." In all probability, Plant's rhetoric was made up to justify his tyranny. The threesome went back to Pond's house where again, Mrs. Pond denied them entry and they continued to tear down the net house. Plant jumped on a panicked Cull and began to choke him and demanded to know where Pond was. Cull was terrorized, but he did not respond.

In the meantime, Pond went to Peter Closs's home and retrieved a loaded double-barreled shotgun. Closs was a nearby neighbor and Pond's cousin. Upon returning to his house; Pond saw Plant and his collaborators tearing down his net house, he finally mustered enough courage to face his tormentors. He told them, "Leave or I'll shoot." They contemptuously ignored his demand and continued to tear down the net house. With confidence and in a strong voice, again, Pond again told them to leave. They didn't.

Plant jumped on a panicked Cull and began to choke him and demanded to know where Pond was.

It was near daybreak and the sun was just peeking over the horizon when a burst from a discharging shotgun resonated throughout the community. Pellets from the shotgun hit Isaac Blanchard. He staggered several hundred yards to a small path near some bushes, and died.

Shortly after the killing, Pond turned himself in to Louis Pond, his brother, who was the village constable. Louis Pond was confused and unsure of what to do—so he did nothing. An exasperated August Pond then sought the help of his two hired hands Whitney and Cull to take him to Beaver Island, where Pond planned to turn himself over to the island authorities. The three began the 25-mile rowboat journey early on Saturday morning. A revengeful Plant and his cohorts didn't want Pond to go to Beaver Island; they wanted him jailed and tried at Mackinac Island. As a result, Plant and four others pursued Pond across Lake Michigan. They caught Pond's boat seven miles from Beaver Island. After Pond's capture they took him to Mackinac Island.

It was near daybreak and the sun was just peeking over the horizon when a burst from a discharging shotgun resonated throughout the community.

Pond's attorney in his trial presented a case of self-defense. At the time, however, the argument that one was justified in killing someone who was threatening in their home was not yet recognized by the courts. As a result, Pond was convicted of manslaughter and sentenced to ten years in prison.

Unhappy with the result, Pond's attorneys appealed the case to the Michigan Supreme Court. The attorneys felt there were sufficient grounds for a ruling of justifiable homicide. In 1860 the court heard Pond's case that advocated justifiable homicide. The court agreed with the their position that the killing was justifiable and threw out the lower court's decision. The Michigan Supreme Court broadened the justifiable defense position and stated, "...that a man assaulted in his dwelling is not obligated to retreat, but may use such means as is absolutely necessary to repel the assailant from his house...." As a result a new trial was ordered for August Pond. Unfortunately, Pond died before his second trial, though in all probability he would have been exonerated of murder. This Michigan Supreme Court ruling, nevertheless, was a landmark decision that not only expanded the right of self-defense in Michigan, but also influenced the national legal system.

The Mackinac Island Court House was the county seat in 1859 when August Pond was tried for murder. In 1882, when St. Ignace became the county seat, the old courthouse was abandoned. It served various entities until it became the island's jailhouse and police department.

Pond, an uneducated fisherman from an isolated fishing community, never lived to know how he played a pivotal role in Michigan law. He lived in a shanty, was a decent man, and in death proclaimed to the world that a "man's home is indeed his castle."

In 1995 a bronze plaque was placed outside of the Mackinac Island Court House and dedicated to the 1860 landmark decision.

Seul Choix, as a village, has vanished and it is no longer a fishing port. Local fishermen, however, still extensively commercially fish the coastal waters. In 2005,

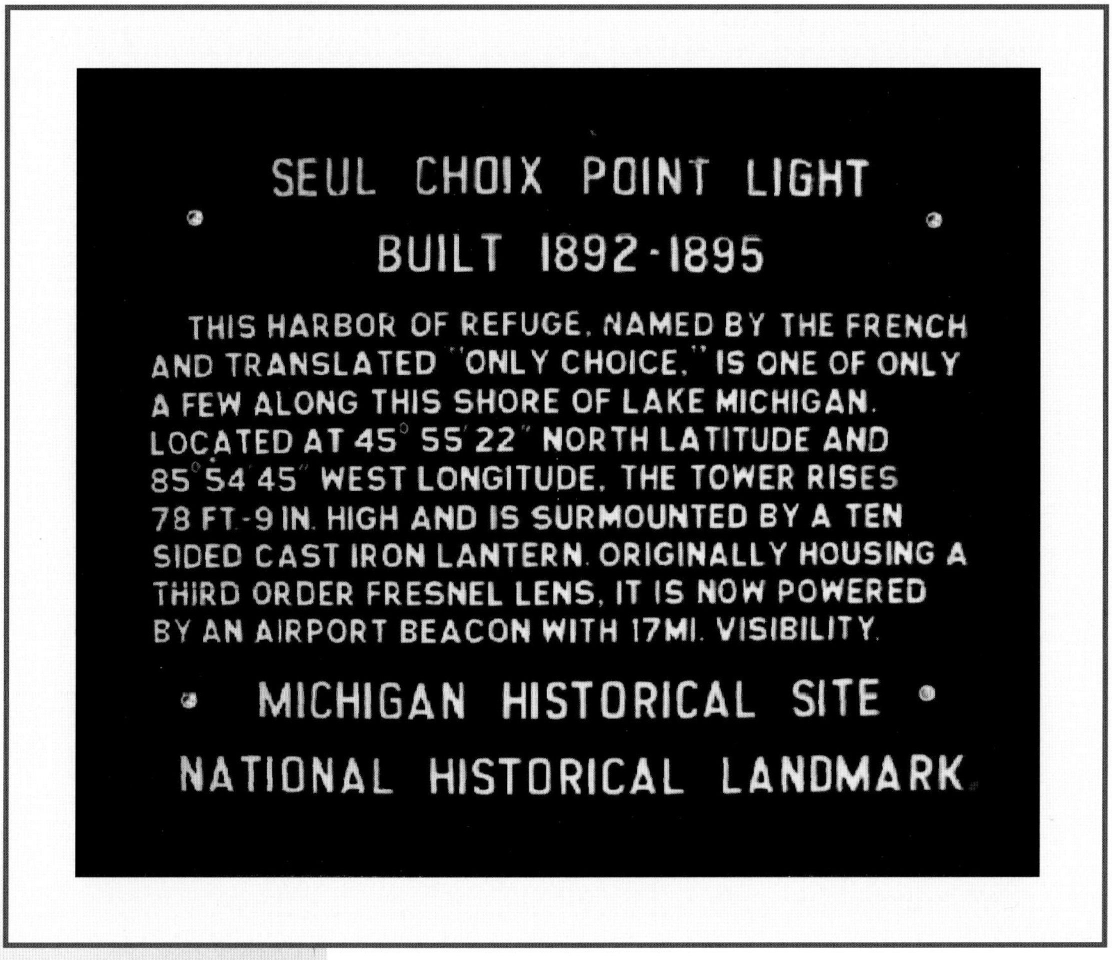

400,000 pounds of fish were harvested from the lake. Pond is long gone, but the fishing that was his life's mainstay 140 years ago, still thrives and continues to support coastal families in Michigan's Upper Peninsula.

Pond, an uneducated fisherman from an isolated fishing community, never lived to know how he played a pivotal role in Michigan law.

VIGILANTE HANGINGS

Frontier justice in the Upper Peninsula in the 1880s resulted in two Menominee loggers swinging from a rope in the town center

> The mob is man voluntarily descending to the nature of the beast.
>
> Ralph Waldo Emerson

In 1880 Menominee was the lumber port capital of the world and home to a rugged lot: lumberjacks—tough, crude men—who worked hard during the week and raised hell on the weekends.

Two of the lumberjacks were Frank and John McDonald. The McDonald cousins were from Nova Scotia, Canada, and had a reputation as bad men, particularly when they were drunk—which was all too frequent.

The McDonalds repeatedly caused disturbances at the lumber camp. On one occasion, Sheriff Julius Reprecht was sent up to the lumber camp where the McDonalds were in the midst of a donnybrook. When Reprecht attempted to quash the disturbance, Frank McDonald, the younger of the two cousins, took offense to the sheriff's interference and pulverized the hapless man unconscious.

Shortly after the beating Deputy Sheriff, Billy Kittson, a burly 200-pounder, arrested and jailed the McDonalds. They were tried, convicted, and sentenced to one and a half years at the Jackson State Prison. They served their time uneventfully and were released early for good behavior. They returned to Menominee where they resumed their old ways: working during the day and drinking and raising Cain at night.

One night the McDonalds began drinking at the Montreal House, a bar in Frenchtown. The bartender on duty was Norman Kittson, brother of the deputy sheriff who was responsible for the McDonald's incarceration. The McDonalds let Norman Kittson know they were out to even the score with his brother. After a short stay at the Montreal House, the McDonalds paid a visit to the Three Chimney House, a nearby and well-known house of prostitution. Fortuitously, the brothers ran across their old nemesis, Billy Kittson. The "ladies" immediately began to shower attention on the McDonald Boys. This angered Kittson and a melee ensued with Kittson hitting Frank McDonald over the head with a bottle and then leaving the Chimney House.

A drunken vigilante mob hung the McDonald cousins on a crossing sign in downtown Menominee for the killing of Deputy Sheriff Bill Kittson.

The vengeful McDonalds followed Kittson to the street, where John McDonald clubbed him with a heavy, metal pipe. Not satisfied with dropping him to his knees, McDonald then plunged a six-inch dagger into his back. Kittson's brother, Norman, witnessing the

Odgen Avenue in downtown Menominee in the 1890s. The McDonald cousins were beaten and kicked as they were dragged down this street.

brawl, sped to his rescue but a McDonald stabbed him. Billy Kittson, wounded and bleeding profusely, got back into the fray to help his beleaguered brother. Norman pulled out a gun and shot Frank in the leg. Billy, the life blood draining out of him, feebly staggered to the Montreal House where he gasped his last breath and fell over dead in the street.

The mob rides an emotional roller coaster and is always on the brink of shedding blood or tears.

Anonymous

With the blood bath now concluded, the McDonalds seized a nearby horse and buggy and went directly to Dr. P.T. Phillips, who attended to their wounds. After getting medical treatment they quickly departed north to Cedar River. On the way they were arrested and jailed by David Barclay, the new Menominee sheriff.

Judge Henry Nason attempted to have a court inquest the next day, but he wisely decided to forgo the proceeding when he learned the citizens of the community were in a rage over the murder the McDonalds had committed. Nason felt that by delaying the inquest he would defuse a potentially explosive situation, a decision he would come to regret.

> *A local priest, Father Heliard, unsuccessfully attempted to stop the mob.*

On Monday, *The Marinette Eagle* speculated on the "...serious threats of lynching the McDonalds," but the night passed without any further violence.

But on Tuesday it turned ugly. Local men gathered at the Forvilly House, a large hotel and saloon, and plied themselves with liquor. By evening the drunken rabble decided that lynching the McDonald boys was the surest and quickest way to have justice. Armed with liquor and self-righteousness, the angry vigilante band marched down the street to the jail and demanded the McDonalds.

When the rabid mob was denied the McDonalds, they grabbed a telegraph pole, and cursing wildly, smashed open the entry door. After a brief scuffle, the deputies were subdued and the McDonalds forced out of their jail cell and clubbed with an ax. With brute force they were taken out of the jail.

Had the McDonalds' murderers been prosecuted, it would have occurred in the stately county court house on 10th street in Menominee. Built in 1875, the courthouse is still functions as the county seat.

A local priest, Father Heliard, unsuccessfully attempted to stop the mob; they cursed and spat on the priest and pushed him into the gutter. The lynch party tied one end of the rope around the McDonalds' necks and the other end to a horse and buggy, then dragged them down Odgen Avenue, then they savagely jumped up and down on the defenseless bodies, ripping off flesh with their lumberjack boots.

Pandemonium spread as a gathering crowd along the route hurled rocks and garbage and cursed the McDonalds. When the lynch party approached an intersection with a railroad crossing, and having spent their energy, they decided it was good a place to hang the McDonalds. They hoisted the two men onto a railroad crossing sign with a rope around their necks and then left the carnage of their handiwork for eager spectators to view. The McDonalds were dead long before they were hung from the sign.

The McDonalds were dead long before they were hung from the sign.

The mob, still in a drunken rage, took the bodies down from the crossing sign and hauled them to a brothel on Belview Avenue. In a further act of debauchery, the necktie party forced a prostitute to lie with the dead McDonalds. Then they burned down the brothel and hung the cousins from a nearby jackpine.

The next day, the McDonalds were still hanging from the tree next to the smoldering rubble of the prostitution house. The drunken frenzy was over.

The McDonalds were buried in an unmarked grave in Potter's field in Menominee's Lakeside cemetery.

A jury indicted several leaders of the mob for murder, but nothing ever came of it. Charges were dismissed for various reasons. One man did eventually go to trial but

Downtown Menominee as it is today. The attractive community located on Green Bay was a thriving lumber port in the 1880s where rugged loggers caroused.

was found not guilty. No one was ever convicted of the McDonalds' murders.

When justice is denied does it seek other avenues to express itself? Perhaps it did in the McDonald case, as several of the men suspected of being involved in the lynching also met a violent death:

Albert Beach, a log driver, fell out of his boat and drowned.

Louis Porter died after apparently being bitten by a rattlesnake.

A mill owner was fatally injured in a lumberyard fire.

A witness named Dunn was later cut into two by a sawmill.

In the 1930s a Federal Employment project renovated the old jail that housed the McDonalds. Bloodstains left from the infamous day over 50 years earlier were clearly visible in the McDonald cell—a reminder of a past when justice in a frontier Upper Peninsula town retreated into the murky depths of mob vigilantism.

No one was ever convicted of the McDonalds' murders.

The McDonalds are buried in an unmarked grave in the potter's field section of the Riverside Cemetery.

The STAGECOACH STICKUP

WANTED: FOR ROBBERY AND MURDER, REIMUND (REINHARDT) HOLZHEY-REWARD $2,800. CONTACT SHERIFF DAVID FOLEY, BESSEMER AUGUST 27, 1889

“You'll get nothing out of me,” a defiant Arnold Macarcher said to Reimund Holzhey who had a .44 caliber side arm jammed into his abdomen. With that, the angry Macarcher pulled out the revolver he had hidden inside of his coat and fired at Holzhey who was attempting to rob him. Macarcher's errant shot went wide and missed his attacker. Twenty-two year old Holzhey responded with a volley from his handgun.

The eight-mile gravel Stage Coach road runs from US-2 to up-scale resorts on the south end of Lake Gogebic. Holzhey thought this road would be the ideal place to commandeer a stagecoach and fleece its wealthy passengers.

One of his shots hit Macarcher in the mouth, seriously wounding him. Macarcher was one of four passengers on a stagecoach near Bessemer in the Western Upper Peninsula.

All that remains on the site of the Gogebic railroad station is this sign. Passengers that arrived at the station on August 25, 1889, departed the train and boarded a stagecoach bound for Lake Gogebic—they never made it to the lake.

In the ensuing confusion, the frightened stagecoach horses bolted and careened down the road. Reimund Holzhey blazed away with his six guns at the departing stage. Two shots hit passenger Adolph Fleischbein in the abdomen, sending him toppling off the stage and crashing to the earth. Two frightened female passengers screamed in horror as they watched the bloody melee. Fleischbein was dead and Macarcher was seriously wounded.

This was the last stagecoach robbery in Michigan. It took place in 1889 on an isolated and primitive stretch of road that ran from the Gogebic Station to the plush Lake Gogebic resorts that were close to the town of Bessemer. It was an isolated area—ideal for a robbery. Highwayman Holzhey knew what he was doing. Both Macarcher and Fleischbein were bankers and probably carrying a good deal of cash. He thought it would be "easy pickins"; after all, he just finished several successful heists in Northern Wisconsin and Upper Michigan. Holzhey didn't think the robbery would end up with him committing murder and having the law hot on his trail.

Holzhey didn't think the robbery would end up with him committing murder.

Reimund Holzhey was a transient German immigrant who had just migrated to the Bessemer area from Milwaukee; he went there believing there were riches to be found in the Gogebic Range. He was bright but uneducated, didn't have any job skills and didn't get along with people. Rumors of gold, silver, and diamonds in the Gogebic area lured Holzhey into a belief that quick riches were soon to be his. He just needed a stake. For Holzhey, robbery was the easiest and quickest way to get his stake.

Republic as it appeared in the late 1890s where Reimund Holzhey was captured after a botched stagecoach heist. Republic at the time was a booming mining community.

After the robbery debacle, he scampered off into the woods with his ill-gotten booty. He lived in the woods for the next several days, eating berries and begging meals from unsuspecting fishermen and campers whom he

A youthful and seemingly unconcerned Reimund Holzhey (center) is handcuffed and guarded by a well-armed sheriff. The German immigrant with an unpleasant personality thought robbing was an easy way to get rich.

encountered along the way. After several days of this nomadic existence, he hopped a train to Republic, some 100 miles from the scene of his holdup.

In Republic, Holzhey's crime spree came to an end. Vigilant law officials from the small mining community would unceremoniously capture the desperado with a price on his head. Historic records vary as to how the actual apprehension took place—some descriptions more colorful, but perhaps less accurate than others.

One newspaper account of the nabbing of Holzhey comes close to describing the "Gunfight at the OK Corral." The article states that Holzhey stepped out of his hotel in Republic on a bright sunny morning, only to be quickly surrounded by an angry mob. The law officers subdued him just before he could reach for his gun, and then he was kicked unconscious by a self-righteous rabble that demanded his immediate lynching. He survived the capture and was incarcerated briefly in Republic and then sent to Bessemer for trial.

The 21-year-old Holzhey was tried in Bessemer's Circuit Court in October 1889. His trial garnered the most attention in the community, even though it was competing with the town's most colorful prostitute on trial for selling whiskey, and a local judge being litigated for embezzlement. The Holzhey incarceration was drawing so much attention that the local sheriff decided to capitalize on the media frenzy by agreeing to have Holzhey photographed in a local studio, wearing a macho ammunition vest and toting a long rifle. The sheriff, with entrepreneurial adroitness, sold the pictures to the curious as well as to souvenir seekers. Young children were shown the photograph of the ominous looking Holzhey and told in stern terms that bad things happen to children who don't obey their parents.

Reimund Holzhey, 22 years-of-age, had a weeklong trial in the Gogebic County Court House. He was found guilty. After a series of failed appeals, on February 5, 1890, he was sentenced to Marquette's Branch Prison for life but only served 24 years.

The 12-man jury convicted Holzhey in 45 minutes in spite of his defensive plea that he had "unnatural feelings" and spells of amnesia after a horse had kicked him in the head. Playing the "victim" card in 1889 did little good, and he was sentenced to a life term at the Marquette Branch Prison.

The 12-man jury convicted Holzhey in 45 minutes in spite of his defensive plea that he had "unnatural feelings."

Holzhey served 24-years in prison for his crime. Prison records reported that Holzhey had recovered from his criminal tendencies following surgery that removed a bone splinter lodged in his brain. He was a model prisoner, eventually becoming the head prison librarian and editor of the penitentiary paper.

Upon his release in 1913, he took a job as a guide for the exclusive Huron Mountain Club, a posh retreat for the wealthy, just north of Marquette. He worked there for the next 20 years, and then at the age of 63 he moved to Florida and began a new career as freelance writer.

Throughout most of his adult life, Holzhey complained of severe headaches and nightmares. Whether these recurring terrible dreams had anything to do with a conscience, weary of 43 years of guilt over the murder he committed, is unclear; but one thing is certain: at the age of 86 he took his own life by putting a bullet through his brain while sitting quietly on a rocking chair on his back porch.

When Death Comes At Dark

Molly Beveridge, a new bride, was slain in the village of Matchwood in 1889

In 1895, Jack McDonald was released from the Marquette Branch Prison after serving five years for the murder of Molly Beveridge. Beveridge was murdered in Matchwood, 30 miles south of Ontonagon on M-28 in the Western Upper Peninsula in1889. Eyewitnesses to the murder were James Redpath and Duncan Beveridge, McDonald's housemates. A jury believed Redpath and Beveridge and convicted a hapless McDonald of murder. McDonald was released from prison when new information came to light that McDonald was duped into believing he committed the murder, when in reality, Beveridge and Redpath were responsible for the killing.

At the time of the murder, James Redpath, Maggie Flaherty, Duncan Beveridge, Molly Beveridge, and James McDonald were sharing a small house in

Matchwood. Today, Matchwood is an unincorporated community with a population of 115. The town was named after the area's largest employer, the Diamond Match Company. Their home with slightly over 500 square feet was cramped, and living conditions were far from ideal for the two couples and McDonald. The Beverages had just been married. Redpath and the 21-year old Maggie Flaherty were not married but living together.

The house was built by McDonald, but later sold to Redpath. Rumors circulated at the time that Redpath did not purchase the home from McDonald, but won it in a poker game. Sleeping accommodations were far from desirable. The couples partitioned off one end of the house into two eight-by-eight cubicles, which served as sleeping quarters. The Beveridges hung a curtain at the end of their cubicle, providing them with a modicum of privacy. Redpath and Flaherty, apparently without a need of privacy, did not curtain their cubicle.

McDonald bought property near the Redpath house and was planning on building a new house. He was a burly

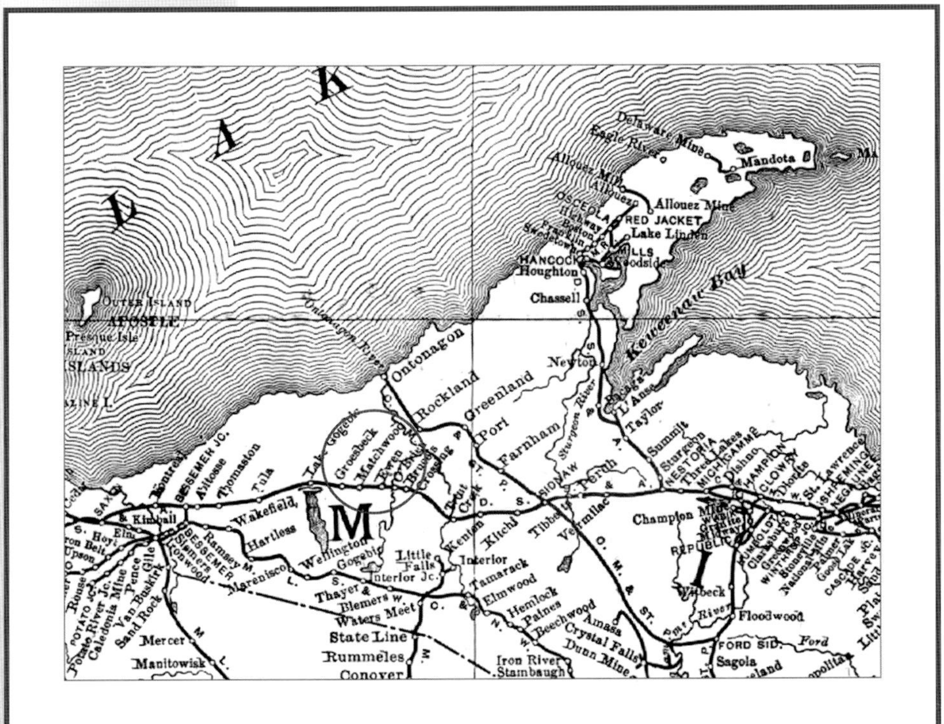

Matchwood in Ontonagon County was the site of the murder of Molly Beveredge in 1889 (circa 1892).

logger, and offered his haying services to Redpath in exchange for a place to live. Redpath and the other house occupants agreed to the terms and McDonald moved in. Far from an ideal arrangement, a cot was set up in the kitchen at night for McDonald. The ladies, somewhat apprehensive about having a rugged bachelor occupy the house, kept the door latched between the kitchen and their "bedrooms."

The harmony was shattered the night of November 11, 1889, when all hell broke loose.

In spite of the congested living conditions, all seemed to be working out for McDonald and the young couples. The ladies took care of the household chores and then assisted Redpath and Beveridge in haying.

The harmony was shattered the night of November 11, 1889, when all hell broke loose. Molly Beveridge was shot and killed and Maggie Flaherty was seriously wounded, McDonald was held accountable for the evening's bloodshed.

Beveridge and McDonald testified against McDonald at his trial. The duo contended that McDonald broke from his bedroom (kitchen) in the middle of the night and began to wildly shoot, killing Molly Beveridge and severely wounding Flaherty. Duncan Beveridge and Redpath easily convinced McDonald that he committed

The Diamond Match Company in Ontonagon in 1885 and one of the area's largest employers was the site where the fire of 1896 started.

The Ontonagon County Court House where James Redpath and Duncan Beveridge were to be tried for the murder of Molly Beveridge. However, the courthouse burned down prior to their trial and they were transferred to Gogebic County for trial.

A panicked Redpath screamed at Beveridge, "My God, Duncan, what have you done?"

the murders. They told McDonald that he was sleepwalking when he did it. A compliant and befuddled McDonald, who was easily duped, agreed that he must have done it, although he said he couldn't remember. No motive was attached to the killing. At the trial, McDonald's attorney used sleepwalking as his client's defense, but to no avail. McDonald was convicted and sent to prison for five years

McDonald's attorney did not have any forensics to refute the witness testimony, thus making the conviction of McDonald a slam-dunk.

However, this was not the end of the case. In 1895, Flaherty, told a new version of events that occurred in 1889. Five years after the murder, Flaherty, now 28, with an apparent desire to clear her conscience, said that Duncan Beveridge and James Redpath were the ones who killed Molly Beveridge. According to Flaherty's new story, she was awakened at 2:30 a.m. by the sound of the

Beveridges rowdily bickering. She heard Molly say, "I'm going away, and when I get away, I'm going to fix you plenty." Flaherty said there was a pause, then the sound of footsteps, and then a gunshot.

Flaherty said she left the bedroom and approached a dimly lit sitting room where she heard the shot. When she entered the room she saw Duncan Beveridge with a Winchester rifle in his hand, standing near his wife's prostrate and bloody body.

An alarmed Beveridge saw Flaherty enter the room, aimed his gun at her and fired, hitting her in the thigh with a life-threatening wound. Redpath, hearing all the commotion, rushed into the sitting room to find one person dead and another seriously wounded. A panicked Redpath screamed at Beveridge, "My God, Duncan, what have you done?" The din awakened McDonald, and he attempted to open the latched kitchen door, but to no avail. Beveridge yelled through the door that he was just shooting at some lynx through an open window. A naive, and somewhat intellectually limited McDonald believed Beveridge and remained in his kitchen/bedroom. According to Flaherty, Beveridge and Redpath decided to hang the murder on an unsuspecting and easily hoodwinked McDonald. McDonald was then called out of the bedroom and told that he must have committed the crime, but he was probably sleepwalking when he did it.

Sources said that Maggie Flaherty was drunk much of the time and caused trouble with the other "working girls."

The devious duo then continued with the crime cover-up by tossing the injured Flaherty into bed and telling her to keep her mouth shut or she, too, would be in trouble. Fearing retribution from Beveridge and Redpath, Flaherty kept quiet for years. The gunshot wound to Flaherty resulted in a broken leg, and it required a year's hospitalization in Marquette.

Why Flaherty came forth with a new version of the murder is not clear. Beyond an attempt to clear her conscience, Flaherty may have sought revenge for the bad treatment she received from Beveridge and Redpath. After she was released from the hospital, she rejoined Redpath and Beveridge in Menominee in their latest business venture—a brothel. Sources said that Maggie Flaherty was drunk much of the time and caused trouble with the other "working girls." Apparently Beveridge got

The Ontonagon County jail (foreground) where Redpath and Beveridge were jailed and awaiting trial. The courthouse is in back of the jail.

Soon the entire village was consumed in flames and terror engulfed the fleeing residents.

tired of her antics and told Redpath to get rid of her. Flaherty said Redpath beat her badly, and she was immobile for several weeks. When somewhat recovered she fled the den of iniquity.

Flaherty married a lumberman from northern Wisconsin in 1895, and that was when she came forth with a new version of the Beveridge murder. Based on her information both Beveridge and Redpath were arrested and jailed in Ontonagon.

It did not bode well for the men; their future looked bleak. Neither had led a faultless life, and it appeared that their nefarious behavior had finally caught up with them. But they had a redeemable side. Unfortunately, it took a catastrophe to bring it to light. While lodged in the Ontonagon jail, the worst fire in the town's history occurred. The summer of 1896 was brutally dry, and by August even nearby swamps were drying up. The Diamond Match Company had stacks of wood and mounds of sawdust everywhere, and with no rain and unbearably high temperatures; it was an inferno just waiting to happen.

Seventy-five-mile-an-hour winds fanned the sawmill's tinder-dry woodpiles. Soon the entire village was consumed in flames and terror engulfed the fleeing residents. The intense heat roasted apples on the trees. The fire's heat was felt a half mile away. After a few hours the town was decimated, more than 344 village buildings had burned down. Ontonagon disappeared from the map.

The fire was a serious problem for Beveridge and Redpath—they were locked in jail—*and the keys were gone!* Sheriff Corbett was off to another part of the county with the cell keys. His wife was left in charge, but at first was unaware that she did not have the keys. During the height of the inferno, Redpath's new girlfriend went to the jail on a rescue mission. She knew they were locked up and feared they would be prematurely cremated. Mrs. Corbett now realized that she did not have the cell keys and began a search for any extra keys. Fortuitously, another set was found, and Beveridge and Redpath were released.

Neither man fled after their heroic act and turned themselves in the following day.

Mrs. Corbett had other concerns after their release. She had to get her children and infirm mother to safety. But the street was thick with smoke and fire. Terrified and

The ruins of the jail after the great fire of 1896. Redpath and Beveridge were locked in the jail at the time of the fire and barely escaped with their lives.

The ruins of the Ontonagon fire of 1896. The village depot once stood here.

desperate, she was unsure what to do. At that moment, Redpath and Beveridge appeared. Redpath helped the children while Beveridge towed the elder Corbett to Pigeon Hill, an elevated area that provided a safe haven for the fleeing party. Neither man fled after their heroic act and they turned themselves in the following day. Their humanitarianism would serve them well as a mitigating circumstance when they went before a judge.

With the Ontonagon jail burned to the ground, Redpath and Beveridge were transferred to the Bessemer jail in Gogebic County. The trial for the murder of Molly Beveridge was held on February 23, 1897. Although Redpath was part of the cover-up plan, he was granted immunity to testify against Beveridge.

Judge Haire advised the jury that even though Flaherty, the primary prosecution witness, had a sordid history, her past questionable behavior was not to be considered when evaluating her testimony. Despite the judge's statements her past might well have led the jury to be suspicious of her credibility.

On March 4, they concluded that Duncan Beveridge was not guilty, and he was set free. One man served five years in prison for a murder that he may not have committed, and one man was exonerated for a murder that he may have committed. The truth will never be known.

Ontonagon as it is today.

Heroes come along when you need them.

Ronald Steel

MENACING DANIEL DUNN

In the 1890s Seney boasted 21 taverns, three brothels in town, and two on the Fox River.

Seney brothel and bar owner Daniel Dunn killed several men before Jim Harcourt took his life in a Trout Lake shootout

The Wild West depicted in movies and dramatized in books had nothing on Seney, a small town in the middle of Michigan's Upper Peninsula. Seney, in the 1880s and '90s was to have an influx of lumberjacks who raped the wilderness of vast stands of virgin white pine. Capricious loggers decimated more then a million acres of pristine forest. Loggers thought the abundant forests would yield precious timber *ad infinitum*. They were wrong. It took only 20 years to render the land naked. The 3,000 lumbjacks who flooded the small community didn't care much about how much timber was harvested. Whiskey, women, and fisticuffs were their only concerns, and these they pursued with a reckless zeal.

In the 1890s Seney boasted 21 taverns, three brothels in town, and two on the Fox River. The most opulent of the in-town brothels was the Grotain. Lawlessness was rampant, and violators were often ignored. The county court at Manistique was too far away to be involved in minor fracases; as a result, a local informal court was created. It was usually in the back of a bar, and it became the place where the judicial process played out. The highly illegal arrangement served the community of Seney for misdemeanor infractions. Petty crimes like larceny, drunk and disorderly, and indecent exposure were often the kinds of cases that were handled by bar room justice. Anything short of murder the locals felt they could handle. In this quasi court, perpetrators frequently went unpunished or had lenient sentences. It was thought that the local entrepreneurs and others in power could easily manipulate the system to their advantage.

Seney, once a bawdy thriving logging town is now a quiet village on the barren "Seney Stretch."

At a court convening, the judge was usually nominated by those in attendance, or seated by self-proclamation. Juries were selected from bystanders, and the defendant frequently was his own lawyer. The prosecutor, like the judge and jury, was selected from those in attendance. After the prosecution presented evidence against the defendant, the jury would decide guilt or innocence (most often guilty), and the judge would determine the sentence. Often it was a fine. The court had no legal basis, but in spite of that, it did, at times, hold those who violated community standards accountable for their behavior and had some success in keeping crime from becoming too rampant.

Seney was ripe for corruption and Dunn thrived in iniquity.

Rape, however, was a more serious matter and the Seney court dealt much more harshly with rapists. "Watering" was the rapist's punishment; it was humiliating and painful. The perpetrator was bound with rope and brought to the nearby Fox River. He was then forced to disrobe, and with the removal of each piece of clothing he was lashed with a stout switch. The lashing continued even after he was nude. Then he was driven across the river naked, receiving a lashing during his trek through the shallow water. When he reached the other side, he was left to find his own place of shelter and some clothes. He was banished from Seney. Banishment has been used as a form of punishment since biblical times. The Jews felt social isolation was a justifiable retribution for violating community norms. To the Jews, there could be no worse punishment than being rejected by your peers and driven into the desert.

Daniel Dunn was a paradox: he never smoked, drank, or cursed, yet, he ran a saloon and whorehouse.

One resident, Daniel Dunn, tested the limits of Seney's justice and moral standards. Seney was ripe for corruption and Dunn thrived in iniquity. The bar and brothel owner was not a likeable man. He had thick eyelids, bushy eyebrows, and looked more the part of respectable banker than a nefarious criminal. The former Roscommon resident was a paradox: he never smoked,

Seney in the 1890s. In its heyday, over 3,000 lumberjacks, when not in the woods, drank, fought, and sought comfort in the village brothels.

drank, or cursed, yet, he ran a saloon and whorehouse and contemptibly trod over anyone who stood in his way. Dunn left downstate Roscommon when a warrant was issued for his arrest. After leaving he had an old man return to the village and burn down his brothel in order to collect the insurance. He paid his beguiled accomplice $50 for successful arson. He took the insurance money and then borrowed more money from a Roscommon druggist and built a bordello in Seney.

Typical of Dunn, he borrowed money easily but was reluctant to pay it back.

Typical of Dunn, he borrowed money easily but was reluctant to pay it back.

The druggist appealed to Dunn many times for the money; Dunn never responded. Exasperated, the druggist threatened Dunn with a lawsuit, and then he went to Seney to force him to pay. When the druggist arrived, the wily Dunn told him that he had discovered bog ore on an island in the middle of the Seney swamp, and that he would soon have enough money to pay him back. Dunn had indeed discovered some bog ore, but its

The popular Grondin Hotel and bar in Seney in the 1890s was a competitor of Daniel Dunn's and the Harcourt brothers' saloons. The hotel burned in 1918, one year before Ernest Hemmingway made his legendary fishing pilgrimage to the village.

ore content was not sufficient to interest any mining company. Dunn took the unsuspecting druggist to the site and proudly showed him the ore that he had earlier strewn on the small island. When the druggist bent over

The Seney train station was busy during the 1880's and 1890's when the town was a thriving logging community.

to sample the ore, Dunn unceremoniously shot him in the head, pushed his body into the bog and covered it with branches. Much later, remnants of the body would be found at the site. Dunn was never prosecuted for the murder.

Dunn shot the old man in the back and briefly examined him to make sure he was dead.

Dunn's accomplice in the arson of his Roscommon whorehouse fared no better. He kept coming back to Dunn for more money. Dunn knew he would spend it on whiskey and that might loosen his tongue and make him brag about burning down the bordello. Dunn solved the collaborator problem like he solved the druggist problem—with a trip to the island in the swamp. When they arrived at the island, Dunn shot the old man in the back and briefly examined him to make sure he was dead. Without missing a beat Dunn went back to Seney, retrieved a shovel, and he then returned to the bog. He dug a grave in the spongy sand and buried the trusting old man. These grisly murders fed the rumor mill in Seney, but again, Dunn was not prosecuted.

Main Street in Trout Lake in the 1890s. The town was at the junction of the South Shore and Soo railroads and getting the reputation as a den of robbers and confidence men.

Murder continued to follow Daniel Dunn. Six Harcourt brothers owned another Seney bar; they were loyal to each other and a tough bunch. They never backed down from anyone, but they were also likeable and honest. They were rivals of Dunn in the Seney saloon business, and they detested their nasty competitor.

Dunn feared revenge by the Harcourt brothers.

In June 1891, 20-year-old Steve Harcourt went to Dunn's saloon, probably on a dare, and ordered a drink for himself and the other bar patrons. A furious Dunn said, "No God-damned Harcourt can drink in my saloon." Harcourt then derided Dunn, telling others in the bar about Dunn's lawlessness. After angry words were exchanged, Dunn picked up a whiskey bottle and smashed it over Harcourt's head. Not content to just smash his skull, Dunn retrieved a gun from under the bar and shot Harcourt in the face. Harcourt desperately tried to defend himself and pulled a gun out of his pocket that was wrapped in a red handkerchief. He managed to get off one errant shot that missed Dunn and ricocheted into a picture that was hanging at the back of bar.

The brothers drew straws to see which one would extract revenge.

Dunn fired a second shot at Harcourt, hitting him in the abdomen. A seriously wounded Harcourt staggered out the barroom door and into the street, where his stunned eight-year-old nephew happened to be. The boy assisted his uncle to Harcourt's mother's house where she, to no avail, picked glass out of his skull. Harcourt died within a few days.

After the gunfight, Dunn was arrested for manslaughter and brought to the Manistique court where the judge dismissed the felony charges and declared Dunn's actions to be in self-defense. Dunn had a charmed life—four times he was brought to court on serious charges—and four times he got off scot-free. But his time was running out.

Dunn feared revenge by the Harcourt brothers—and for good reason; the brothers' loyalty to each other had no bounds. The brothers drew straws to see which one would exact revenge. Jim Harcourt drew the short straw. Dunn was evil, but not a fool, and was well aware of what the Harcourt brothers were up to. He packed his bag and fled

In 1891, the Nevins Hotel and Saloon was the site of the shootout between Daniel Dunn and James Harcourt. Dunn was killed much to the delight of the Harcourt brothers.

The IGA store in Trout Lake was the site of the Nevens Hotel where Daniel Dunn was gunned down by James Harcourt.

to St, Ignace, where he had a keep-peace warrant issued on the Harcourt brothers. Essentially, this was a preventive procedure that would enable the law to clamp down on the Harcourt brothers before any violence occurred.

Sheriff Dennis Heffron journeyed to Seney, where he served the warrant papers to the uncontesting brothers. The brothers accompanied Heffron to Trout Lake, where the party would change trains and then head to Manistique where the court hearing would be held. They arrived early at Trout Lake and went to the local tavern for refreshments during the layover. Little did the Harcourt brothers know that above the saloon on the second floor were Dunn and his wife. They were staying there as guests of bar owner Jack Nevins. Dunn was also waiting for the next train to Manistique. From the second floor he saw the Harcourts enter the tavern. Without any fanfare he stuffed a revolver in his shirt and went down to the bar.

In the tavern, Dunn pulled out his gun, but not fast enough. Jim Harcourt quickly reacted to Dunn and fired four quick shots into him, one striking Dunn in the heart.

His body fell lifeless to the barroom floor; a fitting exit for a man who led a violent life.

Harcourt turned himself over to the sheriff who was standing nearby. Trout Lake is in Chippewa County, and as a result, Harcourt's murder trial was held at Sault Ste. Marie. Half of Seney's population was in attendance. Most thought that Jim Harcourt deserved to have a bronze statue erected in the Seney village square for ridding the town of the scoundrel. The judge, however, did not see it that way, and he found Harcourt guilty and sentenced him to seven and a half years in Marquette's State Prison. Harcourt, when asked by the judge if he had anything to say, replied, "I'm sure that Dan will not kill any more of my brothers."

Jim Harcourt was a model prisoner and through the efforts of James T. Hurst, a state representative, was pardoned by the governor after serving only three years. He returned to Schoolcraft County, greeted by a jubilant crowd. The respected and talented Harcourt embarked on a civic career where he was elected township supervisor, deputy sheriff, and conservation officer. Eventually, with his wife and children, he moved to downstate Houghton Lake where he operated a gravel pit until his death.

"I'm sure that Dan will not kill any more of my brothers."

James Harcourt

After the turn of the century, when the white pine forests were depleted and the loggers were just a footnote in history, Seney faded into near oblivion. The hot summer sun peeled paint off vacant and tired buildings as overgrown grass and weeds slowly consumed the once busy streets. Today, a yellow caution light blinks forlornly on Highway 28, and it's often the only sign of life in the now sleepy hamlet. Truck drivers in 18-wheelers and tourists in shiny sport utility vehicles streak through the village, unaware of its colorful and bawdy history.

The days of rowdy, rough-hewn loggers celebrating a weekend in the village are gone, and all that remains are the tales of what once was the peninsula's wildest settlement.

The Dally home shortly after the ambush. The white marks on the house indicate bullet entry locations.

Out of nowhere, a cacophony shattered the stillness as an avalanche of soft-shelled 30-30 bullets penetrated the boarding house.

A DEADLY AMBUSH

Three slain in a Painesdale boarding house in the midst of the 1913 Keweenaw copper strike

It was December 7, 1913, 2:00 in the morning on a typical cold, blustery December night in Painesdale, a small Upper Peninsula mining community located just south of Houghton. Mrs. Dally had prepared tea for a late arriving boarder and then retired to read quietly in a room that once was a parlor. Her husband, Thomas Dally, slept quietly in an adjacent bedroom. The Dallys ran a boarding house for English immigrant miners who labored in the Calumet copper mines. It was a "double house" in that it had an attached but separate house. Located near the woods at the end of Baltic Street in the miners' village, the Dallys occupied half of the house and five boarders occupied the other half, while in the attached dwelling lived the Adna Nicholson family. The Nicholsons had five children who ranged in age from three to sixteen. Nothing was out of the ordinary on that cold December evening, and Christmas was just around the corner. The holiday spirit was in the air.

Out of nowhere, a cacophony shattered the stillness as an avalanche of soft-shelled 30-30 bullets penetrated the wood-framed boarding house, piercing the thin walls and sending lethal splinters in all directions. Thomas Dally, sleeping contentedly in his bed, was slammed with a 30-30 bullet that ripped into his skull. His wife rushed to the bedroom only to find her husband seriously wounded. He looked pathetically at his wife and said, "Can't you do something for me?" But the wound was mortal and he died. Frightened and grief stricken, Mrs. Dally wept as she watched life slowly ebb from her husband's body.

Frightened and grief stricken, Mrs. Dally wept as she watched her husband take his last breath.

On the second floor, the Jane brothers, Arthur and James, lay sleeping when one of the bullets tore through Arthur's head and continued its deadly journey, striking James, who was beside him. They were killed instantly.

A barrage of bullets also penetrated the Nicholson household. Two bullets hit 13-year-old Mary Nicholson; one grazed her head while the other inflicted a more serious wound in her shoulder. Two other Nicholson children, Marcia (16) and Rozanne (11), although not physically injured, narrowly escaped death when bullets

The Dally house as it is today on Baltic Street in Painesdale.

passed through the pillows that they were sleeping on.

The Methodist Episcopal Church near the Dally home where the Jane brothers planned to attend Christmas service.

The Jane brothers, both in their 20s, and in the prime of their lives, had just returned from Canada the day before and were eagerly anticipating returning to work in one of the copper mines that was still operating, despite a large, regional union strike.

Earlier that evening they and a dozen immigrant miners were in a festive spirit and singing Christmas carols, and planning to attend morning worship services at the Methodist Episcopal Church. It was a good time for the brothers who were pleased they could finally leave Canada and return to their home in the Copper Country.

Why was there a lethal assault in the middle of the night on the Nicholson and Dally homes? It turned out that the Dally house was known to have "scab" laborers, miners who were willing to cross the union picket line and continue to work. The Western Federation of Miners (WFM) considered the Jane brothers scabs.

John Huhta, Nick Verbanac, Hjalimer Jallonen, and John Juuntunen were responsible for the killings and were active members of the WFM. Verbanac, an Austrian, and Huhta, a Finn, were friends for some period of time, and at one time were roommates. Huhta was the local WFM, secretary earning $75 a month, while Verbanac was a union organizer and made $125 a month. These were considered decent jobs, and the pay was commensurate with working full time in the mine and a lot less backbreaking than toiling underground ten hours a day. They were angry with those who supported the mining companies by going back to work. For the most part, it was the English immigrant miners (Cousin Jacks) who

In the joviality of the evening the Jane brother and other miners planned to attend morning worship services at the Methodist Episcopal Church, but death snatched their plans; the Jane brothers would be dead in a few short hours.

Michigan's National Guard (125th Infantry) was called in to keep peace during the 1913 strike. The troops (2,500) encamped throughout the mining community, including churchyards and schools.

wanted to work, regardless of the strike. The English were more experienced miners in that many had worked the coal mines in their homeland of Cornwall, England. In the Copper Country mines, the English had the better jobs; they were the captains and shift managers. The Dally household had five English immigrant residents, making it an easy mark for the angry unionists.

That infamous evening, the four plotters armed with 30-30 rifles walked three miles to the Dally house and stealthily concealed themselves in the woods not more than 50 yards from the house. In the early morning hours they rested their weapons on tree branches, took aim, and unleashed a volley of bullets into the house.

The mining community was outraged at this turn of events. They blamed the WFM for putting Huhta and his cohorts up to the killings. The locals felt that the union was controlled by outside agitators, primarily socialist and communists who created an "assassin squad." In addition, it pitted ethnic group against ethnic group. Animosity between English, Slavs, and Finns was already a problem, and the killings exacerbated an already potentially explosive condition.

The four plotters concealed themselves in the woods 50 yards from the Dally house. In the early morning hours they unleashed a volley of bullets into the house.

Huhta's murder trial was held in Marquette in 1914, some nine months after the killings. The judge not only charged the jury to decide Huhta's guilt or innocence, but also determine if there was a conspiracy by the WFM in the murders. Huhta, who had confessed to the murders, pleaded innocent at his trial. His lawyers contended that his companions had talked him into confessing so they could collect reward money. In addition, Huhta's lawyers maintained that he was intoxicated at the time of his confession and had been so for several weeks. Several months after his arrest, Huhta spoke ill of the union and felt that he had been duped and blamed them for the mess he was in. Regardless of the defense's arguments, the jury in only 38 minutes of deliberation, found Huhta guilty of murder in the first degree and sentenced him to life in prison.

John Huhta was found guilty of murder and sentenced to life in prison. He died in prison four years later.

Huhta died from tuberculosis at the Marquette prison in November 1918. At the time of his death he had been incarcerated for four years; he was only 28. Ironically, his sentence had been commutated and he was scheduled to be released in November 1924.

John Huhta, (second from left) confessed killer of the Jane brothers, marches with members of the Western Federation of Miners during the 1913 copper miners strike.

Horse drawn hearses travel down Sheldon Avenue in Houghton during the Jane/Dally funeral procession.

Murder charges against Verbanac, Jallonen, and Juuntunen were dismissed, as were the conspiracy charges against the WFM.

Most of the upheaval during the 1913–1914 copper strike was between labor and management. The WFM were locked in a death struggle with the mining companies, Calumet & Hecla and The Copper Range Company. The Jane/Dally murders, however, were not the result of labor versus management, but of a division in the labor union itself. There were those who aligned themselves with the WFM and honored the strike, while others felt that working to support their families was a higher calling.

Like it or not, there was an ethnic class caste system that was fundamental to the Copper Country's social structure.

The Jane/Dally murders clearly pointed out that in addition to miners having differing views on the strike, ethnic differences contributed to the conflict. The English did not consider themselves immigrants, but an extension of the indigenous English population that colonized America. They were the skilled workers with better jobs in the mines and were considered elitists, while the Croatians, Slovenians, and Serbs had the more menial jobs and were relegated to a lesser position in the informal caste system.

The Jane and Dally murders, however, were not the result of labor versus management, but of a division in the labor union itself.

Like it or not, there was an ethnic class caste system that was fundamental to the Copper Country's social structure. The Jane/Dally murders were more than just a struggle of workers pitted against management, but also an ethnic struggle that set mining brother against mining brother.

In the early 1820s when Henry Schoolcraft found copper in the Keweenaw Peninsula, he likely never dreamt of how that rich ore body 90 years later would become the site of an embittered strike that spewed blood on the Keweenaw landscape.

The Italian Hall the day after the disaster in 1913. Note the half-mast flag on the top of the building.

A STAIRCASE to DEATH

Seventy-three die in Calumet's Italian Hall during the infamous copper mining strike in 1913

Five hundred children gaily pranced about, their eyes dancing with delight and reflecting a rainbow of colors from the lights on a nearby Christmas tree. The children on the second floor of the Italian Hall eagerly pressed forward toward the stage at one end of the room in anticipation of a gift from Santa, who was positioned prominently at the front of the stage. It was 1913 on a snowy Christmas Eve in Red Jacket, a thriving copper mining town in the Keweenaw Peninsula that was renamed Calumet. For the children this was the best of times.

Then the unbelievable happened.

Someone yelled, "Fire!"

Panic was rampant in the Italian Hall as the alarmed adults and children quickly scurried to an exit that led down a staircase to the first floor. Those that first reached the staircase bottom exited with ease; however, after the first few had escaped the doors swung shut. The surging throng of Christmas merry-makers were pushed together at the bottom of the staircase with nowhere to go. In the ensuing melee, the terrified victims became stacked like cordwood—one on top of the other. The only sound was the crying and weeping of dying children. The pile of bodies on the stairs was six feet high and extended 30 feet. Seventy-three people died there, 62 of them children.

What caused the congestion in the staircase? No one knows for sure, but two theories have been put forth. The most accepted theory is that the doors at the bottom of the staircase turned in and could not be opened when a mass of people was pushed against them. The second theory is that someone had fallen on the staircase and those that followed tripped over the downed body and were unable to get up.

There were three sets of doors at the bottom of the staircase: one immediately at the bottom; one that exited out of the building on to the street; and one that led into Vairo's Saloon on the first floor. While it has been long believed that the first set of doors opened in, subsequent analysis of the doors has not supported that position. Photographs indicate that both sets of exiting doors opened out. The space at the bottom of the staircase only permitted the doors to swing out.

Regardless, this evidence is not widely accepted. A plaque at the site of where the Italian Hall once stood is dedicated to those who lost their lives. The memorial inscription declares that the tragedy partially occurred by inward opening doors. The plaque placed at the site by the State of Michigan requires correction.

Dominic Vairo, owner of the saloon on the first floor, rushed to the second floor when he realized what was happening. He assisted as best he could during the pandemonium taking place above his tavern. When he returned to his tavern he found that the till had been emptied and liquor was stolen.

That Christmas Eve there were close to 700 miners, miners' wives, and their children on the second floor of the brick building. It was an ethnic mixture of Finns, English, and Italians. Multiple languages provided the backdrop for the yuletide music that filled the evening air. A requirement to enter the Christmas celebration was union membership. Those attending had to show a Western Federation of Miners (WFM) membership card.

The gathering that evening was supposed to be a joyous celebration in the otherwise bleak and impoverished world of the local miners.

With chairs lying on their sides, the Italian Hall as it appeared the morning after the worst calamity in Upper Peninsula history.

The gathering that evening was supposed to be a joyous celebration in the otherwise bleak and impoverished world of the local miners. Six-foot, two-inch strike leader, Annie Clemenc, had gathered $58 from local merchants to buy stockings, toys, and candy for the children who attended the Christmas Eve festivities. It wasn't much, but these were hard times, and it did provide some delight for the children.

It is remarkable that more people didn't die when one looks at the number of people that were on the second floor. Many were aware of a fire ladder attached to the side of the building, and hundreds scurried down the escape ladder, while still others jumped out of windows to the roof of an adjacent building.

The catastrophe was for naught—there wasn't any fire. No one knows for sure who falsely yelled fire, but blame was placed on "strike breakers." The miners had been on strike for five months and there was no end to the walkout in sight. They felt the tragedy was the result of the mining company's attempt to disrupt their Christmas Eve.

Several witnesses that evening said they saw a man wearing a dark coat with a cap pulled down and wearing a Citizens Alliance button, and that he was the one who yelled fire. The Citizens Alliance was a group of local businessmen and community leaders who sought to be strike arbitrators, in hopes that they could settle the strike—so they said. The Alliance purported to be neutral, but most knew they were aligned with management. No one knows who the man with the Alliance button was—he just disappeared. Even though he was wearing an Alliance button, it could have been a ploy used by anyone who wanted to disrupt the union's Christmas party and blame it on the Alliance.

In the ensuing melee, the terrified victims became stacked like cordwood—one on top of the other.

One thing is for certain: the responsible person was never found.

The aftermath of the catastrophe sent shock waves not only throughout the Copper Country, but also throughout the nation. The bodies were taken to a temporary morgue. Someone noticed a hand moved on one of the children. Resuscitation was immediately initiated and miraculously, the child recovered. It is one of the few positive stories in an otherwise heartbreaking tragedy.

Most funerals and burials took place on December 28. Six churches in the community were at capacity for the funerals. Children's white caskets were in short supply and many had to be obtained from churches in nearby communities.

The burial of 62 children, most in Calumet's Lakeview Cemetery, broke even the most hardened man. So immense was the task, it took 100 miners to dig the graves. Men who used their shovels to extract copper from the earth were now digging graves to bury their children. Horse-drawn hearses transported the coffins to the cemetery. The sight of 62 white coffins headed toward the graveyard, each one shouldered by four men, was more than most could bear. The two-mile long funeral procession was paved with tears.

Children's white caskets were in short supply.

The Western Miners Federation (WMF) felt the person who yelled fire knew what he was doing, knowing full well it could have resulted in the loss of human life. It is also possible that whoever yelled fire, did so as a harmless prank, never anticipating the deadly disaster. One will never know.

The strike was finally settled on Easter Sunday 1914, some four months after the Italian Hall disaster. By then, it was too late for many of the hard–working miners who had left the Copper Country by the thousands for Henry Ford's burgeoning car factories in Detroit. They were not only making $2 a day more at Ford's, but also leaving behind the sickening memories of the fateful Christmas Eve.

Famed folk singer and left-wing activist Woody Guthrie wrote a song about the disaster called "The 1913 Massacre." The song's narrative chronicles the

White, flower-draped, children's caskets at a church service after the Italian Hall disaster. Sixty-two children died in the cataclysm.

Families, friends, and miners gather at the gravesite of those who died in the Italian Hall disaster.

catastrophe. Not all were partial to the song; many believed it was inaccurate and only designed to create class-warfare…the rich against the poor. Guthrie's emotional and inaccurate lyrics said the miners were making one dollar a day, but that was not true; they were making two dollars and fifty cents a day. He cites that thugs were the ones who yelled fire and relished the aftermath; yet, there is no documentation to support either of Guthrie's positions. But the song did serve Guthrie's agenda of depicting copper laborers as nothing more than chattel who were subjected to the whims of greedy and inhumane mine owners.

Christmas 1913 will long be remembered as the time the rugged Keweenaw wept.

Men who used their shovels to extract copper from the earth were now digging graves to bury their children.

The doorway arch is all that remains of the Italian Hall. A memorial plaque behind the arch recalls the tragedy.

LAKEVIEW
CEMETERY

VICTORIA BURCAR
1904 — 1913
ITALIAN HALL

JANOS
ONDER
MEGHALT 1914

JESSIT
MOTHER
BARBARA
1891 — 1913
DAUGHTER
ROSIE
1908 — 1913

IN MEMORY OF
THE ITALIAN HALL
GONE BUT NOT FORGOTTEN
CALUMET WOMEN'S CLUB
1989

Christmas 1913 will long be remembered as the time the rugged Keweenaw wept.

SLAUGHTER *In* SEEBERVILLE

Two striking miners are slain in a Seeberville boarding house during the bitter 1913 Keweenaw copper strike

The history of labor strikes in the United States is replete with bloodshed and violence, and the Upper Peninsula was no exception to the carnage created by the rift between labor and management. One of the most bitter and deadly strikes was the great copper strike of 1913–1914. Fifteen thousand miners labored in the copper mines; they struck in order to secure better wages and safer working conditions. Although long past, the residents of the Keweenaw Peninsula still remember the catastrophic strike over the rich copper veins that lasted nearly a year.

Thousands of European immigrants were lured to the copper-laden land with the promise of jobs.

Thousands of European immigrants were lured to the copper-laden land with the promise of jobs in the underground mines. In the later half of the 20th century, Croatians, Poles, Czechs, Slavs, Finns, and English flooded a 60-mile stretch from Delaware to Painesdale in the hope of making a better life. Often the miners'

The house in Seeberville (now Painesdale) where Steven Putrich and Alois (Louis) Tijan were murdered during the 1913 copper strike.

Poverty level incomes forced families to live in cramped conditions in company housing, while single men were herded into ethnic boarding houses.

meager wages were sent back to their homeland to remaining family members to secure passage to the United States.

Copper mining began in earnest in the peninsula in1848, but was discovered earlier in the 1820s by Henry Schoolcraft and geologist Douglass Houghton. By the turn of the century, mining companies employed thousands who toiled underground in harsh working conditions. In the bleak winter months the dank caverns were home for immigrant miners; daylight was a rare and precious commodity that miners saw little of. Death lurked around every corner in the subterranean shafts.

Poverty level incomes forced families to live in cramped conditions in company housing, while single men were herded into ethnic boarding houses. Miners were aware of the huge profits that the corporations were reaping from their backbreaking labor and they wanted a larger piece of the pie, something they felt the mine proprietors owed them…and could easily afford. Recalcitrant mine owners were adamant: there would be no negotiations with any labor union over wages and working conditions. A precipitous chasm between labor and management grew larger—something had to give.

The day of reckoning came on July 23, 1913. On that day, renegade miners, without approval from their union, the Western Federation of Miners (WFM), went on strike. They were disgruntled with their paltry $2.50 a day wage and long 10–11 hour work day, but mostly they wanted the deadly "widow maker" to continue to be a two-man operation. The widow maker was a copper extract tool that mining company officials converted to a one-man operation. The miners felt that a one-man operation would not only be dangerous, but would reduce the number of miners needed to operate the mine. The name alone (widow maker) is telling and ominous. In addition, the miners wanted the recognition of the WFM. Calumet & Heckla, the owners of the mine, refused to acknowledge the strike, to do so would have been to recognize the union and legitimize the strike, something they vowed they would never do.

Steven Putrich, a Croatian copper miner, was murdered by Waddell-Mahon security guards during the bitter copper strike.

An unlikely strike leader emerged during the crisis: six-foot, two-inch Anne Clemenc, a miner's wife and household servant, led thousands of strikers in protest marches through the streets in Red Jacket (now Calumet). As with many strikes, arrests were common and violence inevitable.

Alois Tijan (on right) was murdered in a Seeberville boarding house when security guards unleashed a volley of gunfire into the house of unarmed occupants.

But on August 14, 1913, things got worse—much worse—the conflict turned deadly. Events took a grave turn when two Croatians, Alois (Louis) Tijan and Steve Putrich were gunned down in a miners' boarding house in Seeberville by men from the sheriff's department and their hired security guards (miners called them strikebreakers and worse), the Waddell-Mahon men.

Earlier that day, 10 strikers, with nothing more to do, had gathered in a Seeberville park and leisurely drank beer on the grass. They consumed 24 quarts of beer before they disbanded and headed back to their boarding house.

Miners John Kalan and John Stimac straggled behind the others and decided to take a shortcut though mine property. In an anticipating sabotage, mine owners declared mine property off limits to the non-working miners. Kalan and Stimac were told to stop by company guard Humphrey Quick. Not drunk, but perhaps a tad tight, they defied Quick's warning and continued on. In a parting shot, Kalan turned to Quick and said, "Lookout for yourself you son-of-a bitch, I fix you…I fix you for sure [sic]."

Quick told nearby Waddell-Mahon guard Thomas Raleigh what had just happened. Waddell-Mahon guards were private security guards hired by the sheriff's office to keep peace during the strike. The miners, however, viewed the Wadall-Mahon men as nothing but goons and strikebreakers. Earlier, Calumet & Heckla General Manager James MacNaughton rejected Waddell-Mahon guard service, believing that hiring private security guards may only heighten an already tense situation. MacNaughton felt the militia that was sent to Calumet could adequately keep the peace. But County Sheriff Steve Cruise said he was understaffed and couldn't get local men to intervene in the strike. As a result, he felt he had no choice but to hire the Waddell-Mahon men. After speaking with Raleigh, Quick then alerted his supervisor, Edward Polkinghorne, who decided that they should pursue the trespassers and arrest them.

In an ensuing melee, the miners attempted to rescue Kalan, who was being beaten with a billy club by Thomas Raleigh.

Quick, Raleigh, Polkinghorne, and Harry James, along with other Waddell-Mahon men went to the nearby boarding house to find and arrest Kalan and Stimac though no arrest warrant had been issued. But this did not deter the determined party from pursing the trespassers.

The armed guard party, now numbering six, were only 500 feet from the mineshaft when they spotted Kalan. The boarding house, erected in 1902 as a temporary structure, was a rickety building that unbelievably housed 17 people. Ten occupants were miners crammed into the

Houghton County Sheriff James A. Cruise hired Wadell-Mahon security guards to assist in maintaining the peace during the 1913 copper strike in the Keweenaw Peninsula. The workers' union (Western Federation of Miners) considered the security guards as thugs and strikebreakers.

The funeral procession for Steven Putrich and Alois Tijan proceeding along Fifth Street in Calumet.

A number of investigations followed. From the start, each side pointed a finger at the other side as instigators of the fracas.

second floor of the story-and-a-half house. It was wall-to-wall beds. Joseph Putrich and his wife, Antonia, headed the house. The Putrichs and their four children all slept in the same room at the front of the house. All of the occupants were Croatian.

The enforcement party yelled at Kalan that he was under arrest. Kalan responded by saying, "Me no go." Two of the arrest party grabbed Kalan and yelled, "Come with us you son-of-a-bitch." In an ensuing melee, the miners attempted to rescue Kalan, who was being beaten with a billy club by Thomas Raleigh. During the scuffle someone threw a tenpin (bowling pin) that hit one of the sheriff's guards. The guard pulled out his pistol and fired hitting Steve Putrich, a miner near the boarding house on the fringe of the turmoil. Alarmed, the other armed security guards dashed to the boarding house, and from all sides randomly fired into the house through open windows and doors at the defenseless miners and their wives and children. The miners did not have any guns. Pandemonium broke loose inside, with everyone frantically scurrying for cover.

The firing continued until all ammunition was depleted. Alois Tijan was hit in the back while climbing a staircase and suffered a mortal wound. Putrich, who had been shot outside, died in the hospital the following day.

A number of investigations followed. From the start, each side pointed a finger at the other side as instigators of the fracas. The sheriff said they had a legitimate right to pursue the trespassers and that they were only doing their job although, it was not the trespassing duo that ended up being killed, but two innocent bystanders. The sheriff's party claimed the miners shot first and that they were just protecting themselves. Evidence, however, disputed that claim as no weapons were found at the boarding house.

The miners felt the assault was unprovoked and brutal, particularly in light of an insignificant trespass. County Prosecuting Attorney Anthony Lucas said the Seeberville tragedy was "wanton murder." Joseph Cannot, a prominent union official, said, "Sheriff Cruise's hands dripped with blood." The emotional rhetoric polarized the factions even further and made attempts to end the strike more remote.

On August 16, Harry James and Edward Polkinghorne were arrested and charged with first-degree murder. At first, the four Waddell-Mahon men who were in on the shooting were nowhere to be found. They showed up a week later after failing to convince the prosecutor to reduce the charges. The six men were charged with second-degree murder and were released shortly after raising the $60,000 bail.

The trial for the accused men took place on February 15, 1914. Three Waddell-Mahon men, Joshua Cooper, Arthur Davis, and William Groff, were convicted of manslaughter (third degree murder) and sentenced from 7 to 15 years in the Marquette prison. Judge R.C. Flannigan recommended that the trio serve the minimum time. Polkinghorne received the stiffest penalty with a 12-year minimum. Harry James was acquitted while Thomas Raleigh jumped bail and left the area.

The four convicted felons embarked for the Marquette Prison on February 17. Polkinghorne and his father openly wept as the prison-bound train departed the Houghton depot. This brought closure to the Seeberville murders, but the sordid event only further fueled the hostility between the immigrant miners and the mining companies. Peace was yet to come.

In a Croatian funeral custom, Tijan, a bachelor, was followed in the procession by ten women dressed in white, with one of the women marching directly behind the white casket dressed in a bridal veil. The women signified that Tijan's life ended unfinished.

Alois Tijan's funeral was held in the Catholic Croatian church, St. John the Baptist, in Calumet. Five thousand mourners paid their last respects to the fallen miner. In a Croatian funeral custom, Tijan, a bachelor, was followed in the procession by ten women dressed in white, with one of the women marching directly behind the white casket dressed in a bridal veil. The women signified that Tijan's life ended unfinished. The impressive and heart-felt procession, accompanied by the Humu Finnish Band, solemnly wound through the streets of Red Jacket, with the men carrying boughs of evergreen and the women toting bouquets of flowers, to the Lake View Cemetery. In a union gathering after the graveside ceremony, Joseph Cannon, a WFM official, stated that the tyranny of the mine owners was worse than the repression that the Croatians experienced in their native land of Austria.

When the strike ended on April 12, 1914, the miners had won some modest concessions, but not nearly what they wanted. Their union would not be recognized and the infamous widow maker would continue to be a one-man operation. However, wages were increased fifty cents a day and the workweek was shortened to 40 hours.

Tijan and Putrich were unknown Croatian miners and small cogs in a contentious strike that shaped the Copper Country's history.

The grave in Calumet's Lakeside Cemetery of copper miners Steve Putrich and Alois Tijan, who were murdered during the 1913 strike in the Keweenaw Peninsula.

"GYPSY BOB'S" REVENGE

In 1921, murderer and bank robber Robert Harper kills the warden and deputy warden at the Marquette prison

Bold swatches of ink intertwined with intricate patterns of fluid lines blanketed the body of slightly built Arthur "Gypsy Bob" Harper. His body was a sea of ink. It was said that he was the most tattooed man in all of Michigan's prisons. If he hadn't chosen a life of crime to make money, he could have easily earned a living working in a circus sideshow. Even his face was etched with a star on his forehead. And he was as menacing as he looked. At 5'7" and 147 pounds he hardly looked like a hardened criminal—but he was. He murdered, robbed banks, and took what he wanted. By the time he was 19 he was a hardcore criminal.

The tattooed criminal with dark skin and jet-black hair received the moniker "Gypsy Bob" from his nomadic life.

Ironically, Arthur Harper, a career bandit, was born in 1882 to a father who was a respected Philadelphia policeman. Not much is known about his mother's early life, but when Harper was a teenager she was sent to prison for murdering an acquaintance. His criminal exploits made him legendary, even to the point of folklore. One of the tales was that Harper was born while his mother was in prison. Not true. Harper was a teenager when his mother was sent to do time. But the tale made for interesting reading, and many journalists published it without reservation.

After his mother was sent to prison, his highly regarded father was left to raise Arthur, but he had little luck in successfully bringing up incorrigible Arthur. When he was of military age his dad convinced him to join the Navy. Harper enlisted in the service but was kicked out for non-conformity and rejecting rules. Harper never listened to anyone.

The tattooed criminal with dark skin and jet-black hair received the moniker "Gypsy Bob" from his nomadic life. Although his home base was Detroit, he wandered around the country, committing crimes and plying his trade as a tattooist.

"Gypsy" Bob Harper, the tattoed inmate at Marquette's Branch Prison, served 17 consecutive years in solitary confinement.

One of Gypsy Bob's early brushes with the law was in Binghamton, New York, in 1899; he was nineteen at the time. A series of house invasions with the homeowners being brutally beaten spread terror throughout the rural community. Gypsy Bob was arrested on suspicion of committing these crimes, but it was never proven and he was released.

The following year he was arrested for nearly killing a grocer in a hold-up in St. Louis, Illinois. Harper was convicted and sent to a Southern Illinois penitentiary where he escaped and eluded capture for some time. By now burglaries had become the staple of his crime life. For the most part, Harper was a loner; however, that all changed when he went to Detroit.

In 1918, Gypsy Bob assembled a group of five thugs in Detroit and began a succession of bank robberies. This crime escapade lasted close to a year before he was again apprehended and sent off to Jackson Prison.

Because of his lifestyle, Gypsy Bob had alienated his police officer father, G.W. Harper. While he was in Jackson Prison, his father wrote a letter to the warden that said, "…As I am the father of Arthur Harper, I do not understand why you gentlemen show any mercy to such characters…" Gypsy Bob's dad was clearly disgusted with his criminal son.

"…As I am the father of Arthur Harper, I do not understand why you gentlemen show any mercy to such characters…."

G.W. Harper

Harper even failed to get along with his disreputable friends. Roman Kubiak, a former member of Harper's gang, and a fellow inmate, quarreled with Harper and they became bitter enemies. Not to be outdone by attempting to kill each other in any conventional manner, they scheduled a duel to the death. Weapons of choice were not mentioned in the account, but unbelievably, this duel was to take place while the two were confined in prison. One day, however, prior to the scheduled duel, Harper jumped Kubiak from behind in the mess line and fatally stabbed him. While dying, Kubiak called Harper a sneak and said, "…The only way he could get me is from behind…." With an already lengthy criminal history, Harper now had a prison murder rap added to his list of crimes. With that murder, Gypsy Bob sealed his fate: he would spend the remainder of his life in prison. After the Jackson incident he was sent to the Marquette Branch Prison, a remote penitentiary in Michigan's Upper Peninsula, where hard-core, non-redeemable felons are sent. He would spend the next 34 years there.

Amazingly, the volatile Harper adjusted without incident in his new Marquette prison home. Warden Russell put Harper in the outside trustee division where he had limited privileges. Not only was he a trustee and an exemplary prisoner, but a role model for new, youthful offenders coming into prison. Harper frequently took neophyte inmates under his wing and unreservedly advised them to go straight; he was a beacon of hope to many young delinquents. He worked in the library and

Harper, a tattooed life-long criminal, spent the majority of his life in the Marquette Prison.

On December 11, 1921, Gypsy Bob Harper and two other inmates unleashed a reign of terror in Marquette's prison.

began a spiritual journey; he was frequently seen toting his Bible. It was hard to believe that recalcitrant and unrepentant Harper had turned over a new leaf but he had—at least for the time being.

Harper's criminal life was not over. He had more fish to fry, and in so doing he would enhance his already infamous reputation as one of Michigan's most dangerous felons—an image that he loved.

On December 11, 1921, Gypsy Bob Harper and two other inmates unleashed a reign of terror in Marquette's prison. Harper was upset with the new warden T.B. Catlin. Catlin had taken away some privileges that Harper was granted under warden Russell. No one was going to take anything from Gypsy Bob and Catlin would be no exception.

Harper was determined to kill him and selected the movie theater as the place to do it. Unsuspecting of any trouble on a peaceful Sunday afternoon, Warden Catlin, along with Deputy Warden Menhennett, seated themselves comfortably near the front of the theater, which previously was the prison chapel. During the film, Harper moved quietly from the back of the theater to the front along the wall until he approached Catlin. Reaching his prey, Harper proceeded to stab Catlin and then attacked Menhennett who attempted to intercede. Menhennett's son, a prison guard, and sitting nearby, also entered the fray only to be stabbed in his lung. Harper was joined by his two accomplices, Jasper Perry and Charles Roberts, who continued to knife the weaponless victims. As soon as other guards in attendance saw what was happening they turned the lights on, only to see 400 inmates scurrying about the theater.

Catlin was seriously wounded, but managed to escape the grasp of Harper. Charles Anderson, one of the guards on duty in the chapel, gave the warden his cane to fight of his attackers, but it was of little assistance against Gypsy Bob and his knife-wielding accomplices. Catlin then ran down a flight of stairs only to have Harper follow him. He grabbed a nearby blanket to ward of his attackers and then staggered into the deputy's office and barricaded himself by positioning his feet against the door. Prison guard Charles Muck was alerted to the melee and rushed into the deputy's office. He saw Catlin on the floor and his assailants at the door. Muck commanded Gypsy Bob and his cohorts to back off. Muck was joined by inmate Tofi Leon who also had a gun. Harper, Perry, and Roberts were herded by gunpoint into the west wing where they were locked in. The pandemonium finally ceased.

Marquette Branch Prison Warden T.B. Catlin died from a heart attacked brought on by a deep knife wound he received from inmate "Gypsy" Bob Harper in a 1921 attack. Catlin lingered for 45 days before succumbing to the fatal wound.

Gypsy Bob Harper (left) with fellow inmates Jasper Perry and Charles Roberts in the Marquette Prison court yard.

Menhennett died the day after the attack. Initially, it was thought that Menhennett's wounds were not as serious as Catlin's and he was sent home where he died within 24 hours.

Catlin, who had been sent to the hospital, slowly recovered over the next month and began to assume some of his previous duties as warden. He appeared to be recuperating; however, his recovery was short-lived and he died on January 26—45 days after the assault—from a heart attack. It was speculated that Catlin went back to work before he was fully recovered and that may have contributed to the cause of his heart attack. Catlin's death certificate stated that he died of a coronary occlusion. Harper became aware of the official cause of death and protested that he would be tried for a murder that really wasn't a murder. State authorities found a quick way to correct the problem—change the death certificated to "death by knife wounds." This was done, but it was all an exercise in futility. The state eventually ceased the prosecution of Harper, Roberts, and Perry. They came to the conclusion that it wouldn't serve any purpose to prosecute men who were already serving life sentences. A trial would have been a waste of time and money. Some state officials cried for a state constitutional amendment to legalize capital punishment when one commits a second murder, but their outrage was dismissed, and Michigan continued its ban on capital punishment.

This was 1921, and retribution for inciting insurrection in a prison was severe.

This was 1921, and retribution for inciting insurrection in a prison was severe. Harper, Perry, and Roberts were subjected to flogging, a painful punishment and designed to curtail any thoughts about causing more trouble. The prisoner was placed over a barrel and covered with a brine-soaked sheet and then whipped with a thick, leather paddle. Harper and Perry each received 30 lashes while Roberts received 25. Flogging could be shortened at any time by the prison physician—if he felt it was warranted. Reports vary on how Harper withstood the flogging. One report said that he begged for the flogging to be stopped, while other reports said he endured the extreme punishment and did not crack. The latter seems more in keeping with Harper's persona.

The prisoner was placed over a barrel and covered with a brine-soaked sheet and then whipped with a thick, leather paddle.

Prison authorities allowed flogging to lifers who had nothing to lose by committing a crime in prison. It was the only way authorities felt that they could curb prison violence. Obviously, with today's gentler standards, flogging would be considered "cruel and unusual punishment" and in violation of the U.S. Constitution. Today, the litigious American Civil Liberties Union (ACLU) would probably prosecute prison employees for using corporal punishment.

The worst of Harper's punishment was yet to come. He was put in solitary confinement or what was called the "bull pen." While in solitary confinement, Harper did not have contact with other prisoners and was allowed yard time only one hour a day. He served 17 consecutive years in solitary confinement, the most time ever in a Michigan prison.

While in solitary confinement, Harper did not have contact with other prisoners and was allowed yard time only one hour a day.

Catlin always denied Harper's allegations that he stripped him of his trustee status, and in fact said he was over-solicitous to Harper by allowing him to raise canaries in his cell and to sell pictures of other inmates. Records are unclear as to what the truth of the matter was.

Harper was returned to the general population in 1938 and served the remainder of his time uneventfully. In January 1953, Gypsy Bob Harper complained of chest pains and was sent to the prison hospital. He died of a coronary occlusion shortly after arriving. He was 73. Gypsy Bob left a legacy of violence and bloodshed in his early years, but as he advanced in age and inside the restrictive confines of a prison, he unobtrusively slid peacefully away—in an eight-by-ten foot cell.

Gypsy Bob's gravestone in Marquette's Park Cemetery deserves an explanation. The grave has an American flag marker behind the headstone; this is emblematic of the deceased having served in the U.S. military. It is ironic that Harper was honored with this patriotic insignia when he was dishonorable drummed out of the Navy at the turn of the century. Also, the emblem on the flag holder identifies Harper as a World War ll veteran. However, records are quite clear: Harper was in Marquette's prison and 60 years old when the war started. But he would be delighted to know that those who view his gravesite see him as a defender of democracy and not as a notorious and incorrigible criminal.

A Saturday Running Red

Deerton's Oscar Lampinen goes on a shooting rampage in 1924 in Marquette, killing two police officers and one of their sons

Nineteen twenty-four was the era of flappers, bootleggers, and mobsters, a time when insatiable appetites for pleasure and profit were quenched by violent men who raised havoc in the Windy City. Gangsters Al Capone, Dion O'Banion, and Bugs Moran spewed blood in Chicago's alleys, side streets, and warehouses and never gave it a second thought. It was a killing field where thugs as well as cops were struck down in Chicago's dark recesses, black holes that lurked with anguish and death during the racketeer's reign of terror. Bloodshed like this could never happen in a small town located on Lake Superior in Michigan's remote Upper Peninsula—or so the residents of Marquette thought.

But on August 23, 1924, that all changed. It was a quiet summer day, just like a hundred other days in the peaceful city.

But death was in the air.

Patrolman Thomas Thornton was found in bushes in front of the Harlow House on Fourth Street after being shot by Au Train's Oscar Lampinen.

It was a quiet summer morning, but death was in the air.

Before the day was over, two policemen and a policeman's son were gunned down, their bodies leaving a trail of blood between a Washington Street alley and a Harvey riverbank.

Patrolman Thomas Thornton had just finished his shift late Saturday afternoon. He picked up a *Mining Journal* to read in the alley behind Washington Street while he waited for his friend and fellow officer Walter Tippett to pick him up and give him a ride home.

Suddenly, all hell broke loose. Oscar Lampinen, who had just burgled Boucher's Drug Store on Washington Street ran into the alley. Thornton, seeing Lampinen scurrying down the alley by Boucher's was suspicious and ordered him to stop. Lampinen responded by shooting at the officer and running across the railroad tracks to Harlow Clark's front yard. Thornton pursued him and ran into a hail of bullets.

Tippett heard the commotion and ran to Thornton's aid. He found 26-year-old Thornton lying in a clump of bushes, severely wounded. "Oh Tipp, help me, help me; he shot me," said Thornton. Tippett asked if he knew who it was who shot him. Thornton said he didn't know, but he described him as a man about five-feet nine inches in a blue suit with a brown hat, and weighing about 150–160 pounds.

Others had arrived at the scene by this time. Recognizing that Thornton was in critical condition, they loaded him into a car and took him to St. Mary's Hospital. Despite valiant efforts to save his life, he died from the gunshot wounds in the early hours of the morning. In his last moments, cradling his two small sons in his arms, Thornton told his friend, "I did my best, Tipp. That's all I could do."

Tippett heard the commotion and ran to Thornton's aid. He found 26-year-old Thornton lying in a clump of bushes, severely wounded. "Oh Tip, help me, help me; he shot me," said Thornton.

Duluth, South Shore &Atlantic railroad agent, E.E. McIntosh, who assisted Tippett in getting Thornton to the hospital, ran over to the sheriff's office and notified Sheriff Johnson of the calamity. Johnson immediately contacted 50-year-old Marquette Police Chief, Martin Ford, who was at home. Ford's son, Lloyd, who had just graduated from high school and was planning on going to college to be a lawyer, asked if he could go with him. Lloyd was probably more excited about driving his dad's new Nash than he was about pursuing a criminal. Ford bought the car in hopes of fulfilling a life-long dream of driving it to the Atlantic Ocean.

The pair set out in pursuit of the then unknown assailant.

They first went to the hospital to see Tippett and then went over to Clark's yard to search for any evidence the criminal might have left behind. They found nothing. The Fords and Tippett then left to talk to the night turnkey at the jail. He reported that a man fitting the description given to Tippett had been seen walking down the South Shore railroad tracks toward Harvey.

The man they were pursuing was Oscar Lampinen, a 20-year-old Deerton native, who was known as a crack shot and an expert in self-defense. Because of his skill with weapons and expertise in the martial arts, he was idolized by many of Marquette's teenage boys. A friend said that Lampinen liked to read cheap books on Western adventures and Indian tales.

The Marquette City Police Force in 1915. Martin Ford (top row second from left), was the Police Chief in 1924 when he was killed by Oscar Lampinen.

Marquette's thin blue line just became thinner.

A year before the shooting, Lampinen had enlisted in the Army. Not suited for military service, he spent much of his time in the guardhouse and was soon drummed out of the service. When he returned to Deerton, he told friends, "Deerton is too small for me; I'm going to the cities [sic]." Lampinen wanted to head west to Duluth and then to the wheat fields in the north Midwest.

Arriving at Harvey, the pursuing party spotted Lampinen walking down a railroad track. They opened fire and chased him into the woods. Lampinen ducked down behind a riverbank and returned the fire. He hit both Chief Ford and his son Lloyd. Lloyd managed to get off one shot before he was dropped. Tippett, searching a nearby swamp, heard the shots and came running. He rushed to Ford's aid, but to no avail. Chief Ford gasped, "He got me, Tipp." Reluctantly, Tippett left Lloyd who was severely wounded to doggedly resumed the chase.

Lampinen fired at Tippett, one bullet narrowly missing him and lodging in a tree near his head. Tippett then spotted Lampinen swimming across the Chocolay River. In the water he was an easy target. Tippett fired and Lampinen went down and then resurfaced. Tippett fired again. Lampinen sank and did not resurface. His body was later retrieved by the Coast Guard within 20 feet from where it went down.

Lampinen fired at Tippett, one bullet narrowly missing him and lodging in a tree near his head.

Bloody Saturday was over. Two of the city's finest were dead. Marquette's thin blue line just became thinner.

The largest funeral in memory was held in St. Peter Cathedral for Martin Ford and Thomas Thornton. In a show of support, hundreds of cars formed a cortege that serpentined through town to the Holy Cross Cemetery.

Lloyd Ford tenuously clung to life in St. Mary's Hospital, which was only three blocks from St. Peter Cathedral. Lying in his hospital bed, Lloyd heard the bells ring at the Cathedral. In a quiet but knowing voice said, "Is that for Dad?" He knew for whom the bells tolled.

Lloyd Ford died the day after his father's wake. His funeral was held two days later. Stores were closed to honor the memory of the three men.

The *Mining Journal* established a $5,000 memorial fund for the families of Ford and Thornton. The largest

The site on the Chocolay River where Oscar Lampinen was shot by officer Walter Tippett.

Martin and Lloyd Ford grave headstones in Marquette's Holy Cross Cemetery.

single contributor was Louis Kaufman who gave $1,000. In addition the city authorized the pavilion concession stand at Presque Isle Park to be managed by Martin Ford's widow, Mary. It was the city's effort to financially assist the widow, who now had to raise two of her three children by herself. Ford left three surviving daughters, Lyda, 25, Remona, 11, and Eileen, three. Thornton left his wife and two small children, Edward, three, and one-year-old James.

The home of Martin Ford in south Marquette as it appears today.

Eileen Kroken, age 88, is Martin Ford's last surviving child and lives in Marquette. Eileen said on the day her dad died, Marquette Mayor Clark came to the house and told her mom about Dad's death. Eileen said, "I remember running to my Dad's car when it was driven to our home, hoping it wasn't true, there was a stranger in it—it wasn't my Dad."

Although only five at the time of her father's death, Eileen vividly remembers his playful nature. On one occasion he good-naturedly shaped the mashed potatoes on her plate in the form of a house. She said,

Eileen Kroken holding a memorial plaque honoring her father Martin Ford. It was given to her in 1992 on National Police Officers' Day.

"Later on in life others told me that he was a 'witty Irishman.'"

Eileen said, "Mom took Dad's death real hard, she went to her bedroom and stayed there for a long time. She led a lonely life after he died. She never talked much about his death". Mary Ford never drove the new Nash; it remained in the garage for years collecting dust on its once shiny finish, never having the chance to spin down the highway in quest of distant shores.

The newspaper noted that a quiet service for Lampinen was held at his home in Deerton.

Martin Ford wanted to drive his new Nash to the Atlantic. Ocean.

The Marquette City Commission went on record as favoring the state compensation law for police officers families killed in the line of duty. Both Ford and Thornton families would receive $4,200 over 100 weeks under the state provisions.

Walter Tippett was unsettled after killing a man, justifiable as it was. He later worked at the prison and then went to work in Ishpeming's underground mines. He had several brothers who were working in the mines, and it seemed like a natural fit and a safe place where he did not have to worry about death being around the nearest corner. Providence, however, interceded, in a cruel twist of fate, Tippett was killed within hours of starting his first day at the mine on November 3, 1926. This occurred only two years after the bloody shoot-out in Marquette.

Marquette's retired Police Chief, George Johnson with Martin Ford's nightstick.

Tippett died in the worst mining disaster in Michigan; a catastrophe at the Barnes-Hecker mineshaft that claimed 52 lives in 1926.

On May 5, 1990, Eileen Kroken received a plaque honoring her father the late Martin Ford in a ceremony at the Holy Cross Cemetery. Eileen said, "I was honored, but really nervous about being in the public eye—I'm really quite shy." On that day, The National Police Officers' Day, all slain police and conservation officers from the Upper Peninsula who died in the line of duty were honored.

Lampinen was known as a crack shot who was idolized by Marquette's teenage boys.

Eighty-five years have passed since that infamous day. Marquette has been relatively peaceful since then. There have been other murders over the years, but not of the magnitude that claimed the lives of two police officers and a young man. Relative tranquility has returned, and that's just fine for the citizens of the peaceful lakeshore city.

Twenty-year-old Oscar Lampinen was quietly buried in the Au Train Cemetery, located 15 miles east of Marquette.

The SENSELESS SLAYINGS

Two Marquette conservation officers were slain when a poacher is threatened with a citation

To game wardens Arvid Erickson and Emil Skoglund the weather didn't matter.

Fall in Michigan's Upper Peninsula not only brings a collage of spectacular color, but a burst of activity by deer hunters as they prepare for opening day. To many Upper Peninsulans (Yoopers), hunting season rivals Christmas as the year's most sacred day. The hunting ritual breathes life into the peninsula before the winter's snow blankets the earth. Fall is a confused season, it is not quite sure if it wants to wrap itself in the lingering warmth of summer, or prepare the inhabitants for the bitter cold months that follow.

To game wardens Arvid Erickson and Emil Skoglund the weather didn't matter—gray and nasty, or pleasantly brisk, they were busy doing what they usually did prior to the opening of hunting season: looking for violators.

On September 29, 1926, Erickson and Skoglund were on a routine patrol in the Sands Plains, a jack pine covered area located between Gwinn and Marquette, when they found a salt lick. Salt licks are deer appetizers that are often used by hunters to lure deer. Attempting to snare a violator hunting before the season began, Erickson and Skoglund obscured themselves in a bush near the salt lick.

In a short time Roy Nunn and Joseph Contois arrived at the site. The officers recognized Nunn; he was a habitual game violator. Erickson and Skoglund came out from their cover and surprised the two men. Nunn had a gun but Contois was weaponless. It is illegal to carry a firearm in the woods just prior to hunting season without a permit. A surprised Nunn could not produce a permit. Erickson told Nunn that he was in violation and would be taken to Gwinn for arraignment. Erickson then directed Skoglund to drive his car to Gwinn and that he and Nunn would follow in Nunn's car. When they approached Nunn's car, Nunn went to the back and pulled out a 22-caliber pistol. He ordered Erickson to put his hands up. Contois, seeing what was happening, panicked and quickly fled. While running away he heard a gunshot. Contois did not look back or stop but continued to sprint home. Because of his abrupt exit, he didn't know what happened to Skoglund.

Contois arrived home breathless at 7 p.m. and told his wife what had just happened. Perhaps fearing he would be in trouble, or not wanting to get his friend in trouble, Contois told no one else. He feared Erickson and Skoglund were dead.

In 1926, World War 1 veteran and Marquette County Game Warden, Arvid Erickson, was shot in back of the head while attempting to arrest game violator Roy Nunn.

Strawberry Lake on Sands Plains is located ten miles south of Marquette and not far from the murder site of conservation officers Emil Skoglund and Arvid Erickson.

Thirty-year-old Arvid Erickson was born in Finland but came to the United States when he was six years old. He knew danger only too well; twice he was wounded while in the military during World War I. Erickson was a family man with a wife and two children under the age of ten.

Erickson's partner, Emil Skoglund, was a 30-year-old bachelor who resided in a camp south of Ishpeming owned by another game warden, Andrew Schmeltz. Skoglund loved the outdoors and only went to town when he had to.

Contois feared Erickson and Skoglund were dead.

The next day, October 1, when the officers failed to show up for work, there was concern in the department that something may have happened. When they were still missing the next day, authorities began one of the largest manhunts in Upper Peninsula history. Hundreds of volunteers, including game wardens, trappers, and area residents took part in several massive searches for the missing game wardens. By now it was feared they were dead.

On October 4, searchers found a significant amount of human blood on Sand's Road, not far from picturesque

Strawberry Lake. Discovered close to the dry blood were two spent .22 shells. They were significant finds but still did not yield information as to the whereabouts of Erickson and Skoglund.

Little progress was made in the case even after the discovery of the blood and the shells. In an attempt to shake something loose, state conservation officials offered a $1,000 reward for information leading to the capture and conviction of a suspected killer(s). Marquette County matched the $1,000, which swelled the pot to $2,000, a tidy sum in the 1920s.

Was it the reward that enticed 45-year-old Joseph Contois to come forward with critical information, or was it because he had a feeling of civic responsibility? Mrs. Contois claimed neither. She asserted that she was the one who encouraged her husband to go to the police and tell what he knew about the murders. In any case, on October 13, nearly two weeks after the slaying, Contois went to the police with his incredible story.

Contois said that Nunn came to his house on the afternoon of September 29th and asked him to join him deer hunting. Contois, aware that it was not yet deer season, went with Nunn, but did not take a gun. They proceeded to the site on the plains where the salt lick was located. When Erickson and Skoglund showed up, all hell broke loose, and Contois said he quickly fled the area.

It was discovered that after Contois left, within minutes, Nunn shot Erickson and then Skoglund when he came to assist Erickson. Both died instantly. Nunn now had a problem—what to do with the bodies. His first thought was to toss them into Pickerel Lake (now Harlow Lake) just 15 minutes north of Marquette. Nunn, however, could not find a deep enough location on the small, shallow lake to effectively dispose of the bodies. He then opted to submerge them in Marquette's lower harbor. He tied brick anchors to the bodies and dumped them off a dock into the icy waters of Lake Superior and was confident they would not be found.

After Contois's remarkable revelations about the murders, the police immediately went to Nunn's gun repair shop in Marquette and arrested him. Although Contois did not witness the shootings, he placed Nunn at the site of the crime.

Little progress was made in the case even after the discovery of the blood and the shells.

Nunn emphatically denied any involvement in the mystery of the missing game wardens.

After killing Arvid Erickson and Emil Skoglund, Roy Nunn dumped the bodies near the dock in Marquette's south harbor. He failed in an earlier attempt to submerge the bodies in Harlow Lake. To insure they were not found he anchored the bodies with bricks.

He tied brick anchors to the bodies and dumped them off a dock into the icy waters of Lake Superior.

Nunn emphatically denied any involvement in the mystery of the missing game wardens. Even after numerous interrogations he stuck to his story. He told police that he had encountered Erickson and Skoglund that morning near Strawberry Lake, and that he did not have a gun permit with him, but he did have one at home. Nunn said he and the officers drove to Marquette where he produced a gun permit he had purchased earlier. A check of the records verified that Nunn did have a valid gun permit.

According to Nunn, after showing the officers his gun permit they all went back to Sands Plains. Nunn claimed, "I left them. I don't know what happened later."

Nunn was a scurrilous character. He began his crime career at 17 when he was sent to prison for killing his uncle. He was sentenced to life for the murder, but only served 17 years when Governor Woodbridge Ferris pardoned him from the Marquette Branch Prison. Little did prison authorities know at the time that Nunn would chalk up two more killings before finally receiving a permanent life sentence.

After his release from prison, it didn't take Nunn long to again be in trouble. Within a year he robbed a store in Gwinn and was sent back to prison, this time for one to 15 years. He served five years on that sentence and again was turned loose. He remained a free man for the next six years—until he killed again.

Nunn was a scurrilous character. He began his crime career at 17 when he was sent to prison for killing his uncle.

In the murders of Skoglund and Erickson, the evidence on Nunn began to mount. The police not only had direct evidence provided by Contois's description of what happened, but also circumstantial evidence of a screwdriver found in Nunn's car that belonged to Skoglund.

The police felt they had a solid case against Nunn and began to put the heat on. They took him to the site of the murders and produced a blood-soaked coat that belonged to Nunn. Detectives then began to intensively grill him about the murders. Under repeated pressure, Nunn cracked and confessed.

On December 7, Nunn pleaded not guilty to murder in Marquette County Court. Early in the trial Nunn

Skoglund and Erickson were employed by the Marquette Conservation Department in the early 1920s. The agency was renamed the Department of Natural Resources in 1969.

A memorial plaque citing Upper Peninsula conservation officers who died in the line of duty. Skoglund and Erickson are the first two cited on the plaque.

recanted his earlier confession. He said the only reason he confessed was because the state police had tortured him. In an unsuspecting defensive move, Nunn said it was Contois who killed the officers. The jury didn't buy any of Nunn's desperate last-minute arguments. After deliberating a little more than a half hour they found Nunn guilty of first-degree murder. [Second degree probably would have been more appropriate.] With Nunn's previous criminal record, Judge Richard Flannigan wanted to make sure that Nunn stayed in prison for the rest of his life and sentenced him to a life of hard labor at Marquette's Branch Prison.

These senseless killing of two conservation officers occurred over a suspected minor hunting infraction that would have resulted in no more than a fine. Struck down in the prime of their lives, the two 30-year old conservation officers were doing what they loved—protecting the Upper Peninsula's precious natural resources.

Ironically, Nunn had a permit at home—he killed for nothing.

Blood Bath In The Big House

In 1931, six were killed in a botched escape from Marquette's prison on the bloodiest day in the prison's history

Andrew Germano callously and gratuitously murdered Dr. Hornbogen in a botched prison escape.

A long line of cars stretched down Spruce Street on a gray Saturday morning. It was a sad occasion and grieved mourners had gathered at the house of esteemed physician A. (Alfred) W. Hornbogen to pay their last respects. That afternoon one of the longest funeral cortèges the city ever saw, serpentined through the city to the Park Cemetery where Dr. Hornbogen was laid to rest.

Hornbogen came to Marquette to practice medicine in 1899, and for 32 years he faithfully served the medical needs of the citizens of the community. In addition, he provided medical services for Marquette's prisoners—at no charge. His humanitarian efforts cost him his life. Marquette prison inmate Andrew Germano callously and gratuitously murdered Hornbogen in a botched prison escape on August 31, 1931. Hornbogen would not be the only one to lose his life that day; five other lives would be snuffed out on the bloodiest day in Marquette's prison's history.

On the last day of August, Dr. Hornbogen volunteered to fill in for vacationing physician Youngquist. The day started no differently than any other day that Hornbogen worked at the prison. Dr. A.W. Hornbogen and his brother Dr. Dan Hornbogen, who was also a physician, planned on driving to the prison together, when at the last minute Dan received a phone call from a patient on Lake Street in need of immediate attention. Dan told A.W. to go without him and that he would join him at the prison after he treated a patient for a severe nosebleed. Dan went to Lake Street and packed his patient's nose, then proceeded to the prison, arriving there a short time after A.W. By the time Dan got there, A.W. had been murdered. Had Dan gone to the prison with his brother, he too, may have been killed. As fate would have it, a nosebleed saved Dr. Dan Hornbogen's life.

Dr. A. E. Hornbogen was slain in a botched 1931 escape from Marquette Branch Prison. He was 65 years old.

Dr. Hornbogen was treating patients in the infirmary on a routine Thursday. In his waiting room were three inmates, Andrew "Tony" Germano, Martin Duver, and Charles Rosbury, all former Detroit residents. Germano, who was serving 30 to 35 years for armed robbery, complained of stomach pains. Hornbogen asked Germano to remove his shirt so he could begin the examination. But Germano had a revolver in his waistband under his shirt, and he had not anticipated that Hornbogen would ask him to strip. He knew that taking of his shirt would reveal the gun. Not knowing what else to do, Germano retrieved the gun and shot Hornbogen in the heart. He died almost instantly.

The escape had just started and already things were going awry. Killing Dr. Hornbogen was not part of the plan.

In the same room with Hornbogen and Germano were Head Inmate Nurse, Frank Oligschlager and Inmate Assistant Leo Bolger. Quickly responding to the situation, Oligschlager knocked the gun out of Germano's hand. Hearing the commotion inside, inmate Martin Duver, who was in the hall waiting room, rushed into the examining room. Duver also had a revolver and without hesitation shot Oligschlager in the stomach. Oligschlager hung on to life for the next 16 hours, and then he, too, died. Within minutes one man was dead and another dying—and the melee had just begun.

Nurse Leo Bolger picked up a porcelain rod and swung it at Germano. Duver, recognizing how badly the situation was playing out, shot Bolger. He was wounded, but it was not a life-threatening injury.

It was the early stages of an escape and things were not going according to the plan. The three conspirators quickly left the medical facility and entered an open area between A-Block and B-Block. While leaving they encountered Warden Corgan and Deputy Warden Newcombe near the prison barbershop. With guns blazing, the fleeing prisoners sent a hail of fire at the two wardens. With bullets ricocheting off prison bars, Corgan and Newcombe somehow managed to escape uninjured and retreated to the gunroom. Corgan sounded the prison riot alarm that was housed in the gunroom. Guards immediately encircled the prison, and all prisoners were directed to return to their cells. In sounding the alarm Corgan was hopeful that whatever was occurring would not spread to the general population.

With bullets richoeting off prison bars, Corgan and Newcombe somehow managed to escape uninjured and retreated to the gunroom. Corgan sounded the prison riot alarm that was housed in the gunroom.

The desperate inmates continued on a reign of terror in their escape attempt. They came upon the hall master's office where Deputy Warden Joe Cowling and his secretary were conducting the day's business. The terrorists fired into the office and wounded Cowling. The convicts then grabbed Lieutenant George Hurley, the prison fingerprint expert, from the office and held him hostage.

Dr. Hornbogen lived in a quiet neighborhood on Spruce Street in Marquette at the time of his murder.

It was made clear to the hostages that any attempt to escape would mean their life.

The gunmen with hostage Hurley advanced to the prison yard where they took another hostage, guard Alonzo Hulett. With the two hostages ahead of them the three inmates scurried across the yard. It was made clear to the hostages that any attempt to escape would mean their life. Hurley knew once they reached the entry gate that the convicts could exit to freedom. With that in mind Hurley made a break for it when they reached the corner of the greenhouse. A barrage of bullets pursued Hurley on his gambled escape. Miraculously, he didn't get hit and made it to safety. One of the rogue inmates put a revolver to Hulett's head and pulled the trigger, but the weapon misfired. The gun misfired because the weapon had been stored in a gravy can. All the weapons the inmates had were smuggled into the prison earlier inside chicken and gravy cans. The three convicts then futilely pursued Hurley; in doing so it gave Hulett a chance to escape.

The desperate threesome then entered the box factory; from there they went into a three-story industrial building. Charles Arnez, the guard on duty in there was taken hostage. They advanced to the third floor which housed 30 inmates. Another guard, Charles Alvord, was also taken hostage. The inmates and their new hostages were encircled not only by the prison guards, but also by the State Police, and the Marquette and Negaunee City Police. The police and the guards now rained down a volley of fire through the open windows into the industrial building. The two hostages were ordered to close the building's windows with a broom, and then forced to barricade the doors with inmate cots. The convicts returned the fire whenever they could see a guard or police officer through one of the windows. Panic enveloped the entire third floor and everyone scurried about looking for cover. Germano, the leader of the escape group, compelled guard Arnez to write and sign a note that demanded prison authorities provide an escape car to be driven by Warden Corgan. Corgan's reply was swift and certain: he emptied a salvo of tear gas into the building. Tear gas filled the room and the escapees knew that their chance for freedom was now doomed. Germano and Rosbury decided the only way out was suicide. They had agreed on suicide if their escape failed and that time was now at hand. Duver was reluctant to join them in suicide, but he finally consented to the "final solution."

Tear gas filled the room and the escapees knew that their chance for freedom was now doomed.

The unobtrusive sandstone entry leading several blocks to the Marquette Branch Prison where the Hornbogen murder took place in 1931. Foot traffic is forbidden beyond the gate.

The Hornbogen family headstone in Marquette's Park Cemetery. Dr. A.E. Hornbogen is buried a short distance from the primary marker while his brother, Dr. Dan Hornbogen, is interred near the headstone.

Recalcitrant Duver, however, did not go easy. He wanted to kill Alvord prior to taking his own life. One of the bunked inmates, who was not part of the plot, prevailed on Duver not to kill Alvord because he had eight children. The pleading inmate was not sure how many children Alvord had, but he correctly guessed it would spare Alvord's life. Duver pulled back the revolver he had aimed at Alvord's head.

Rosbury was the first to take his life. He inserted a revolver into his mouth and then blew his brains out. Germano did the same. Duver, the last of the trio, expressed one regret just before he took his own life: that he had not killed Hurley when he had the chance. Five were now dead and the fracas was still not over.

Inmate Frank Hohfer, who was housed in E Block, had a weapon and was suspected to be a part of the escape group, but was barred from going to sickbay with the other escapees because Warden Corgan wanted Hohfer kept away from Germano. He knew if those two were together that trouble would follow. Hohfer was in his cell when he heard three shots ring out and rightly suspected that the other three had taken their lives. When Hohfer saw guard Al Fingel in his block, he fired at him with a revolver he had hidden in his cell. Fingel returned the fire and wounded Hohfer in the leg. After the initial exchange of fire Hohfer took his own life as his compatriots had done earlier. The blood bath was finally over, leaving strewn in its wake, four dead inmates, one dead physician, one dead inmate nurse, one wounded inmate, and one wounded deputy warden.

Revenge may have played a role in the escape. Several weeks before the blood bath, Edward Wiles, a close companion of Germano, went to the prison hospital with a severe heart problem. On his deathbed at the hospital he said to an attendant, "If I die, my buddies will clean out this place." Wiles' friends didn't succeed in cleaning the place out, but they did succeed in leaving a bloody trail through the prison.

How the dangerous inmates got the four guns was at first a mystery. An extensive investigation by the police, however, determined that a tinsmith in Detroit was responsible for smuggling the weapons into the prison. The guns and ammunition were hidden in cans of ready-cooked chicken. The cans, with the weapons inside, weighed the same amount they would have weighed when filled with chicken. Eventually, several other inmates, along with the tinsmith were indicted for transporting weapons into the prison. Those convicted of the gun smuggling were sentenced from 20 to 40 years.

Hornbogen was trusted and well respected by the prison inmates.

Michigan's Governor, William Brucker, recognizing the contribution that several inmates made in assisting the prison guards to quell the escapees, justifiably and posthumously commuted the sentence of Frank Oligschlager, while inmate Leo Bolger's sentence was commuted to immediate release pending employment. It was the only time that Brucker ever commuted prisoners' sentences during his tenure as governor.

Hornbogen not only enjoyed the admiration of the Marquette community but also was trusted and well respected by the prison inmates. Had the foursome not committed suicide, their life in the prison would have been tenuous. Inmate Jim Burton, who was serving a double life sentence, remarked about the inmate's suicide, "They saved me the trouble." Such was the esteem that Hornbogen had with the 800 inmates who were housed in Michigan's toughest prison.

Dr. Hornbogen's moss covered and difficult to read grave marker is not far from a tranquil pond in the cemetery.

The DYNAMITE DISASTER

Killer attempts to eradicate evidence of murdering a Marquette conservation officer by using 70 sticks of dynamite

The team slogged through tag alders and mud before coming across a grizzly scene.

Shortly after midnight in a wooded sanctuary just north of Negaunee, a brilliant light flashed across the darkness. Accompanying the illumination was an explosion that shattered the night air. Then all was still.

One hour later another, louder eruption cracked the quiet evening. Then all was still.

Within hours a third and final burst occurred, accompanied by a flare of intense light that danced into the darkness. Then all was still.

It was October 20, 1936, and not far from where the explosions occurred, S.O. Hoff and two conservation officers from Marquette were huddled in a car waiting for the morning light to see if they could find missing conservation officer Andrew Schmeltz. Hoff was a good friend of Schmeltz.

Shortly after midnight the threesome heard the first explosion. Alarmed, two of the conservation officers sped to Marquette for assistance, while Hoff manned the site from where they heard the explosion.

Hoff heard the next two explosions before the search party returned. When help arrived it was the middle of the night and too dark to begin searching for Schmeltz or the cause of the blast. But when the sun pierced the early morning, the search began. The team slogged through tag alders and mud before coming across a grizzly scene. Stunned, they entered what looked like a scene from World War I's trench warfare where scarred land was pockmarked with water-filled craters. Near the craters, trees were draped with pieces of bloody flesh that dangled like grapes on a vine. Hoff and the others assumed that the defoliaged landscape and earthen holes were created by the dynamite blasts.

Conservation officer Andrew Schmeltz (46) was murdered in 1936 by trapper Raymond Kivela. Kivela attempted to hide the murder by dynamiting the body.

Amidst the carnage, they found Schmeltz's revolver and holster and 19 illegal muskrat traps. Unbeknownst to the search party, they were being carefully watched through binoculars by a young man who had concealed himself in the thick underbrush.

The search for the killer began immediately and several suspects were picked up, but later dismissed. However, it did not take County Prosecutor John D. Voelker and Sheriff Rudolph Franson long to identify a logical suspect in the case—Raymond Kivela. Kivela was a 27-year-old trapper who lived with his parents, not more than a half mile from the site of the murder. Kivela hardly looked like a criminal, much less a murderer. Slightly built at five feet eight inches and weighing 155 pounds, the bespectacled and hunched Kivela would have gone unnoticed in a crowd.

When Kivela was arrested on October 23, he scoffed at the insinuation that he had murdered Schmeltz. After several interrogations, he continued to proclaim his innocence. But when State Trooper N.H. Modders searched the Kivela farmhouse, he found evidence that implicated Raymond as the murderer. In the attic of the home, Modders found a pair of overalls still damp with blood and pieces of human flesh stuck to the fabric. Further examining the coveralls Modders found a receipt in a pocket for 100 sticks of dynamite dated the same day as the murder. But there was one problem with the name on the dynamite receipt; it wasn't Kivela's. In an attempt to establish that the handwriting was Kivela's, the police asked him to write his name and the name that appeared on the receipt. That was it—his writing matched the one on the receipt. He knew he was trapped by the evidence and confessed to the murder.

In the attic of the home, Modders found a pair of overalls damp with blood and pieces of human flesh stuck to the fabric.

There was a mountain of evidence that Kivela had committed the murder. In addition to his confession and the bloody overalls, the dynamite at the scene of the killing matched the dynamite that was found in his home. Fingernail parings and paraffin casts taken from Kivela clearly showed that he had recent contact with nitrates.

The slain officer, 45-year-old Schmeltz, was a lifelong Yooper. Born and raised in Ishpeming, he loved the outdoors and was well suited to be a trapper for Michigan's Department of Conservation. He was a dedicated guardian of the wilderness. The veteran of World War I was tough and violators didn't get any breaks.

The night he was murdered was just like every other night that he went out to find poachers. Poachers were usually doing one of two things: either setting traps out of season or trapping without a license. On October 20, at 9:00 a.m., Schmeltz and Hoff left for the Carp River just north of Negaunee to check on recent reports of illegal muskrat trapping. Hoff was physically disabled: he had an artificial left leg and a disfigured right foot. Although he was crippled, Schmeltz relied on Hoff to accompany him on remote patrols. Besides being a trusted companion on the isolated road searches, Schmeltz felt that Hoff could give him assistance if he ever needed it. Hoff was restricted in what he could do, but keeping his buddy company in his pursuit of violators provided him with a life purpose. He didn't know it at the time, but accompanying Schmeltz that day was significant for law enforcement.

Schmeltz had a job to do, and he did it with determination.

It was a typical cold, bleak, October day, when one would rather be snuggled up next to a warm fireplace than sitting in the woods looking for violators. However, Schmeltz had a job to do, and he did it with determination. He was on a stake and not too far from his car. Hoff waited patiently for Schmeltz in the car as he had done many times before. He became concerned by mid afternoon when Schmeltz had not returned. This was untypical. As darkness edged out the receding daylight, Hoff became alarmed. He didn't have the car keys, but he knew he had to get help. Hoff tottered painfully down the Carp River Road to the main road to Negaunee. He then hitched a ride to town to report that Schmeltz was missing. Two other

The memorial plaque on this boulder at the entry of the Department of Natural Resource building located two miles south of Marquette on US-41, bears the name of conservation officer Andrew Schmeltz who was killed in the line of duty.

Andrew Schmeltz's grave marker in Ishpeming's cemetery. Raymond Kivela killed Conservation officer Schmeltz fearing that he would take his hunting traps for violating.

conservation officers drove Hoff back to the site where in a short time they heard the explosions.

Kivela related to authorities what happened the night of the murder. He said that he was walking along a ridge by the Carp River when he encountered Schmeltz. Kivela said he was carrying a 22 rifle when Schmeltz asked him if he had a gun permit. He said that he could not produce a gun permit because he left it at home. As a result, he said Schmeltz was about to confiscate his gun. Kivela said he did not want to lose his gun and that's when he struck Schmeltz and knocked him to the ground. Kivela turned the gun on Schmeltz and shot twice, both times striking him near the heart. He said that he completely lost his head when he killed Schmeltz. The killing took place about 11:00 a.m. After he murdered Schmeltz he towed the body to a nearby swamp and covered it with brush. Kivela was now concerned that someone might find the body and that it would lead to his arrest.

To prevent being found out, Kivela quickly came up with a plan—he would dynamite the body, thus eliminating evidence. He went back to his farm, got his car and went to Ishpeming where he purchased 100 sticks of dynamite. Then he returned home and finished his farm chores. Later in the evening he played the customary checkers with his dad, and then he went to bed around 9:00 p.m. But his day was far from done. At midnight he stealthily left the house and slipped into the night. He returned to the murder site where he placed 70 sticks of dynamite on the body and ignited it. Kivela thought a large blast would drive the body down deeper into the swamp—he was mistaken. Instead, the blast spewed human flesh 250 feet in all directions. He was now in a worse predicament. Kivela went back to his farm only to return a short time later to see if he could clean up the mess with two more charges of dynamite.

Instead, the blast spewed human flesh 250 feet in all directions. He was now in a worse predicament.

Judge Frank Bell sentenced Kivela to life in prison on December 14, 1936. He served time in four Michigan prisons before he was placed in the Newberry State Hospital (which was an institution for people with psychiatric disorders). Prison officials said Kivela had a long history of mental Illness. In 1981, when Kivela was 74, Governor William G. Milliken commuted his sentence. He spent his last years in a nursing home in Upper Michigan.

The Lieutenant With A Luger

Army Lieutenant Coleman Peterson guns down Mike Chenoweth, a Big Bay tavern owner

On a warm summer evening on July 31, 1952, Lieutenant Coleman Peterson looked solemnly at his wife and said, "I want you to swear on this rosary what you just told me was true." Without hesitation, Charlotte Peterson placed her hand on the sacred beads and swore that she was telling the truth.

Attractive, auburn-haired Charlotte just told her husband that Mike Chenoweth, owner of the Lumberjack Tavern in Big Bay and former state trooper, had raped her. With his wife's testimony documented to his satisfaction, he retrieved his 9-mm lüger and proceeded to the Lumberjack Tavern. The tavern was only a quarter-mile from Peterson's trailer in Big Bay's Perkins Park. At midnight, Peterson reached the tavern and went to the bar where Chenoweth was working. Without wavering, he reached over the bar and pumped five bullets into defenseless Chenoweth, who fell to the floor in a pool of blood; he died almost instantly.

Chenoweth was an excellent shot and kept guns at the bar, but the surprise attack didn't give him time to go for a gun. Peterson was probably unaware that Chenoweth was an expert marksman, but it is doubtful that would have made a difference. He committed the murder in a heat of anger and nothing was going to stop him. Bartender Bud Wentzel stopped Peterson leaving the tavern. Peterson stared coldly at Wentzel and said, "Do you want one in the head?" Wentzel wisely let Peterson continue on.

Peterson stared coldly at Wentzel and said, "Do you want one in the head?"

The firing of the pistol sent bar patrons scurrying in all directions. Ken Goldsdworthy, who just moments earlier had been sitting with Chenoweth, said, "All hell broke loose and people were running everywhere. Several men ran into the women's bathroom."

Peterson returned to his trailer and told his wife that he just shot Chenoweth and that she should call Sheriff Marsh.

Former state trooper Mike Chenoweth was gunned down in his bar, the Lumberjack Tavern, in 1952 by an angry husband.

The events leading to the murder were provocative and sizzled the public's imagination. The tantalizing details wrapped the community in both horror and delight. Wanton sex, a jealous husband, and a stunning lady were all the ingredients needed to stroke the shameless curiosity of the locals.

Earlier on that fateful evening, near 9 p.m., Charlotte Peterson bid her husband goodbye, left their trailer and walked to the Lumberjack to get a six-pack of beer. At the bar, Charlotte decided to have some drinks and play shuffleboard with Chenoweth. Peterson took off her shoes to gain leverage at the table to the delight of the male patrons. Bud Wentzel said her behavior

Marquette resident Ken Goldsworthy revisited the Lumberjack Tavern in 2001 where he witnessed the Chenoweth murder 50 years earlier.

was considered "unladylike." The early 1950s was not Victorian in moral values, but by later standards Charlotte's behavior would not have been given a second thought.

After two and half hours in the bar, Peterson was ready to return home. According to her, Chenoweth offered her a ride, and at first she declined, but later agreed to his offer. According to her, he did not take her home, but instead pulled into a side road near the park and raped her. She said that she told Chenoweth that her husband would kill him if he found out. Chenoweth replied, "He doesn't have the guts. I'm not worried about him—he's just a sissy." She said she left the car with a flashlight and with George, her short-haired terrier, went back to the trailer.

Coleman noted the disheveled and bruised condition of his wife.

Charlotte said she was screaming and crying when she entered the trailer. This woke her sleeping husband. According to Coleman Peterson he noted the disheveled and bruised condition of his wife; her skirt was torn and her panties were missing. He asked her what happened and she told him. It took a half-hour for her to tell her husband. It was then that he incensed Peterson took out the rosary.

The murder trial was held in September 1952 at the opulent, Beaux-Arts Marquette County Court House. The elegant sandstone building constructed in 1904 sits on a knoll overlooking Marquette's picturesque harbor. The building's 26-foot solid granite Doric columns at the entrance stand as able sentries, jealously guarding the building's portal. Inside, a white marble staircase

The opulent Marquette County Court House where the Peterson murder trial took place and later became the site for the filming of a movie based on the trial.

gracefully sweeps up to the second floor. Impressive stained glass windows and a detailed cornice frieze provide an elegant backdrop to the stair landing. At the end massive dark-stained mahogany doors lead to the most imposing courtroom in Michigan's Upper Peninsula.

John Voelker, an Ishpeming attorney, and former district attorney, was hired to defend Peterson. Voelker had served for 14 years as district attorney, but was defeated in a 1948 election. He felt empty and forlorn after this defeat and had the feeling the community had conspired to ridicule and humiliate him. In retrospect, the defeat was a blessing in disguise. Had he continued as a prosecuting attorney, he would have been on the opposite side in the Chenoweth murder, and his great blockbuster novel based on this case, *Anatomy of Murder*, may have never been written.

John Voelker, an Ishpeming attorney, and former district attorney, was hired to defend Peterson.

Voelker was facing Edmund Thomas, his nemesis, and the upstart attorney who beat him in the last election. Leaving nothing to chance in this high-profile murder trial, the prosecution solicited weighty Lansing Assistant Attorney General Irving Beattie to assist in the case. For Voelker, the trial was fraught with both vindication and fear. If he won the case against his adversary, glory would be his, but if he lost there would be humiliation.

Peterson played into the insanity defense with deftness.

Voelker had a difficult case. He had a defendant whose killing of a bar owner was witnessed by bar patrons. Voelker realized the only workable defense would be insanity. It was a long shot, but if it worked, the most his client would have to serve would be a period of time in a mental hospital.

Peterson played into the insanity defense with deftness. He said he remembered going to the bar with his gun and seeing Chenoweth at the bar, but did not remember shooting him. The only way that he knew that he must have killed Chenoweth was when he got back to the trailer and discovered his gun was empty. To Voelker, Peterson's statements solidified the defense of temporary insanity. The insanity plea might just work.

Lieutenant Coleman Peterson in defending his wife's honor, took his Luger and sought revenge.

Voelker needed verification though, that a rape did occur. However, that didn't happen. A medical evaluation did not show any evidence of a rape. Voelker was searching for anything that could make a jury sympathize with Peterson—a man who was simply defending his wife's honor. Charlotte's black and blue eyes were convincing, but were they inflicted during a rape, or could her husband have done it in a fit a jealously? In addition, Peterson had a history of jealous rages when it came to his wife. If this were so, how could a defense attorney get around the crime not being premeditated? Voelker had an uphill battle.

Charlotte Peterson went to the tavern where she shed her shoes and provocatively played pool to the delight of the male patrons.

On September 15, the trial began with the prosecution charging first-degree murder. They contended that 40-50 minutes had elapsed between the time Peterson heard his wife's story and the time that he shot Mike Chenoweth. This, the prosecution argued, gave Peterson time to plan the murder—a clear case of premeditation.

Voelker, in his opening statement said, "The defense will show that the defendant was suddenly awakened, saw his wife in a dazed condition, sobbing, screaming, hysterical, her skirt ripped and her underpants missing; that his mind was in a turmoil...and that he decided to seek out Chenoweth and take him into custody...That he had legal right to go to the tavern, and...carry a loaded pistol; and that he was suffering from temporary insanity; that he was suffering from an irresistible impulse, and that he now has recovered." Voelker's phrase, "irresistible impulse," would become legendary in legal circles.

Peterson had a history of jealous rages when it came to his wife.

Tempers flared in courtroom exchanges between Voelker and Beattie. In one instance, Voelker objected to Beattie's manner and line of questioning. Voelker let the jury know that Beattie was a hired gun—a big city lawyer—and not one of their own. Beattie quickly shot back. "Just for the record, my home town is Marine City, Michigan, a smaller town than Marquette."

Ten days later, on September 25, after deliberating five hours, the jury of eleven men and one woman returned with a verdict of not guilty. Two Marquette physicians, Dr. Warren Lambert and Dr. Andrew Swinton, testified to Peterson's sanity and were satisfied that it was perfectly safe to have Peterson set free. Neither Lambert nor Swinton had psychiatric degrees.

John Voelker, the country lawyer with a homespun demeanor, just won his greatest court victory.

John Voelker, the country lawyer with a homespun demeanor, just won his greatest court victory.

To some, the verdict was a case of jury nullification—the prosecution had proved their case, but the jury chose to ignore the evidence and based their judgment on the position that Peterson was a man who was justified in defending his wife's honor.

The sensational 1952 murder trial quickly developed a life of its own. Voelker's novel *Anatomy of a Murder* was

Attorney John Voelker was hired to defend Coleman Peterson in what appeared to be an unwinable case; however, the "country lawyer" was not to be out dueled.

published in 1957, under the pen name of Robert Traver, and director Otto Preminger turned the best seller into a hit movie in 1959. Filmed in Marquette and its environs, the city basked in the glory of being the temporary "tinsel town." Although the murder occurred over 50 years ago, it is something that Marquette and Big Bay residents still talk about at coffee clutches and cocktail parties.

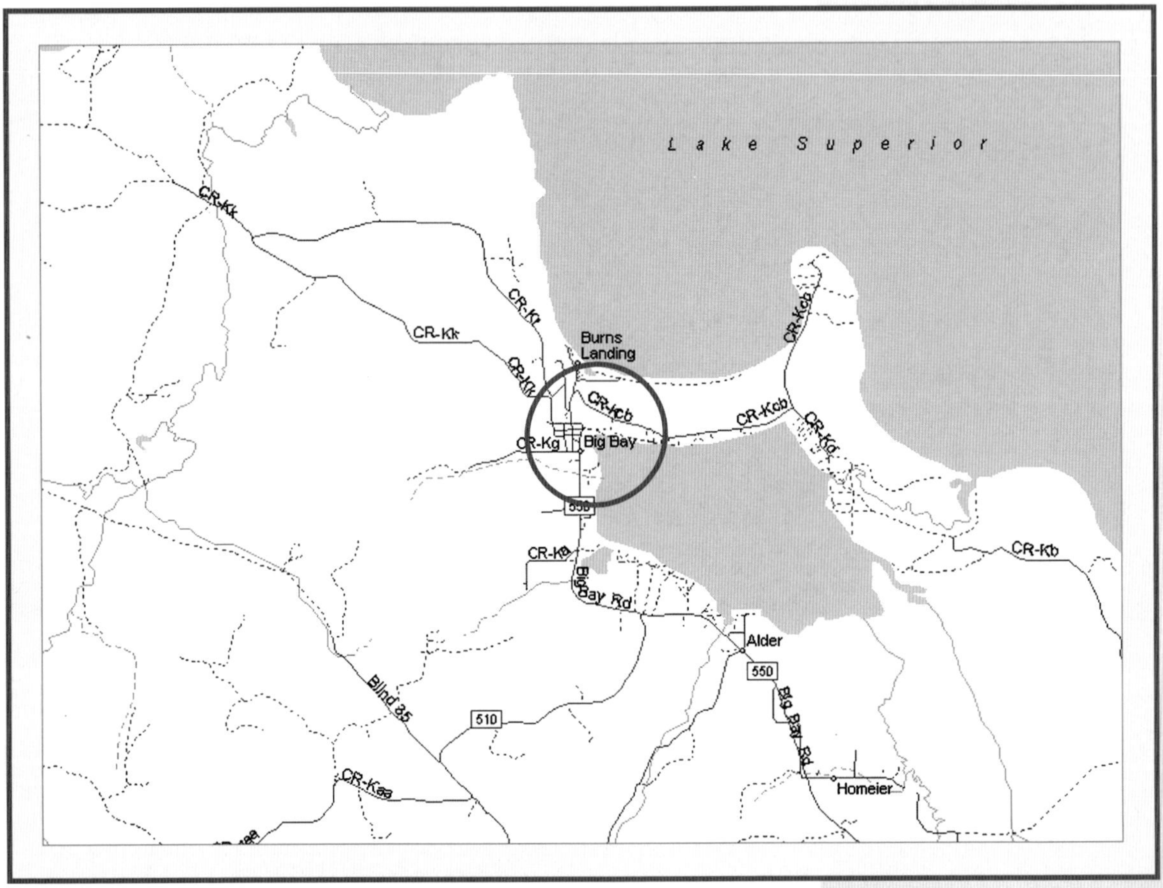

Big Bay nestled close to the shore of Lake Superior.

A DEATH ON WILDERNESS ROAD

In 1956, Patricia Burdick, an attractive second grade teacher in Grand Marais, was murdered by Marquette Prison parolee Leonard Lundberg

Grand Marais, is a quaint hamlet that at one time was a burgeoning fishing and lumber village.

Highway M-28 in Michigan's Upper Peninsula is a long, barren corridor of blacktop that winds its way across the north side of the isolated region. A particularly desolate and uninhabited stretch on this highway is from Seney to Munising. In that expanse there is one paved highway off of M-28 in Seney that heads north to Lake Superior's rugged shore. It is highway M-77, a 26-mile wilderness road that is columned by a lush forest of mixed hardwoods and evergreens.

At the terminal end of M-77, or the road to earth's end, is Grand Marais, a quaint hamlet that at one time was a burgeoning fishing and lumber village. The out-of-the-way village hugs the shoreline where a breakwater protects the town from Lake Superior's brutal, ripping winds that ravage the village on bitter-cold December days.

Summers, however, are idyllic. There aren't any theaters, box stores, or gambling casinos, to distract one from inhaling the summer stillness that satisfies tourists seeking solitude. Life pivots around outdoor activities.

In the summer and fall, fishing and hunting are the recreational pursuits, but in the winter, high school basketball games become the community's focal point. Fishing is still important in the lazy summer months, but now it is mostly left to tourists and local die-hards who seek fresh lake trout and whitefish. Grand Marais has the quiet rhythm of a community going about its business, impervious to the outside world. The extraordinary residents brave the stark winters and hard economic times, conditions that normally drive people to sunny retreats but here create a bond.

Patricia Burdick, an attractive 21-year-old Grand Marais teacher, was murdered near Seney after visiting her mother in Sault Ste. Marie.

The Grand Marais school has 90 students and seven teachers. The residents are proud of their diminutive but high quality school, which also serves as the focal point for community activities. For years, Friday night football games and neighborhood fish fries were about the most excitement one would find in the village. And that was just fine with the 350 year-round residents.

But all that changed on April 26,1956, when a teacher was found bludgeoned to death. The murder of attractive 21-year-old Patricia Burdick shocked the town's peaceful citizens and put them on notice that their secluded world was no longer safe from the violence of urbanized America.

Burdick, unlike most working women her age, did not have a car and depended on others to provide transportation for her weekend jaunts.

Burdick had been a first year grade school teacher for eight months. She was described as reserved and did little to draw attention. Her unassuming demeanor, though, did not shield her from predator and prison parolee, 35-year-old Leonard Lundberg.

On Sunday, April 22, Burdick returned from her weekend trek to her mother's, Eva Burdick in Sault Ste. Marie, a town 100 miles east of Grand Marais. Unlike most working women her age, she did not have a car and depended on others to provide transportation for her weekend jaunts. On that Sunday, William Dolozel, a Marquette resident who was transporting four girls from the Sault to Northern Michigan University in Marquette, offered Burdick a ride to Seney. She took the ride and was dropped off at the M-77 and M-28 intersection in Seney, after which Dolozel continued on to Marquette with his other passengers.

Burdick taught a first and second grade combination class in the Grand Marais K-12 School in 1956.

The Seney site on M-77 where Burdick was hitchhiking north to Grand Marais when she was picked up by prison parolee Leonard Lundberg.

A short time later, George Niemi and his wife stopped to pick up the hitchhiking Burdick, wearing a red jacket and khaki slacks. The Niemis were only going part of the way to Grand Marais; as a result, Burdick declined their ride offer, perhaps fearing that she would be stranded in a place with little traffic.

Marquette prison parolee Leonard Lundberg was visiting relatives in Seney the Sunday night that Burdick was there. Sometime after 8:30 he spotted the stranded Burdick hitchhiking and picked her up. En route to Grand Marais he pulled into a side road in the remote area with the intention of having sex with the young women, but she resisted. Lundberg then had a burst of anger, he retrieved a tire wrench from the car trunk and smashed in Burdick's skull. Then he left her clothed body under a pine tree with some brush and straw thrown over the corpse.

Marquette prison parolee Leonard Lundberg was visiting relatives in Seney the Sunday night that Burdick was there.

Lundberg then headed to Marquette and along the way deposited his bloody clothes in a ravine under a bridge near Munising. This was a critical mistake. In the pocket of his bloody clothes a laundry ticket with his name on it would be discovered.

The next day when Burdick didn't show up at work, school personnel immediately called her mother. Mrs. Burdick, suspecting something was wrong, immediately contacted the police.

The next day when Burdick didn't show up at work, school personnel immediately called her mother.

For the next two days, sheriff's deputies, state police, and conservation officers combed the woods in search of Burdick. Joining the search party of over 100 were lumbermen, villagers, and servicemen from nearby Kinchloe Air Force Base. A helicopter and two airplanes from the Civil Air Patrol augmented the ground search party. But the massive search was fruitless.

On the third day, Lundberg's bloody clothing was found. This was the first solid lead that investigators had, and it was a good one. A subsequent check on Lundberg found that he was a parolee from the Marquette Prison, and he was in Seney the previous weekend. A further assessment found that he did not report to work at Munising Wood Products that Monday. Red flags were popping up everywhere. With substantial evidence now in hand, the police went to Lundberg's home in Marquette to question him about Burdick. He denied that he knew anything about her. A subsequent examination of his car,

Grand Marais, a peaceful lakeside community of 350 residents, was shocked when in 1956 one of their school teachers was bludgeoned to death.

however, revealed fresh bloodstains. This along with verification that he was in Seney the night of Burdick's disappearance was enough to arrest him.

At first Lundberg told the police that the blood was from a deer that he struck with his car, and that he tried to put the deer carcass in the front seat. A bleeding deer in the front seat of the car? The police didn't buy his almost laughable explanation. They continued to confront him and soon he confessed to the murder of Patricia Burdick.

The following day, Lundberg directed the police to the isolated spot where he left her body. He agreed to take the police to the scene of the murder as long as he didn't have to get out of the car and look at her.

Lundberg agreed to take the police to the scene of the murder as long as he didn't have to get out of the car and look at her.

While lodged in the Schoolcraft County Jail and awaiting arraignment and trial, Lundberg attempted suicide. He slashed his arm with a piece of glass that he had hidden. The slash opened two large veins in his upper arm, causing profuse bleeding and then shock. He needed immediate medical attention and was transported to the Schoolcraft County Hospital, where he received two plasma transfusions and a pint of blood.

Lundberg said of his failed suicide attempt, "I guess I didn't succeed."

Schoolcraft Prosecutor William J. Sheahan said Lundberg's attempted suicide was phony, and that he was only trying to establish an insanity defense. However Lundberg had anticipated success in taking his life and left three letters. In one to a relative he wrote, "There was no reason for killing that girl, but sorrow won't bring her back."

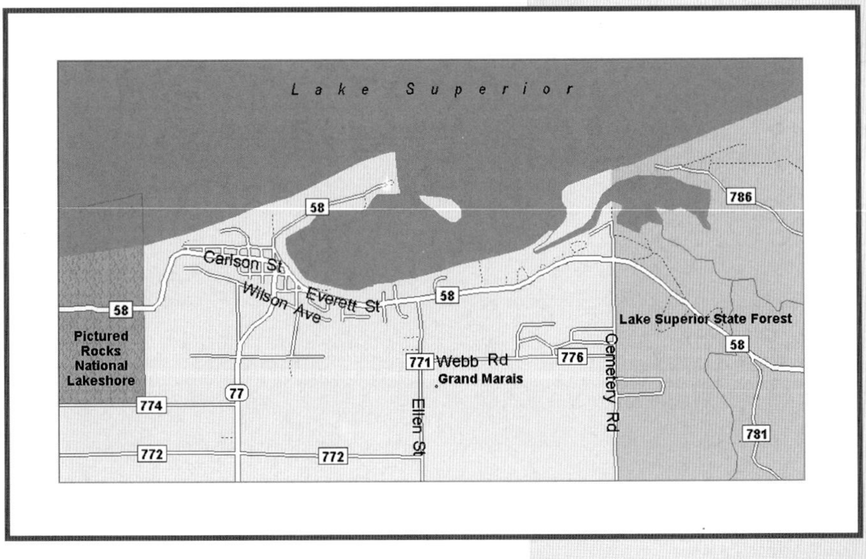

Map of Grand Marais on the south shore of Lake Superior.

Lundberg opted for a bench trial at the Schoolcraft County Court House. This meant there would not be a jury, and that Judge Nebel would decide Lundberg's guilt or innocence, and if guilty the length of his sentence. It was a swift trial lasting only two days. The charge was first-degree murder, but Lundberg protested the charge and said it should be second-degree. First degree necessitates premeditation and Lundberg said the murder was not premeditated but an "explosion of anger." Lundberg's assessment was legally sound; however, the prosecution and citizens were in no mood to entertain anything that may give Lundberg anything less than a life sentence. His court appointed attorney G.S. Johnson apparently did not contest the charge.

After serving 21 years in Marquette's prison, Lundberg was released in 1977 and moved to New York with his wife who he married while in prison. He died in 1990 just short of his 80th birthday.

One of the key witnesses for the prosecution was forensic expert Dr. Clarence E. Muehberger, who testified that the red hair fibers similar to those in the coat worn by Burdick when she was killed were found on a pair of Lundberg's blue trousers.

A guilty decision was a forgone conclusion. In administering the sentence, Judge Nebel said, "You are a waster both with yourself and the people around you" [sic]. When Nebel asked if he had anything to say, Lundberg responded, "The slaying was not premeditated, but done in a burst of anger." It didn't matter what he said, he was going to prison for life. Eva Burdick wept quietly in the courtroom as the guilty verdict was read.

Lundberg was sent to the Marquette Branch Prison to serve out his time. Guards who supervised Lundberg while he was in prison said he was a model prisoner and never gave them any trouble.

What became most remarkable is what Lundberg did while in prison. From being a burglar and murderer he became an astute legal scholar. In spite of the fact that he only had an eighth-grade education, he immersed himself in law and became a respected and serious legal advocate for other inmates. Other prisoners sought him out to prepare legal documentation for appeals or whatever legal advice they may have needed. Attorneys marveled at his competency, and many said that his lawyering skills were superior to some lawyers who were practicing law on the outside. If anyone reinvented himself for the better it was Leonard Lundberg.

What became most remarkable is what Lundberg did while in prison: he became an astute legal scholar.

In addition to working as a clerk in the prison store, Lundberg found time to become an ordained chaplain. When he was not busy clerking, lawyering, or serving the spiritual needs of other inmates he made quality jewelry that he sold in the prison gift shop.

His jewelry sideline led to outside contacts, one of those was Patricia Montresor, a woman from upstate New York who had polio and who was also a jeweler. She began corresponding with Lundberg while he was in prison. This eventually blossomed into a romance that led to a marriage that took place in the Marquette prison chapel in 1973. While in Marquette the new Mrs. Lundberg stayed in the convent of The Sisters of Saint Paul De Chartres. She remarked to resident nun Sister Mary Ann

The prison gift shop where inmate Leonard Lundberg sold his hand crafted jewelry and leather goods. The shop is no longer in operation.

Laurin, "I'm probably the only woman alive who spent her wedding night in a convent."

With a diligent effort by his wife and his attorney, Lundberg, after serving 21 years in prison, was released in 1977. Mrs. Lundberg attributed prayer as the single most important thing that made the parole happen. The couple left Marquette and moved to Brooklyn, New York. Later they moved to up-state New York. She saw her husband as a bright and caring man who after release from prison gave much time to charitable causes.

In 1999, Leonard Lundberg died in New York at the age of 79.

In Loving Memory
Leonard H. LundBerg
Feb. [illegible] 1920--Dec.18, 1999

"I asked God for all things that I might enjoy Life
He gave me Life, that I might enjoy all Things"

Fisherman, Airplane Pilot, Nurse, Carpenter, Welder,
Master Millright, Practical Joker, Storyteller,
Ferry Boat Pilot, Roller Skater (dancer), Ski Jumper,
Lumberjack, Boat Builder, Phlebotomist, , Hospice
Worker, Parachutist, Underwater Diver, Motorcyclist,
Member FGBMA, Coffee Lover, Dental Hygienist,
Leather Craftsman, Jewelry and Plastic Carver,
Cost Accountant, Prolific Letter Writer
Beloved Husband, Devoted Father, Loving Grandpa

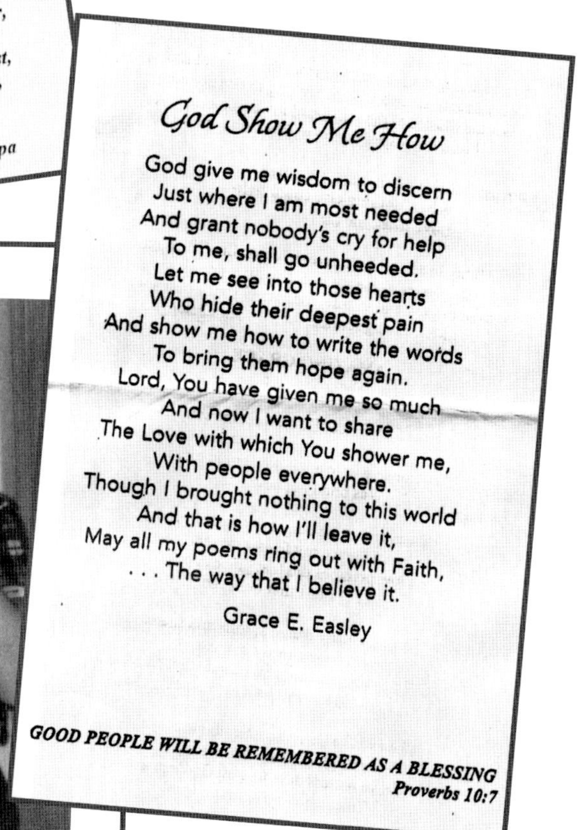
God Show Me How

God give me wisdom to discern
Just where I am most needed
And grant nobody's cry for help
To me, shall go unheeded.
Let me see into those hearts
Who hide their deepest pain
And show me how to write the words
To bring them hope again.
Lord, You have given me so much
And now I want to share
The Love with which You shower me,
With people everywhere.
Though I brought nothing to this world
And that is how I'll leave it,
May all my poems ring out with Faith,
. . . The way that I believe it.

Grace E. Easley

GOOD PEOPLE WILL BE REMEMBERED AS A BLESSING
Proverbs 10:7

The UNSOLVED SLASHING

The mutilated body of Paul Girard was found on a gravesite with his throat slit and over 40 gash wounds

Paul Girard died in the prime of his life (34) in 1988. He was murdered on a cold autumn night in Marquette's Presque Isle Park.

The mutilated body of Paul Girard, 34, was found lying face up, not far from Charlie Kawbawgam's grave at the east side of the Presque Isle Park in Marquette. Over 40 gashes mutilated his body and his throat had been slit. The pattern and number of wounds suggested that the killer was frenzied, stabbing over and over again. Evidence indicated that a struggle had taken place 15 to 30 feet from the body.

Girard had been murdered sometime after 3:30 a.m. on September 30, 1988.

An elderly woman had seen the body earlier but failed to report it, saying she thought it was a manikin, part of a college prank. Another passerby reported it to the police at 10:15 a.m.

Mechanically inclined Paul Girard graduated from Gwinn High School in 1971.

Little physical evidence was found at the scene. A jackknife near the body was determined to be Girard's, but it was not the murder weapon and didn't provide any clues. Girard's car was nearby in the Presque Isle marina parking lot. His car keys and wallet were never found. There was considerable blood, but it was all Girard's. The lack of evidence and no witnesses made the murder a nightmare to solve.

Then, the police received a break: Someone reported seeing a man between 20-24 years old wearing a dark jacket and tan pants walking down Lakeshore Boulevard at 4 a.m. the night of the crime. The same man, later identified as 5 foot 10 inches tall, with dark hair and a moustache, had been seen a second time that night further down the same street. Police quickly identified the suspect.

Interrogated at length, the suspect (whose name was never released) provided information, which the police felt that only someone at the scene could possibly know. His home and workplace were meticulously searched for evidence. But nothing was found.

Paul Girard lived in this modest two room tin building located on Division Street in South Marquette. Often drive-bys bellowed epithets at him in the middle of the night.

The Michigan State Police forensic laboratory evaluated hair fiber and blood samples taken from the murder site. Enlisting all possible resources, the Marquette police consulted with a University of Michigan forensic pathologist to review the skimpy evidence. All available department personnel were marshaled in what became the most extensive investigation in Marquette's Police Department history. Most non-violent police cases (bad checks, theft, etc.) were assigned to a single detective so the remaining detectives and officers could concentrate on the Girard case. More than a dozen detectives spent long hours trying to solve the murder. Marquette Police detective, Sal Sarvello, said the police followed up on over 200 tips, but with little success. The case was difficult to solve because of little physical evidence. Sarvello said, "It occurred in the middle of the night, so there's less physical evidence."

Drastic changes in behavior are not uncommon for someone who just committed a crime.

Sarvello believed that whoever committed the crime might have altered his behavior. Drastic changes in behavior are not uncommon for someone who just committed a crime. Sarvello said that perhaps his drinking increased, or that he quit his job.

Paul Girard's body was found not far from Charlie Kawbawgam's grave in Presque Isle Park in Marquette. The murderer was never found.

Detective Mike Angeli, who was on the city police force about a year when the murder occurred, said, "Because of Girard's gay lifestyle he was well known to the police. He was often victimized by those that opposed the way he lived."

To stimulate community responses for information a $2,000 reward was offered that authorities hoped would lead to an arrest. The reward was never collected.

The police theorized the murder was linked to Girard's life-style. He was openly gay and was known to police, often as a victim. Neighbors near his home on South

Paul Girard was buried in the Gwinn cemetery in October 1988. Twenty years later the police are still optimistic that the killer will be found.

Mary said, "We were just a normal family and didn't see ourselves any different from other families."

Division Street reported guests coming and going at all hours. They also heard epithets shouted at his home from passing cars. Authorities felt the murder was a result of "gay bashing." In 1984, there were four confirmed gay murders in the state of Michigan. Some crime experts felt someone who had repressed homosexual desires may have committed the murder.

Girard grew up in a close-knit family farm near Carlsend, a small settlement 20 miles south of Marquette. His parents, Ernest and Adeline, raised beef cattle and had vegetable gardens in the idyllic setting. Although farming was not the primary source of income, it did provide the family with meat and vegetables. Girard's sisters, Sue (Girard-Jackson) and Mary (Stiles) described their upbringing as typical in rural Upper Michigan. Mary said, "We were just a normal family and didn't see ourselves any different from other families." While growing up Paul, often helped his father at a sawmill that was on the property. Sue and Mary said Paul was industrious and his father was pleased when Paul labored with him at the mill.

Charlie Kawbawgam lies in stoic silence just feet below where Paul Girard was murdered. The secrets of what happened on the night of the murder may well be in the possession of the Ojibwa spirits.

The sisters had a close attachment to their brother. Sue said, "Paul was a great brother and he would give anyone the shirt off his back." As a child he loved to play with cars and enjoyed tinkering with anything mechanical. This interest served him well in adulthood. At B&D, a rental and sales shop in South Marquette, he repaired small engines. It was the ideal setting for using his mechanical skills. Girard could take an old and broken lawn mower and have it purring in no time.

Sue and Mary said Paul was a joy to be around and this was particularly true when they shared Sunday dinner. Mary remarked, "He was witty and with an infectious laugh; he was fun to be around." The sisters had a deep affection for their brother and view what happened to him over 20 years ago a travesty to which there is no closure.

Months passed and then years—the trail got colder.

Months passed and then years—the trail got colder. No new evidence has been uncovered and police activity diminished, but the case remained an active, unsolved murder.

Speculation is that the murderer's identity is known, but police lack evidence to bring the case to the county prosecutor. The suspect, police say, has since moved out of the area.

Below the surface of the murder site, Ojibwa Chief Charlie Kawbawgam rests in stoic silence. Two decades later, after that cold autumn night, the cutthroat is still at large, enjoying what life has to offer. Maybe periodically he glances uneasily over the shoulder, unsure of when the police may come knocking.

An unsolved murder always irks and frustrates law enforcement, but unsolved murders are common.

An unsolved murder always irks and frustrates law enforcement, but unsolved murders are common. Forty-eight percent of all murders in the United States are not solved. In a recent year in San Francisco, only 26 per-cent of the city's murders were solved. The Marquette police are unhappy that they did not bring Girard's murderer to justice, but they are not alone in failing to find a killer with only minimal evidence.

What left the Marquette police most exasperated was they almost had the killer in their grasp, but lack of evidence prevented an arrest and trial. Twenty years later it still sticks in the department's craw.

Mike Angeli, Marquette's Chief of Police, was a one-year rookie on the police force when the Girard murdered occurred. Angeli said, "The Girard murder is still an open case and we will continue to follow any new leads."

The sensational headlines that dominated the papers only told part of the Paul Girard story. He was more than what the headlines blared; he was a decent human being who worked hard and had a loving family and caring friends.

Sal Sarvello, who was a detective on the case, said, "I believe there are at least one or two people in this area that still have knowledge of the murder. It hasn't been put away and forgotten."

Assistant prosecutor Peter Plummer, who worked the case, said, "Sometimes it takes years to develop evidence. Hurrying these cases does more harm than good." Perhaps there still is a chance the "night slasher" will be caught.

PORTAGE CANAL CARNAGE

David Allen Goodreau, a church going man of God, had a secret—a dark secret

Houghton—(June 26,1991) a decomposing female body was found by a fisherman in the Portage Canal yesterday. The canal is a waterway that cuts through the Keweenaw Peninsula, with both entry and exit on Lake Superior. Her nude, decaying body, had been floating in the waterway for 15 days. The U.S. Coast Guard recovered her body from the canal after receiving a tip from a fisherman. She was identified as Kathy Nankervis, 20, a L'Anse resident and the mother of two young children. She had cerebral palsy and was moderately disabled.

Kathy Nankervis & Jodi Watts were murdered in the early 1990s by a prominent social worker.

Houghton—(January 21, 1992) On a frosty winter night in Houghton, the body of Michigan Technological University (MTU) coed, Jodi Watts, 19, was discovered in the early hours

Watts had been raped and stabbed in a parking ramp near the Subway restaurant in downtown Houghton.

of the morning. Watts had been raped and stabbed in a parking ramp near the Subway restaurant in downtown Houghton. Watts, bloody and near death, managed to crawl in the snow 150 feet to a nearby, street where a passerby on a bike discovered her. The biker covered her partial-clad body and then reported the incident to police. When the police arrived, Watts was still alive, but died shortly after being transported to the Portage View Hospital.

Attractive Jodi Watts, a former high school track star and nighttime jogger, was raped and murdered in Houghton on a cold winter evening.

He never drank; he never smoked; he raised two delightful children; he faithfully attended church; he had a job that helped others; and he had amiable chats with the neighbors. But David Allen Goodreau had everybody fooled—he was a killer; he would kill and then kill again. Kathy Nankervis and Jodi Watts were victims of the mild-mannered and unassuming David Allen Goodreau, a state social worker and caring father from Hancock.

He hardly looked or acted like a serial rapist and killer. A spiritual man, Goodreau and his wife attended the Calvary Baptist Church and played softball in the church league. He had been employed by the state since 1978, and he was one of two field workers in the Houghton County area.

He hardly looked or acted like a serial rapist and killer.

Goodreau graduated from Houghton High School in 1973 where he was an honors student and excelled in basketball and golf. He then attended Michigan Technological University (MTU) where he obtained a baccalaureate degree in forestry. Shortly after graduation, he married and left the area. He held jobs in Aurora, Ill. and in downstate Michigan before returning to the Upper Peninsula. But Goodreau had a dark side that he hid for years. He buried his demonic nature, but

The downtown parking ramp in Houghton where the body of Jodi Watts was found in the early morning hours of January 21, 1992.

The Lily Pond area of the portage Canal where the body of Kathryn Nankervis was found by a fisherman on June 26, 1991.

eventually his sinister side emerged.

Kathy Nankervis stood 5'2" and weighed 115 pounds. She was a Social Security recipient, the mother of two children, and a client of Goodreau's. He abducted Nankervis from her home on June 12, 1991 after peeking through her window and seeing her sleeping naked on a couch. He entered her house and bound her with duct tape and then took to her to the Lily Pond area of the Portage Canal. Goodreau said that he drowned her in the Lilly Pond, but her body resurfaced. He took her out of the water and repeatedly stabbed her, assuming that a release of air in her body would allow her to sink. He did not, however, puncture her stomach and the gasses that it contained, which later raised her to the surface. Two weeks later, a fisherman discovered her floating body in the canal.

Goodreau buried his demonic nature, but eventually his sinister side emerged.

When Nankervis was first reported missing by her family, authorities were not sure if they had a missing person case, a homicide, or a suicide. Friends reported that Nankervis was recently depressed about having two children and little social life. She had cerebral palsy that resulted in slurred speech and an awkward gait. The discovery of her body, however, made it quite clear to the police what they had on their hands.

In January of 1992, just seven months after the Nankervis murder, Goodreau struck again. Jodi Watts was an attractive and popular coed on MTU's campus. The former high school track star was studying biology at the university, where her father was an administrator.

While jogging in the late night hours on a cold winter evening, Goodreau grabbed Watts near the Houghton municipal parking garage, adjacent to the Subway shop on Shelden Avenue. He hauled her further into the garage where he raped and brutally stabbed her. Goodreau suspected that she recognized him and he knew that he would have to kill her to avoid being caught.

Goodreau, if nothing else, had audacity; he murdered Watts within 100 feet of the police station.

Goodreau, if nothing else, had audacity; he murdered Watts within 100 feet of the police station.

This was the second murder in the area in a seven-month period and sent shock waves though the community. Women in the area began locking their doors, something they hadn't always done before the Watts and Nankervis murders.

MTU took quick action in the wake of the Watts slaying. Reluctantly, the university president authorized campus police to carry firearms, feeling it was imperative in order to provide added security on campus. The community was now on high alert.

Grief and shock emanated from the Houghton area with the slaying of Jodi Watts. Pastor of the Good Shepherd Lutheran Church, Chris Heavner, said, "...She was a

Michigan Technological University where Jodi Watts was studying biology and where her father was an administrator.

good person. Bubbly, smiling, didn't let things get her down." Jodi's high school friend, Shannon Hanson, after learning of the murder, said, "I just cried and cried and thought why her...." Steve Markey, a vice-president of Caesar's Pizza in Houghton said, "Jodi did an outstanding job for us, she was great with customers. This is such a terrible tragedy."

Little Caesars Pizza in Houghton where Jodi Watts worked at the time of her murder.

The local Kiwanis Club, in hopes that it would lead to the killer's arrest, offered a $10,000 reward.

Police chief Ralph Raffaelli of Houghton said that these murders were the first in over 25 years in the county.

The FBI was enlisted to assist in solving the double homicide.

With few clues, both murders went unsolved for a longer period than the local police would have liked. As a result, the FBI was enlisted to assist in solving the double homicide. Like others before, an FBI profiler felt that the two murders might be related, only because it was unlikely that you would have two murderers killing at the same time in a sparsely populated area. In addition, the profiler said the perpetrator was probably physically strong, hated women, and was most likely a local resident.

Investigators chased down 500 leads over a 30-state area, but still came up with nothing until June 24, 1993, when a Hancock woman reported a break-in at her apartment at

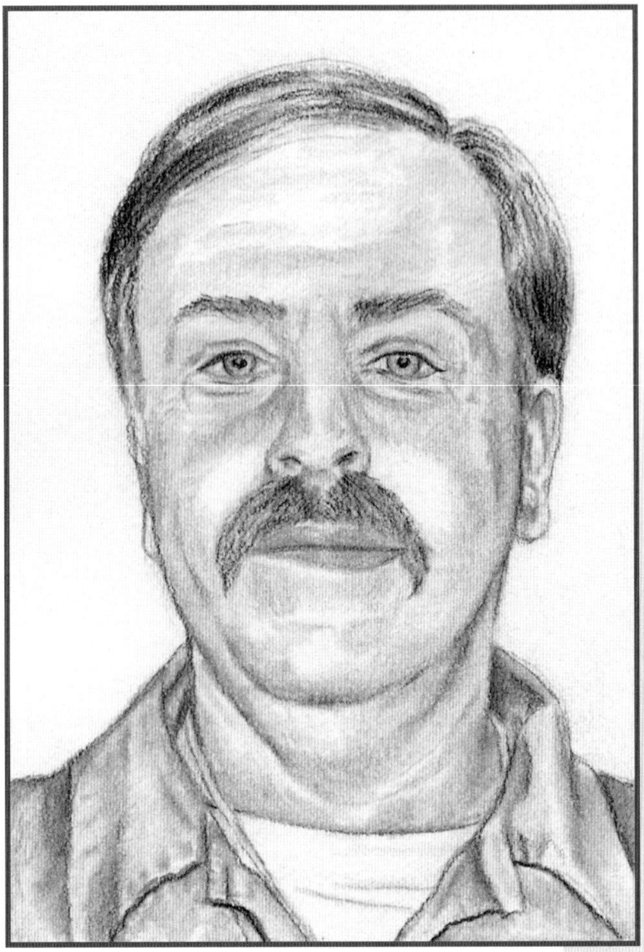

David Allen Goodreau, a Houghton County social worker and a religious man, murdered Jodi Watts and Kathryn Nankervis in the early 1990s.

2:30 a.m. They didn't know it at the time, but that break-in would unravel the Nankervis and Watts murders.

The police quickly responded to the forced entry and found Houghton social worker David Goodreau near the site of the apartment. Goodreau was immediately arrested and within a short time, much to the investigator's surprise, he confessed to the murders. Goodreau's wife and children were at a bible study camp at the time of the apartment break-in.

They play one tune and dance to another.

John Clarke

For his defense, Goodreau hired Marquette attorney Mark Wisti. With Goodreau already having confessed to the murder, Wisti was limited in his options as to a defense strategy. An insanity defense appeared to be the most plausible choice. Insanity is difficult to prove under

"We had a beautiful confession, there was no chance of acquittal."

Prosecutor Douglas Edwards

the best conditions. Few lawyers advocate using a mental illness argument because it is rarely successful and extensive psychiatric evaluations are necessary.

Goodreau's initial exam by the state did not help his position and he was declared competent to stand trial. The defense then had a second psychiatric examination conducted by a Marquette psychologist. This exam refuted the findings of the first psychological assessment. As a result a third exam was conducted, and it affirmed his sanity.

Prosecutor Douglas Edwards said, "We had a beautiful confession, there was no chance of acquittal. The man claims to be religious and he thought it [pleading guilty] was the right thing to do."

The historic Houghton County Court House where David Goodreau pleaded guilty in the 12th Circuit Court to the murders of Jodi Watts and Kathryn Nankervis.

Goodreau pleaded guilty and had a bench trial in Houghton. A bench trial does not have a jury, and the judge makes a ruling on guilt or innocence and determines the sentence. During the trial, Goodreau serenely described the killing of Nankervis and Watts; in his discourse, he was relaxed and indifferent. At the end of the trial, Judge Garfield asked Goodreau if he had reflected on the charges. Goodreau responded, "I felt I was influenced by satanic forces at the time of the crimes."

James Lassila was a co-worker and a social worker who shared an office in Hancock with Goodreau. He lived about a mile from Goodreau, their children often played together, and the men frequently carpooled to work. Lassila was incredulous when he heard about Goodreau's murders. He said, " We never saw this coming because he was so religious. When I was with him he was never anything but a gentleman. He never seemed like a violent person."

Goodreau's wife spoke with skepticism at the arrest of her husband. She said, "I knew he had been arrested, but that's not Dave." Goodreau excelled in keeping his hideous side well hidden—unbelievably, even from his wife.

Goodreau excelled in keeping his hideous side well hidden—unbelievable, even from his wife.

Those who knew him said that he was an upstanding member of the community and no different from themselves. Mitch Lake, news director for WMPL-AM said, "He didn't come across as anything but a perfect upright citizen…friendly, soft-spoken." Goodreau at times was on the radio answering questions about Social Security on a local call-in talk show. Why Goodreau raped and murdered is not known. Most people view a murderer and rapist as just plain evil, or at best a psychopathic lunatic.

Was Goodreau responding to Darwinian logic and was driven by a biological imperative to pass on his genes? Or was he committing these atrocious acts because he hated women and wanted to punish them? Were they acts of a man who was avenging a humiliation that he experienced earlier from a woman? Or was it a power move to show his dominance over women? All of these speculations are open to debate, as his confession did not provide any definitive conclusion.

In rural Upper Peninsula, rape occurs as it does in any metropolitan area, just with less frequency due to the sparse population. Data gathered by the Women's Safety Education Group has stated that one out of every four women on college campuses will be either raped or assaulted with the intent to rape. They state further that only five percent of all college rapes are reported, and that only three out of every 100 rapists are convicted. Tragically, Jodi Watts was one of these appalling statistics.

David Goodreau was sentenced to life in prison and is serving his time in the Straits Correctional Facility in Michigan. He has much time to pray now.

"Everyone who does evil hates the light, and does not come to the light, lest his deeds should be exposed."

Jesus

SPOUSAL-ASSASSIN

Bruce Moilanen attempted to disguise his wife's death as a hunting accident

Bruce Moilanen on August 15, 1993, was convicted of murdering his wife. While jailed, Moilanen failed in an attempted escape. He was sentenced to life in prison.

Ontonagon is a reposeful village located on the shores of Lake Superior in the northwest corner of Michigan's Upper Peninsula. In the winter the hamlet is subjected to driving blizzards when northwest winds howl off Lake Superior and drop several feet of snow. Only the courageous venture out on these stormy days; but they love it. On warm summer days refreshing lake breezes sweep the shoreline and cool the lakeside village. It has the best of both worlds.

Not much happens in this peaceful town. Main Street has a sprinkling of watering holes visited by the locals as well as a few mom-and-pop stores. And in the summer months, tourists visit the quaint village.

Bruce and Judy Moilanen were from Ontonagon, but made their home in

Judy Moilanen's parents lived on Cherry Lane Road, a short residential road off M-38, just east of Ontonagon and not far from where Judy was ambushed.

Marquette. They often visited their parents who still resided in the village. This was particularly true on holidays.

On November 29, 1992, two days after Thanksgiving, the village solitude was shattered when an unheard-of event occurred—one of their own was murdered. Charismatic Judy Moilanen was found dead a short distance from her parents' home on Cherry Lane in rural Ontonagon. Her heart was ripped in half by a 30-06 rifle bullet. Finding Judy's body in the woods was unexpected, but something that could be explained. It was hunting season and an errant bullet that missed its target could have easily traveled beyond its quarry and inadvertently struck Moilanen. It was the time of year when blaze orange is fashionable and accidental shootings are not uncommon.

At 1:30 on a Sunday afternoon, Judy took her five dogs out for a walk. Nearing dusk, she had not returned.

At 1:30 on a Sunday afternoon, Judy took her five dogs out for a walk. Later in the day and nearing dusk, Judy had not returned, and her mother, Mary Ann Blake, was starting to worry. In typical mother discomfort, Mary Ann took a brief walk in the surrounding woods in hopes of finding Judy, but didn't have any luck. She returned to the house and asked Bill Dorvinan, a visiting neighbor, to search with her. It was getting dark and it was not like Judy to be wandering in the woods at dusk. Her dogs were found, but Judy was nowhere to be seen.

They kept searching and spotted what appeared to be a body lying across a remote, sodden trail. Dorvinan and

Blake cautiously approached the motionless form. They were horrified at their discovery; it was Judy Moilanen. Her feet were in a pool of water. Dorvinan turned her over and examined her blood-covered chest; she was dead. Mary Ann Blake shrieked in horror.

Judy Moilanen left her parents house in November 29, 1992, and took her dogs for a walk down a dense trail that ran parallel with Cherry Lane. It was the last time anyone saw her alive.

Judy Moilanen was born and raised in Ontonagon by religious parents. She had a normal upbringing in rural Upper Michigan. She loved the outdoors, and was a skilled downhill skier and spent considerable time at nearby Porcupine Mountain Ski Hill, where she met her future husband, Bruce Moilanen.

They began a courtship that blossomed into marriage in June 1978. Judy's mother, Mary, was not enamored with her daughter marrying Bruce, but there was little she could do. Judy attended Northern Michigan University in Marquette and after graduation went to work at Marquette General Hospital. She was employed as an assistant to the hospital administrator, and by all accounts she was a valuable and well-liked employee.

Bruce Moilanen also grew up in Ontonagon and graduated from the local high school. His high school career was unremarkable, and the only evidence that he attended the school is a lone graduation picture. He attended Northern

Bruce and Judy Moilanen both attended Ontonagon High school. The only place that Bruce appears in the yearbook was his 1973 senior picture. Judy was two years behind him in high school.

Michigan University and earned certification as an emergency medical technician. He was eventually employed by the EMS Department at Marquette General Hospital. His employment record was far from stellar. He was often late, and at times he failed to show up. He was not well-liked by other employees, nor by most who encountered him; he grated on nearly everyone. Whether he was aware of how unpleasant other people perceived him is uncertain. Shortly after Judy's death he was fired by the hospital. He let others believe that he quit the hospital, and that within a short period of time he would soon be wealthy.

Bruce and Judy Moilanen were employed at Marquette General Hospital. He was an emergency medical technician, while she was a secretary in the administrative division.

Any death by firearms is investigated by the police. The Moilanen case was no exception. It appeared Judy's death was just one of those unfortunate hunting accidents, but a police investigation would have to substantiate that prior to certifying the cause of death.

State Police crime investigator Bob Ball from the Calumet State Police post was the lead detective in the shooting, and was ably assisted by Lt. Richard Goad and Sergeant Don Poupore of the Marquette post. In spite of these state police posts being in the remote Upper Peninsula, where few murders occur, these officers were highly skilled and determined.

The Moilanen home in Beaver Grove near Marquette. Bruce Moilanen attempted to kill his wife in the home in what were "staged accidents." He failed in two attempts.

Examining the crime scene at first yielded little information. There wasn't any forensic evidence—no gun, no bullets, no fingerprints, and no DNA. What Ontonagon Sheriff Tom Corda observed, however, was a bullet blaze on a tree not far from where the shooting occurred. But no bullet or shell casing was found near the tree. The police then sought the services of Dan Castle, an Ontonagon mine employee, who had a hobby of searching for hidden treasures with a metal detector. Castle repeatedly scanned the site, but failed to find a bullet or a shell casing. Undaunted, Castle tried an unusual and creative method to find a bullet. He took a slingshot with marbles and fired them at the tree. Castle then observed where the marbles ricocheted. Over and over again he searched the ground where the marbles had fallen and found nothing—finally his luck changed. Not far from the tree, he unearthed a foliage-covered 30-06 caliber bullet. At last the police had something to work with.

A further investigation found that in the months prior to his wife's death, Moilanen had been making overtures to other women.

In cases of a spouse death the partner is always investigated. When a woman is murdered, 57 percent of the time either a husband or someone who knew her intimately is responsible. Red flags surfaced early in the Moilanen investigation.

One of the first things to ascertain was the time of death. Forensic evidence placed the time of death about 3 p.m., with a moderate open window at both ends. Bruce Moilanen easily established his whereabouts earlier in the day and also for later that day, but he had difficulty verifying where he was at this time.

In cases of a spouse death the partner is always investigated.

Investigators and others noted little remorse in Moilanen, and when there was sorrow, it looked contrived. A further investigation found that in the months prior to his wife's death, Moilanen had been making overtures to other women. Gayle Lampinen, a nurse at Portage Hospital, and Lee Ann Wsysocki, a Marquette resident and an employee at Marquette General Hospital, were the recipients of Moilanen's gratuitous attention. Wsysocki was a single parent raising a child and a good friend of Judy Moilanen. Neither Wsysocki nor Lampinen had any interest in Bruce Moilanen and considered him an annoyance. Regardless of the rebuffs he received from the women, he persistently contacted them.

The Moilanen murder trial was held in the Ontonagon County Courthouse on November 19, 1993.

The more the police investigated, the more it appeared that this was more than a hunting accident—and the evidence was clearly pointing at Bruce Moilanen. He knew the investigation was zeroing in on him and he complained the police were harassing him. He continued to proclaim his innocence. Moilanen balked at taking a polygraph test. Arrangements were made several times for a lie-detector evaluation, but Moilanen never showed up or canceled just prior to the exam.

Finally, he took the test on April 23, with predictable result—he failed. Although not admissible in court, the results further convinced the detectives of Moilanen's guilt and increased the pressure on him. They continued to prod him when they told him they knew that he committed the murder. A broken man, Moilanen finally confessed to killing his wife. He was then jailed and a trial date set.

Prior to his trial, Moilanen attempted an escape from the Ontonagon County Jail, when he threw a powdery substance into a corrections officer's eyes and face. Moilanen then fled the jail to a nearby wooded area. Within a half hour he was spotted on a dirt road and was pursued by the Ontonagon police. Moilanen did not give up without a fight. Gerald Kitzman, Ontonagon County Sheriff, said, "He never really gave up. We had to tackle him and bring him down."

The Moilanen trial began in Marquette on November 19, 1993; it lasted until December 15th. Prosecuting attorney Beth Paczesny, only 26 years of age, presented the case against Moilanen, while renowned attorney Tom Casselman was the defense attorney. Casselman's court presence is frequently abrasive and confrontational, while Paczesny's demeanor is low-key. As a neophyte prosecutor trying her first big case, she must have felt somewhat intimidated by experienced and tenacious Casselman. But if she was she didn't show it. Paczesny held her own and methodically presented her case.

Paczesny presented evidence that Bruce Moilanen had both motive and opportunity. She traced the acquisition of a 30-06 rifle to Moilanen's ownership, a weapon he acquired from a friend. She provided evidence as to his insolvency, and how he would receive over $300,000 in death benefits should his wife die an accidental death. Also, Paczesny pointed out that he was unable to account for his whereabouts at the time of his wife's death. The suspected love interests Moilanen had in Lampinen and Wsysocki was frosting on the case. Most damning,

Paczesny presented evidence that Bruce Moilanen had both motive and opportunity.

Moilanen showed no emotion at the verdict. He impassively stared ahead.

however, was Moilanen's confession to Bob Ball. The defense would have a difficult time explaining this. Casselman discredited the confession as one that was extracted from a tired and besieged defendant who would have confessed to anything to end the interrogation.

When the prosecution rested it was Casselman's turn to present the defense case. He subpoenaed 29 witnesses and the trial was expected to take another week. Casselman, however, surprised everyone, when he was asked by Judge Gotham to present his case. Casselman replied, "The defense rests." Even Judge Gotham was taken aback at this turn of events. Up to this point, Casselman's case consisted largely of attacking prosecutor witnesses. This was how it would remain.

Ontanogan is peaceful community of 2,000 that hugs the shore of Lake Superior. The quiet village was abuzz in late 1993 when the Bruce Moilanen murder trial was the talk of the town.

After six and one-half hours the jury reached a verdict. Court clerk Julienne Takala, in a voice quivering, read the verdict: *"Bruce Robert Moilanen guilty of first degree premeditated murder."*

Moilanen showed no emotion at the verdict. He impassively stared ahead. When he killed his wife a year earlier, he sealed his fate. He would now spend the remainder of his life housed in the Marquette Prison with no possibility of parole. Ironically, his prison residence was just two miles from the home where he once lived in freedom.

DELUSIONAL DEFENDANT *Gets* LIFE SENTENCE

Nathan Hanna, a motor route driver for the "Sault Evening News," gunned down a colleague at work

> *The behavior of the insane is merely sane behavior, a bit exaggerated and distorted.*
>
> *Aldous Huxley*

> They were saying, like I said, bondage and putting people in slavery and for sexual—people getting—okay, and then they loaded up and then they would get in debt to these people and then they would turn around and these people would take them over to a place across the sea where the main islands are over there. Then once they got them over there they had no rights as a citizen of the United States so they—turned them into bond slaves. Then they came back here. There are people back here that was already set up that if they got out of line or something they would work like the Mafia and they kill them if they didn't do what they did.

That was the incoherent rambling of Nathan Hanna at his murder trial on July 23, 1998, in Sault Ste. Marie. Hanna's attorneys were pursuing an insanity defense for the man who had shot one of his colleagues while at work at the *Sault Evening News.* The prosecution, however, refuted the insanity plea and charged Hanna with first-degree murder.

On a warm day in July, Hanna, a motor route driver for the *Evening News*, calmly approached *News* employee and circulation manager Anthony Gillespie in the newsroom. He then unleashed two shotgun blasts at Gillespie, killing him almost instantly. Richard Beadle, an advertising manager for the Sault paper, whose desk was near Gillespie's, witnessed the homicide. Beadle said he observed Hanna enter the room with a 12-gauge shotgun and approach Gillespie's desk. Beadle said he didn't give it much thought as Hanna made small talk with him as he went by.

Nathan Hanna, 39, was convicted of murdering Anthony Gillespie, 48, in July 1998. He was sent to the Riverside Correctional Facility in Ionia. Hanna's case was appealed and in December 2005 he was granted a new trial.

A gun brought to work would send shivers down the spine of most office workers, but this was the Upper Peninsula where hunting is the national sport, and someone proudly bringing a new shotgun to work to show co-workers would not be considered unusual. However, this was not the case with Hanna. Within a few moments Beadle heard a shot and saw Gillespie fall to the floor. Beadle said Hanna then raised the gun and fired a second time, hitting Gillespie in the face. Another observer was receptionist Diane Glaz. Glaz said, "I first heard shots go off and I looked up and saw body parts flying though the air; I was terrified." According to Beadle, Hanna then looked at him and another employee and walked out of the front of the building slowly and deliberately.

After shooting Gillespie, Hanna left the newsroom and hid in the woods for three days. Following an exhaustive three-day search, Hanna was finally located on Baker Side Road, just off Three Mile Road. He did not surrender easily. When the police spotted a muttering Hanna walking down the rural road and carrying a gun, they commanded him to stop. Hanna, indifferent to their commands, turned around and fired at the police. Three officers then returned fire, striking Hanna three times, in his chest, shoulder, and leg. Hanna was seriously injured and was immediately taken to the War Memorial Hospital in the Sault where he underwent seven hours of surgery.

Three officers then returned fire, striking Hanna three times, in his chest, shoulder, and leg.

During Hanna's confinement in the hospital he confessed to the killing of Anthony Gillespie. Hanna's attorney, Elizabeth Church, attempted to have the hospital confession thrown out on the grounds of his physical and mental condition at the time. She also contended that he was deprived of council when she was not provided immediate access to him the day he confessed. In addition, she said he was not properly "Mirandized" (read his rights). The court rejected both defense motions and allowed the confession to be admitted at the trial. The court also said Hanna was properly read his rights. The confession would later provide Hanna legitimacy in requesting a retrial.

The prosecution charged Hanna with first-degree murder. Judge Lambros gave the jury instructions to an open murder charge. Under the open murder charge, the jury could consider six options: not-guilty, first-degree murder, second-degree murder, guilty but mentally ill, not-guilty but insane, or manslaughter. Church agreed that her client committed the murder, and sought a conviction of-not guilty but insane. She was convinced that he is delusional and met the insane criteria. Church said every mental health professional that came into contact with Hanna said he was not competent to stand trial. She said Hanna knew the killing was illegal, but not that it was morally wrong.

Using an insanity defense is dubious at best, and most lawyers know this. It is used in less than one percent of all murder cases, and only one-fourth of those are successful.

The Sault Evening News **building on Arlington Street in Sault Ste. Marie is the site of the murder of circulation manager Anthony Gillespie by Nathan Hanna, a contract motor carrier.**

Insanity as a legal term differs markedly from a psychiatric definition.

There are many problems associated with the insanity defense. First, definitions of insanity vary from state to state and the federal judiciary. Secondly, many of the statutes are confusing and difficult to understand. Furthermore, it is difficult for lay people to make a decision on insanity when attorneys, psychiatrists, and judges cannot agree on what constitutes insanity. Insanity as a legal term differs markedly from a psychiatric definition. One can be psychotic yet be legally sane. To add to the confusion, both the prosecution and defense solicit experts that support their opposing positions.

In the broadest legal terms, insanity is defined by being able to tell right from wrong. In the Hanna case, it was determined by the court that he could tell right from wrong, even though at times his jumbled rambling speech was clearly delusional. Investigators interviewing Hanna felt that he knew he had done something wrong. Prosecutors contended that hiding in the woods for three days substantiated that he knew he did something wrong.

The murder trial began on July 25,1999, and ended three days later. Hanna testified that he believed Gillespie to be the anti-Christ, and the deity had demanded him to kill

Gillespie in order to save the world. The trial brimmed with psychiatric testimony, but little of it made an impact on the jury. The prosecution had a parade of witnesses, most testifying to the events of the day of the murder and the subsequent arrest. Much of this testimony was superfluous, as the defense did not question the mechanics of the murder; they were more concerned about Hanna's state of mind at the time of the slaying.

Gillespie's three children, who had contact with Hanna, said Hanna was not mentally disturbed. Church considered the children's testimony prejudicial.

The jury of nine men and three women deliberated for five hours and arrived at a verdict: Hanna was declared guilty but mentally ill. It was a compromise verdict between guilty, and not-guilty but insane. Observers felt that the jury wanted a conviction that would ensure Hanna would not be set free.

Hanna was sentenced to life without parole. He would be confined to a psychiatric prison with no possible release. Hanna's attorney sought and failed to get the insanity conviction and not the mentally ill conviction. If Hanna had received the insanity conviction he could have been released upon a full recovery.

At the sentencing hearing, Judge Lambros said it was within the jury's right to reject the expert's opinions that Hanna was legally insane. The jury rejected psychiatric and psychological evaluations that concluded Hanna was not competent to stand trial.

The jury rejected psychiatric and psychological evaluations that concluded Hanna was not competent to stand trial.

At his sentencing hearing Hanna said, "I'd like to say I'm sorry to the Gillespie family. I regret there is nothing that can be changed. That's all I have to say."

Hanna appealed his conviction to the Michigan State Court of Appeals. The Appeals court affirmed the trial court's judgment that Hanna was guilty but mentally ill. The court rejected the defense's arguments that Hanna should have been convicted on an insanity charge. The court reasoned that: (1) Hanna knowingly waived his Miranda rights; (2) the lower court did not abuse its discretion in allowing Gillespie's three sons to testify as to Hanna's sanity; and (3) the lower court's decision was sound.

The Chippewa County Court House, built in 1877, was the site of Nathan Hanna's murder trial. The opulent carvings and mansard roof are characteristics of the building's Second Empire architecture.

Hanna's attorney then appealed to the Michigan Supreme Court. Again the court reaffirmed the trial court's decision.

Hanna's attorney, still unhappy with the results, appealed to Judge Robert Bell's U.S. District Court. After a review of the case, Bell found the Hanna trial had a number of rulings that he considered in error. He ruled that Hanna's confession was not voluntary because he was medicated, in pain, suicidal, and had not eaten for days. Bell also stated that former Chippewa County Prosecutor Farrell Elliot had made prejudicial comments to the jury, and that Hanna's defense attorney, Elizabeth Church, failed to object to those statements.

On November 6, 2007, and after serving seven years in Michigan's Ionia State Prison, Hanna was returned to Judge Nicholas Lambros's 50th Circuit Court for a hearing to schedule a new trial. Defense attorney Anthony Mark Dobias of Chippewa County said the trial would probably not take place until 2008. Dobias indicated that he needed time to allow for completion of medical evaluations for Hanna. Dobias replaced attorney Elizabeth Church, who was on leave. The federal court ruled that the trial must take place within 90 days of its ruling, but agreed to give the defense an extension as more time was needed for case preparation.

In the meantime, Hanna sits in the Chippewa Correctional Facility waiting for the next round of legal wrangling that will determine how and where he spends the rest of his life.

A PICTURE PERFECT PLAN For MURDER

Juanita Richardson plummets 140 feet to her death at Alger County's (Munising) Pictured Rocks

Pictured Rocks 140-foot sheer limestone cliffs jut skyward to their leafy crown.

Munising is a vacationer's delight. It's the crème de la crème of Lake Superior beauty. In the pleasant summer months sightseers journey to the lakeside town to board ferry boats that cruise the nearby nationally famous Pictured Rocks Cliffs. The 140-foot sheer limestone cliffs jut skyward to their leafy crown. Their base of forbidding rock estuaries chiseled by relentless waves awe vacationers and are one of nature's wonders. Earth-tone hues on the precipitous cliffs embrace the early morning sun as Superior's icy waters carve intricate patterns on its isolated promontories. Peripheral hills wrap the lakeside village in a snugness that emanates security to its inhabitants. In the winter months, snowmobilers from the Midwest flock to town where more than 250 inches of snow blankets the village.

Nothing much outside of this busy winter and summer tourist trade ever happens here. Murder—well that's something that you see on TV or in the movies, or read about in the city papers that come on Sunday. Crime is minimal. A reckless youth may steal a car for a joy ride, or a hapless soul gets ticketed for drunk driving on Saturday night, but that's about as rowdy as it usually gets.

On June 22, 2006, Juanita Richardson's broken body lay lifeless at the base of a Pictured Rocks lookout.

That all changed on June 22, 2006 when Juanita Richardson's broken body lay lifeless at the base of a Pictured Rocks lookout, where she had plummeted from a 140 foot cliff. It appeared to be a tragic accident and that Richardson had accidentally fallen to her death. It was the first death in Pictured Rocks history.

One of the Pictured Rocks tour boats was cruising the waters off Miners Castle just after Richardson's plunge. It was a blustery day with light rain and white caps battering the boat's bow. On board were Warren, Michigan, resident Doris Crowl and her family. Crowl loved visiting the Upper Peninsula ever since childhood, and was delighted she could share her knowledge of the area with her husband and children. Around 11 a.m. the ship's captain received a message that a woman had fallen from a cliff near Miners Castle. The captain maneuvered the ship as close to the rocky shoreline as he dared. Crowl said, "…We could see this white jacket with all the red on it; this person wasn't moving." The size of the boat and the shallowness of the water prevented a rescue, but a police boat was enroute from Munising. Unfortunately, Crowl

Thomas Richardson, 46, was accused of pushing his wife Juanita off Munising's Pictured Rocks on June 22, 2006.

I am the light of the world. Whoever follows me never walks in darkness but will have the light of life.

Text on a card made in special memory of daughter and sister Juanita.

Juanita Richardson, 43, a secretary in the athletic department McBain High School, was on vacation in Michigan's Upper Peninsula when she met her untimely death.

said of the experience, "Seeing this woman's body at the base of the cliff will be a memory for the rest of their [her children] lives; this is a sad remembrance of our vacation."

Juanita Richardson and her husband, Thomas, McBain, Michigan residents, were vacationing in the Upper Peninsula. Earlier they were in the Copper Country and were heading southeast when they stopped at Munising's Pictured Rocks to revisit what they called their "honeymoon spot." It was a small patch of land, close to Miners Castle with a breathtaking view of Lake Superior.

Juanita, was an active woman who took pride in her home and its surroundings. She loved gardening and landscaping, skills that suited her well in enhancing her family's new log home. Her children, Laceine, Lindsay, and Levi, were a source of joy as was her job at McBain High School as a secretary in the athletic department.

Thomas Richardson was born in Cadillac, Michigan, where he graduated from high school. He had several different jobs over the years from working at Four Winns, a boat company where he repaired boats, to his then current employment as a Federal Express driver in the Traverse City Area.

On the day of the cliff fall, Richardson said that he left his wife near the lookout site and went to the visitor's center for a bathroom break. The visitor's center is approximately one half-mile from the lookout. When he returned to the site his wife was gone. Richardson said he crawled to the cliff's edge and peered over the side, only to see his wife's motionless body on the rocks below. He said he crawled to the edge because he was afraid of heights.

Later that day, Richardson told a different version of what happened. He now said when he returned from the visitor's center he saw her standing near the edge of the

Juanita Richardson was an active woman who took pride in her home and its surroundings.

Miners Castle at Pictured Rocks National Lakeshore, juts into Lake Superior and is close to the site where Juanita Richardson plummeted to her death.

cliff and then she jumped, saying something like, "Oh my God," as she leaped to a certain death. Richardson said the reason that he did not initially tell authorities that she leaped to her death was because he was attempting to conceal her suicide from her children and her employer.

The Clevenger Information Center where Thomas Richardson went for a bathroom break, leaving his wife near a cliff he called their "honeymoon spot."

The following day Richardson came up with a third rendition of Juanita's death. He told police that when he got back to the lookout he saw his wife accidentally fall over the cliff's edge. Richardson was slowly becoming his own worst enemy.

Richardson was slowly becoming his own worst enemy.

Richardson's contradictory stories on how his wife died raised the eyebrows of the police and indicated a further probe was needed into Juanita's death. Richardson at first freely talked with the police and was not aware that he was a suspect. However, within a short period of time he knew that he was being targeted, but he returned home and optimistically thought his name would be cleared. However, as the investigation continued, more information came to light that convinced the police this was more than just an accident. After ten months of investigating, the police concluded that Thomas pushed Juanita off the cliff—it was murder.

On February 6, 2007, Thomas Richardson was arrested while at work and incarcerated in the Alger County Jail in Munising.

Alger County Prosecutor Karen Bahrman said, "There was a lot of risk in bringing this case to trial. You had a non-traditional defendant who had all the trappings of a normal life. This makes prosecution difficult, but I had no choice and had to do what was right."

Prosecutor Karen Bahrman said, "There was a lot of risk in bringing this case to trial."

On February 28, 2007, a preliminary hearing was held in Alger County's 93rd District Court to determine if the state had enough evidence to charge Richardson with murder. Bahrman litigated for the state, while Jason E. Elmore, a Cadillac lawyer with the firm of McCord & Wotila, provided Richardson's defense. Judge Mark E. Luoma presided over the hearing.

Bahrman, 51, was a seasoned prosecutor with 25 years of experience, the last six as Alger County's only prosecutor. Prior to Munising, she honed her skills in Marquette and Escanaba. The veteran barrister had a half-dozen murder cases to her credit, the most recent was an inmate slaying at Shingleton's Camp Cusino. She was widely known as a no-nonsense prosecutor.

Early on there was a question as to who had jurisdiction over the case, the federal government or the state government. It was determined that the state had jurisdiction because the federal lands in question were a unit of the National Park Service and not a national park.

The Alger County District Court building lacks the stately opulence that characterizes other county courts in the Upper Peninsula, but it does serve the needs of Alger County. The court was at capacity at the preliminary hearing with more than 40 people jammed into its oak, church-like pews. Television cameras at the rear of the courtroom unobtrusively recorded the court proceedings.

Juanita (right) and her sister Janette when they were cheerleaders at McBain High School in 1981. Janette delivered a heartfelt impact statement in support of her sister at the sentencing of Thomas Richardson's murder trial.

Bahrman called 23 witnesses at the preliminary hearing to support her contention that this was not a tragic accident, but murder. In addition to Richardson's inconsistent stories on how his wife died, Bahrman submitted collaborative evidence as to motive. The prosecutor's investigation revealed the Richardson marriage was rocky and Juanita was considering divorce. Bahrman also noted that the couple was in serious debt, and that Thomas Richardson was pursuing another love interest.

Attorney Jason Elmore said Richardson did not push his wife off the cliff and it was instead an unfortunate accident.

There wasn't any direct evidence that linked Richardson to his wife's death, but Bahrman felt the circumstantial evidence was enough to warrant a charge of murder.

Elmore said Richardson did not push his wife off the cliff but instead that it was an unfortunate accident. The defense stated further that it was only natural that his recalling the event was inconsistent, as he was in emotional turmoil at the time and inconsistent statements would not be out of the ordinary. In addition, Elmore noted the lack of direct evidence linking Richardson to his wife's death. One of the few facts Elmore and Bahrman agreed on was that circumstantial evidence would be at the crux of the trial. Elmore's

The Richardson murder trial was held in Schoolcraft County's 11th Judicial Circuit Court. The change of venue from Munising to Manistique was due to the pre-trial publicity. Safety and logistics were also factors in the change.

position, however, was significantly different than Bahrman's; he contended that the circumstantial evidence was not enough to charge his client with murder.

Articulate, and well-prepared, 44-year-old Karl Numinen would be trying his first murder case.

Bahrman, with her substantial height and dressed in a conservative black suit, exuded authority. With self-assuredness she bantered with Elmore over a number of issues. Elmore looked boyish with his clipped hair and fair complexion. However, that belied his court presence; it was quickly evident that he was a capable attorney. His questions were sharp and direct, though at times he became mired in paperwork as he searched for information.

Richardson, 45, wore a dress shirt with a hint of yellow and a conservative brown tie. He stroked his neatly trimmed beard and took copious notes throughout the proceeding. He showed little emotion and occasionally bent over and engaged in brief conversations with his lawyer. Richardson wore dark glasses and said he needed them because his eyes were light sensitive due to a brain injury he suffered in 2002. Richardson's casual demeanor during the proceeding made it appear that he had not given serious thought to the possibility he could be spending the rest of his life in prison.

Attorney Karl Numinen examines some 7,000 pages of testimony that the Richardson trial generated.

Judge Luoma in his black robe and thinning gray hair spoke softly yet confidently from the bench. The evidence threshold required at a preliminary hearing is minimal, and after three days of the hearing, Luoma concluded that the prosecution had presented enough evidence to charge Richardson with murder. In hearing the decision, Richardson bent over in anguish and wept. He was bound over for trial and remained in jail. After the preliminary hearing the case was moved to Alger County's 11th

Jason Elmore (center), Richardson's first attorney, was removed by the circuit court, but later reinstated by the appellate court. He was second chair in the trial.

Judicial Circuit Court where Judge Charles Stark presided.

Bahrman surprised the court several weeks after the preliminary examination—she demanded that defense attorney Elmore be removed from the case for intimidating a witness. Bahrman contended that Elmore threatened witness Kelli Brophy with prison and loss of child custody, and that she could be considered an accessory to the murder. The prosecution contended that Brophy was Thomas Richardson's love interest and that her testimony could weaken the defense's case. Bahrman asserted that Elmore was attempting to negate her testimony through coercion. Elmore responded to the allegations by saying that he had a conversation with Brophy on July 31, but he emphatically stated, "There's no way I did anything to intimidate this woman." Judge Stark didn't see it Elmore's way and dismissed Elmore as the defense's attorney.

"There's no way I did anything to intimidate this woman."

Jason Elmore

Elmore was not happy over his dismissal and sought redress through the appellate court. The case went to the appellate court and then to the Michigan State Supreme Court. The higher court tossed the case back to the appellate court and directed them to render a decision.

The appellate court reversed Stark's decision and reinstated Elmore. In Elmore's absence, Richardson hired attorney Karl Numinen of the Marquette law firm of Pence & Numinen. After Elmore's return, Richardson decided to retain both attorneys, with Numinen being the

Karen Bahrman, Alger County's "no nonsense" prosecuting attorney, successful prosecuted Thomas Richardson for murder. It was her greatest court victory.

lead attorney and Elmore taking second chair. Articulate, impeccably dressed, and well prepared, 44-year-old Numinen would be trying his first open murder case. He looked ready for the task.

Bahrman said she wanted Richardson's sunglasses removed because they were a distraction.

Bahrman had additional concerns she brought to the court's attention. She wanted the court records to be sealed, stating that excessive publicity would be harmful to the case. Stark denied the request. Another point of contention that Bahrman had was Richardson's sunglasses. Bahrman said they were a distraction, and that his eyes should be in full view so the jurors would better be able to determine the subtle nuances that eyes often reflect. Stark agreed and Richardson was ordered to remove the sunglasses in court. She also asked the court's permission to bring the jurors to the site of the crime; she wanted them to see the cliff. Bahrman held that the site visitation was important and that just showing the photographs in the courtroom was not adequate. Stark rejected this request.

A cellmate of Richardson, Dylan Bonevelle, 23, testified that Richardson solicited him to kill prosecutor Bahrman.

The combative attorney's duel continued when Numinen requested Stark remove Bahrman from the case. Numinen contended that Bahrman had illegally obtained records from Richardson's cell by using another inmate to steal them. Bahrman derided Numinen's allegations saying it was "transparently retaliatory" after she successfully had Richardson's previous attorney removed from the case. She continued, "It is likely that Numinen's motion was for public consumption." Numinen was unsuccessful in getting Bahrman removed from the case, but he wasn't the only one trying to get rid of her.

In August 2007 Richardson was back in court for a pre-trial evidentiary hearing. A cellmate of Richardson, Dylan Bonevelle, 23, testified that Richardson solicited him to kill Karen Bahrman. Richardson allegedly told Bonevelle, "He wished the pigs and hogs on Bahrman's

Judge William Carmody resided over the Richardson trial in Schoolcraft County Circuit Court. Carmody was appointed trial judge when judge Charles Stark withdrew.

farm would devour her and that he wouldn't cry a tear if she dropped dead." Bonevelle told Bahrman in the court, "He had a Corvette and a boat and was willing to trade for you." No charges were filed against Richardson for attempting to solicit a murder; prosecutors felt there was not enough evidence.

Numinen requested a change of venue because of the extensive coverage by the media. Stark agreed and the trial to Manistique, some 30 miles away. Numinen said, "I would have preferred the trial been moved a further distance from Munising, but Judge Stark kept it within his circuit district." At the same time, Stark removed himself as the trial judge and reassigned it to Probate Judge William Carmody. Numinen and Elmore sought Stark's removal contending he was not up to the trial. Bahrman had no problems with Stark being the trial judge.

Numinen said, "I would have preferred the trial been moved a further distance from Munising."

The trial began on March 3, 2008, 20 months after Juanita's death. With the pre-trial issues finally settled, jury selection was next for the scheduled six-week trial. Numinen wanted jurors who had an education. He said, "They were more likely to examine the facts and less likely to make emotional judgments." Fifteen jurors were selected from 114 that were called. Numinen dismissed 12, the maximum number allowed, and Bahrman dismissed 11. Two of the final 15 had college degrees. Three of the 15 jurors were alternates and would be removed prior to deliberations. The court bailiff drawing names out of a hat would select those removed. Going into the trial Numinen said, "I was very confident that we had a winnable case."

Going into the trial, Numinen said, "I was very confident that we had a winnable case."

The prosecution had the first five weeks while the defense had the remaining week. Bahrman had 169 witnesses scheduled, while Numinen and Elmore had 93 for the defense. Not all would testify. The first week of the trial traced the sequence of events at the Pictured Rocks site. This included testimony from the park ranger, park security, and emergency medical personnel, who were first on the scene.

The heart of the trial, however, was Richardson's character. Bahrman attempted to establish that Richardson wanted his wife dead, while the defense argued that what happened was a tragic accident.

Bahrman said Richardson believed the only way to get out of debt and pursue his new love interest was to kill his wife.

Through numerous witnesses Bahrman explored the Richardson's finances and revealed they had serious money problems. They built an opulent log home on waterfront property that was beyond their means and still owed $191,000 on it. In addition, the Richardsons had $27,000 of credit card and truck payment debt. Their total debt was $237,000. As a Federal Express driver, Richardson had a decent income, but it was not enough to sustain his lifestyle. This debt, Bahrman advocated, was one of the reasons Richardson wanted his wife dead. A $240,000 life insurance policy was just enough to bail him out.

Steve Vanderwall, a close friend of Thomas Richardson whose wife had recently died of cancer, testified to a conversation he had with him. Richardson knew when Vanderwall's wife died that he collected her life insurance and paid off his debts. He was envious of Vanderwall's financial windfall. Bahrman said Richardson believed the only way to get out of debt and pursue his new love interest was to kill his wife.

The Richardsons built a handsome log home on an idyllic river setting in McBain. The home represented $191,000 of their $237,000 debt. Although they had a decent income, they still struggled to make ends meet.

Bahrman continued with a number of witnesses who testified about the couple's rocky marriage. They separated in 1999, and reconciled in 2000. It was known by Juanita's friends that she was planning to divorce him as soon as their last child left the house. In June, their youngest, Levi, graduated from high school. If Juanita divorced Thomas he would be left financially destitute.

Core to Bahrman's prosecution was Richardson's liaisons with Kelli Brophy, a woman he met while having coffee at the Quality Dairy, her place of employment. A number of witnesses testified that Richardson and Brophy had a relationship that was more than platonic. He was serious about the affair and reassured his new love that at some time he'd take care of her Richardson and Brophy made 383 phone calls during the relationship, including one the night before Juanita's death of Juanita. Purportedly, Richardson also told Brophy, "If anything ever happens he'd put a ring on her finger." Bahrman contended that Brophy was another reason that Richardson wanted his wife out of the way. Brophy, however, denied she and Richardson had a relationship and said they were only friends who talked about the Bible and scripture.

Numinen argued for a dismissal of the charges, stating, "There is no evidence of causation."

Marquette County Medical Examiner Randy Smith testified that Juanita Richardson died as a result of multiple injuries suffered during the fall. Smith could not establish whether she died as a result of an accident, suicide, or murder. Juanita Richardson had a fractured neck and a bruised breastbone, Smith reported. "She had a lot of injuries on her neck that could have been caused by a variety of mechanisms," Smith said. His testimony was neither advantageous for the prosecution or the defense, but did establish what she died of, and not how it came about.

Bahrman, in attempting to establish Thomas Richardson's culpability, called Douglas Kehl to testify on how he instructed Richardson in martial arts that included five chokeholds, of which one was a "carotid sleeper hold."

Juanita Richardson's father Don Culver also testified for the prosecution. Culver said after their separation he wanted his daughter to get out of the relationship and

Don Culver, Juanita Richardson's father, had little use for Thomas Richardson. Purportedly, Thomas struck Juanita and left facial bruises. Culver said he would kill Richardson if it ever happened again.

"not look back." Early in the Richardson marriage he said his daughter had facial bruises she got from her husband. Culver said, "I'd kill him if it ever happened again."

After five weeks of prosecution testimony, Elmore and Numinen presented the defense's case. Prior to calling their first witness, Numinen argued for a dismissal of the charges, stating, "There is no evidence of causation." Judge Carmody, however, denied an acquittal, saying that he "was not persuaded a jury could not find guilt beyond a reasonable doubt."

Attempting to discredit the prosecution's case, Numinen and Elmore had several of Richardson's friends and co-workers from Four Winns testify as to Richardson's character. Comments from supporters were positive. "He loved his family," "a man of high integrity," "easy to talk to," and "he didn't have anything to do with her death," were the range of comments solicited from the stand by those who believed in his innocence.

Not an uncommon defense strategy in a murder trial is to try to taint the character of the victim.

Not an uncommon defense strategy in a murder trial is to taint the character of the victim. This was the case in the Richardson trial as well when the defense called Molly Bassett to testify about two affairs that Juanita had during her marriage to Richardson. Bassett said Juanita told her about the affairs in confidence. She was reluctant to testify and only did so when Numinen subpoenaed her.

The defense submitted medical testimony on Juanita's use of the prescription drug Effexor that she once took for depression. A search of the house, requested by the defense, in June 2007 resulted in finding a pill container of Effexor. The defense attempted to establish that Juanita was suffering from depression, thus making suicide seem more plausible. The prosecution countered that Juanita's use of Effexor was long ago and that she was no longer taking the drug. After her death a toxicology exam did not show any drugs in her system.

David Richardson, Thomas's father, with his wife and grandchildren faithfully attended their son's murder trial. David was not always pleased with the news coverage and said, "The media is mostly negative."

The defense called psychologist Dr. Julianne Kirkham, an expert in neuropsychology who works at Marquette General Hospital, to testify on acute stress reaction. "Dilated pupil, rapid breathing, sweating, muscle cramps and nausea are symptoms of someone who is having an acute stress reaction," Kirkham said. She noted a park employee described Richardson as having some of these symptoms at the time of his wife's death. Kirkham said, "All of these symptoms suggest he was responding to something horrifying." She also stated that someone suffering from this disorder might be sensitive to light. Richardson wore sunglasses increasingly after his wife's death. Kirkham said she didn't think his symptoms were related to a traumatic brain injury that Richardson said he suffered years earlier.

Emotional and powerful testimony was elicited from Laceine Richardson, the eldest daughter. In a tearful testimony, Laceine described her childhood as carefree and parentally supportive. "They (her parents) would have done anything to make us happy," she said. Thomas Richardson teared up and put his head down during his daughter's dramatic testimony. Laceine said her father

Laceine described her childhood as carefree and her parents as strongly supportive.

wasn't sleeping or eating much after her mother's death. She noted that she saw him crying one time when he was cutting the grass.

With the trial portion concluded, Carmody gave the jury instructions prior to their deliberations. He said they could consider four charges: first-degree murder, second-degree murder, voluntary or involuntary manslaughter. They must be unanimous in their decision; any split is a hung jury.

Public speculation on Richardson guilt or innocence ranged anywhere from "He's guilty as sin," to "No smoking gun—acquit." It was now up to the jury to decide whether Richardson would spend the rest of his life in prison. The jury began deliberations at 11:30 a.m. on Tuesday April 15, 2008, and concluded at 5:30 p.m. that day with no decision. They took a vote that afternoon with a seven-five, split, seven saying guilty and five not guilty. They resumed deliberations on Wednesday morning, and at 3:10 p.m., after 11 hours of discussion they reached a verdict. When the jury reassembled in the jury box, Carmody asked jury foreman Jeff Bolm to speak for the jurors. Bolm, a veneer mill employee, read from a sheet of paper. "We the jury find the defendant Thomas David Richardson guilty of murder in the first degree."

Laceine Richardson, Thomas's daughter, stood by her father at his trial. She gave a tearful and powerful testimony on the stand in his defense.

Thomas Richardson's children, stunned at the verdict, cried. Not only had they lost their mother they would now also lose their father.

Juanita Richardson's family wept and held each other.

Richardson was noticeably distressed as he exited the courtroom. He was taken to the Munising jail to await sentencing on May19.

Janette Ellens, Juanita's sister, reviews a family photo album that she gave in intestimony at Thomas Richardson's sentencing.

Bahrman said, "I was more optimistic when the jury went into its second day, usually quick decisions are not good for the prosecution. The longer they take, the better."

The trial was exhaustive for both the prosecution and the defense. Numinen and Elmore stayed in Manistique for the duration of the trial. Numinen said, "We often left the courtroom at 6 p.m., went to our motel where we frequently worked until midnight, then slept for a few hours and were back in court by 6 a.m., getting ready for another day." Bahrman also stayed in Manistique for the trial.

Richardson was sentenced at Alger County Circuit Court where a packed courtroom assembled for the last breath of the lengthy trial. Janette Ellens, Juanita's sister, spoke for her family. In measured comments and near tears, she held a large picture of Juanita and said, "God gave her to mom and dad to love and they did," Ellens then looked at Richardson, "She worked hard but could never please you. I only hope that Juanita was oblivious to the evil in your heart."

Richardson spoke for the first time in court when Ellens finished her statements. Responding to her statements Richardson said, "That was inaccurate but touching." He made additional comments on how much he loved

Juanita and how good their marriage had become. He never admitted guilt.

There was little drama to Judge Carmody's expected sentencing, he followed the mandated state guidelines and remanded Richardson to life in prison without the possibility of parole.

Ellens, after the sentencing hearing, said, "I wanted to tell Thomas Richardson what I thought of him, but I was advised to keep it positive—it was Juanita's day. It was very difficult for me to do that with him sitting there."

Immediately after the sentencing, Richardson was transported to Marquette Branch Prison where he was processed and then sent to the Southeast Michigan prison in Jackson.

Elmore and Numinen said they would seek a new trial. Numinen said there were several areas that justified this. "The character issue was the thrust in the prosecution's case, and one cannot be convicted of a crime based solely on their character," he asserted.

The court drama is gone, but few residents will forget the happenings of what was a near picture perfect murder.

There are no winners in murder. Juanita is dead, Thomas will spend the rest of his life in prison, Juanita's parents and sister are disconsolate over their loss, and the children lost both their parents. Murder trials, unfortunately, create alignments of allegiance that disrupt both families and communities.

At the sentencing, Juanita's family wore purple shirts of solidarity with "Justice for Juanita" neatly embroidered over the heart of the shirt. Her children, however, sat on the defense side of the courtroom, with their father's parents, David and Meredith Richardson. The memories of Juanita may dim as the years go by, but those she touched will cherish remembrances, be it only for a lingering moment.

Munising has returned to its casual rhythm, where summer tour boats search out coastal beauty and winter snowmobiles hum in the winter paradise. The Richardson murder trial brought excitement to the city, not unlike what the Chenoweth (*Anatomy of a Murder*) murder did to Marquette over 50 years ago. Chatter about the trial in the coffee shops diminishes as the years pass. And reporters and curious on-lookers have vanished. The court drama is gone, but few residents will forget the happenings of what was a near picture perfect murder.

Juanita's sister,
Janette Ellens

Juanita's mother,
Jeanie Culver

Juanita's father,
Don Culver,

Prosecuting Attorney
Karen Bahrman

After his jailing, Simmons attempted suicide by slitting his throat. He missed the carotid artery in his failed attempt.

check on Levana and found her unconscious. He attempted to revive her, but all efforts failed—she was dead. When the friend told Simmons that she was dead, Simmons became distraught. In despair, he prompted bystanders to resuscitate her, but it was of no use; Levana would suffer no more. Whether it was grief or shame Simmons was feeling is uncertain, but he was distressed over what he had just done. The following day he was arrested and taken to the Wayne County Sheriff's office. Curiously, the sheriff, in Simmons's farm wagon, escorted him with his wife's corpse in the back. This could not have been a pleasant experience for the despondent Simmons. After his jailing, he attempted suicide by slitting his throat. He missed the carotid artery in his failed attempt and survived, only to later have the Michigan territorial government do what he failed to.

Simmons was born in New York City in 1780 to John and Catherine Simmons; he was one of six children. His father owned a popular tavern in New York City, and it was a favorite watering hole for a heady cliental. John Jay, Thomas Jefferson, and Aaron Burr were notables who brushed elbows at the tavern while discussing the state of the new republic. The tavern prospered and the family appeared to be financially sound. Simmons's upbringing was typical of the time; he fared no better or worse than others his age. At age 17 Simmons was described as tall and well built. He enlisted in the military at 18 where he was commissioned a second lieutenant. The military in the late 1890s was in shabby condition. It was a volunteer army that had low morale and nothing to do. But even the dismal army did not have any use for young Simmons; he was drummed out. Official records on his dismissal are slim but the telltale words of "arrest" and "dismissed" are indications that things were not going well for him.

In 1805, at age 25, Simmons moved to Detroit. The city was nothing more than a pioneer town built on a swamp with bad water. But land was cheap and in all probability this is what attracted Simmons.

In Detroit, Simmons married Levana (last name not available) when he was 25. The union produced six children that Simmons supported through farming and a tavern/inn that he bought in 1826. The tavern was located in what is now Wayne. It was one of two taverns on the road from Detroit to Ypsilanti, and it was not a desirable place to either eat or lodge. Simmons did little to improve the run-down establishment, and its fare left much to be desired. The sleeping accommodations in the tavern/inn were primitive at best; it had only two beds that were crudely partitioned off from the dining area. In the cramped quarters of the roadside inn, the women slept in one bed and the men in the other. Even though it was an inn, guests at times had nothing to eat, in spite of having spent the night at the shabby hostel. The isolated tavern had a rustic sign hanging out front that did little to invite a wayfaring traveler in for sustenance and rest.

Simmons drank often and his wife frequently drank with him. They were nasty and aggressive when they drank.

He farmed 110 acres with limited success, mostly due to his shoddy farming skills. By the time he reached 40 he was still struggling to make ends meet and had yet to capture the brass ring. Simmons was a man with few successes in life.

Simmons drank often and his wife frequently drank with him. They were nasty and aggressive when they drank; however, their excessive drinking was not out of character for the time. Up to the1830s, drinking was considered a prerequisite to any social or work activity. If one needed help to harvest a farm crop, an abundant supply of alcohol was a must to maintain a volunteer work force. It was thought that drinking cured many common ills and thus served a higher purpose. Farmers often made whisky from their corn and rye rather than convert it into flour or meal. Simmons, being a part-time farmer and full-time tavern owner, was in the right occupation with his proclivities for drink. Attempts to control or abolish liquor in the United States didn't materialize with any significance until 1826 when the American Temperance Society was founded. By the 1830s the temperance movement gained some influence, and by the time of

Simmons's hanging there were five temperance societies in Michigan.

Less than a month after the murder on July 6, 1830, Simmons's trial began on a hot sultry day in low-lying Detroit. It was not a pleasant day to be confined in a crowded courthouse determining the fate of a man. The trial was held in an opulent Greek Revival courthouse; it was an impressive building, though it is doubtful that Simmons had the time or inclination to give that any thought. Smoking and chewing were permitted in courtrooms. Spitting tobacco juice during the court proceedings was common at that time. But sleeping was not allowed. If the constable, who was keeping court order, found anyone sleeping, he would wrap whomever with a pole that immediately got their undivided attention.

The jurors were faced with convicting Simmons of either first-degree murder or manslaughter. At the time there was no second-degree murder or one of the multiple levels of manslaughter.

Simmons's lawyer was George A. O'Keeffe, an impressive Irish-born attorney who was witty and cultured.

Simmons's lawyer was George A. O'Keeffe, an impressive Irish-born attorney who was witty and cultured. Over six-feet tall, he had a commanding presence in the courtroom, and his skillful repartee did not go unnoticed.

O'Keeffe spent more time picking what he hoped would be a sympathetic jury than he did on the trial. The process is called jury selection, but it should be called jury exclusion. O'Keeffe needed a jury that would view his client with some favor; this would be a difficult task at best. Simmons was looked upon as a drunken brute, and with his crude demeanor he would be a difficult sell to a jury. Juries often had an elitist slant, something O'Keeffe didn't want. Bankers, lawyers, and businessmen were the ones selected for jury duty, and O'Keeffe knew they would not be partial to his client. O'Keeffe wanted farmers and tradesmen on the jury, men that could identify with Simmons's plight.

Doing his best, O'Keeffe disqualified as many prospective jurists as he could. His goal was to shrink the jury pool and thus force the court to select farmers and tradesmen. After the dismissal of 138 jurors, 12 men were finally seated, not totally to O'Keeffe's liking, but as good as he was going to get.

Details of the court proceeding are sketchy as there were not court reporters at that time. Simmons's children did not help; they testified against him. They bore witness to the wretched life they had been living with their drunken father. Even an unskilled prosecutor would have needed nothing more than the children's compelling testimony to convince a jury of Simmons's guilt. The children's court statements hastened Simmons to the gallows.

O'Keefe's defense was simple: Evil drink made him do it. No matter how eloquent O'Keeffe's defense and final summation, he was defending a doomed man. After a day of O'Keeffe presenting a defense, the case went to the jury.

No matter how eloquent O'Keeffe's defense and final summation, he was defending a doomed man.

On Wednesday, July 14, 1830, barely six weeks after Levana's killing, the jury rendered a verdict—*guilty*. Twelve days later he was sentenced—*death by hanging*.

On September 24, 1830, bareheaded Simmons steadily walked to the gallows to a certain death.

The hanging of Stephen Simmons was a gala community event. Detroit and the outlying areas were titillated with the idea of a community hanging. Men, women, and children trekked to the courthouse on horseback and in wagons to see the spectacle. Eager voyeurs camped out on Gratiot Road to ensure they could get a good seat. Over 2,000 Detroiters packed the bleachers that were adjacent to the gallows; others stood wherever they could find a place.

The day of the hanging, Simmons dressed himself and laced on a new pair of shoes. He did not appear apprehensive, and walked with a firm step. A pulsating drum and a shrill-toned fife playing a death march accompanied his macabre march to the gallows.

The day of the hanging, Simmons dressed himself and laced on a new pair of shoes.

On the gallows, Simmons was reported to have made an impassioned plea in which he condemned drink and asked forgiveness. He followed his repentant oratory by melodically belting out in a rich baritone voice a religious song of contrition. The once titillated spectators now wept with unabashed shame over this poor soul going to his death after such a soul cleansing confession. Newspaper accounts of the hanging recalled how witnesses to the hanging were so moved by Simmons's appeal, that they thrashed the scaffolding and tore down the whipping post. Although this account of the hanging was widely reported, author David G. Chardavoyne disputed this claim. In his well-documented book, Chardavoyne clearly states that Simmons's execution was carried out with more dignity than most were at the time. None of Simmons's children attended the hanging. At any rate, the more raucous popular version of the event fueled the anti-capital punishment movement in Michigan.

None of Simmons's children attended the hanging.

Simmons's hanging was one of the last before Michigan became a state in 1837. His was not the first hanging in the Michigan territory, but it would it be one of the last under territorial law. Prior to becoming a state, Michigan had as many as 12 hangings; most of those hanged were Native Americans. Simmons's execution, however, had global impact. Sixteen years after his hanging, Michigan, in 1846, became the first state to ban capital punishment. He didn't know it at the time, but he achieved more in death than he did in life: His hanging was the event that ushered forth the drive to abolish the death penalty in the State of Michigan.

Simmons is believed to have been unceremoniously buried with his wife at their farm, but there is not any evidence to substantiate this.

Perhaps the words of F. Scott Fitzgerald best describe Simmons's life. "First you take a drink, then the drink takes a drink, then the drink takes you."

The KING Is DEAD

Beaver Island's Mormon prophet and king was murdered because of ordering women to wear bloomers

"Of all the plaques which mankind are curst ecclesiastic tyranny's the worst."

Daniel DeFoe

Beaver Island is the poor stepsister to Michigan's major islands. Charming and historic Mackinac Island is a destination for travelers throughout the nation, and remote and scenic Isle Royal in Lake Superior is a haven for outdoor enthusiasts. Beaver Island, however, is not as well known, but it is a secluded jewel and the largest island in Lake Michigan.

Its history, while not as significant as Mackinac Island, is colorful and compelling. Beaver Island is located 31 miles from Charlevoix on Michigan's west coast and is a 30-minute boat ride from the mainland. It is also only 30 miles from Naubinway, a small fishing community located in the southeastern Upper Peninsula. Beaver Island is an archipelago of 13 islands that are a fertile area for commercial fishing and attract fishermen from both the Upper and Lower peninsulas.

The island is 14 miles long and three to six miles wide and for the most part is relatively sandy and flat. Approximately 600 residents make this their home year-round, and in the summer months a sizeable tourist trade treks to the remote island. Fishing, logging and farming at one time were the mainstays of the economy, but now government services, tourism, and home construction provide the majority of the island's income.

Beaver Island is also known as the "Emerald Isle" because of the large Irish population that fished there long before James Jesse Strang arrived.

King James Jessie Strang moved his flock of Mormon dissidents to Beaver Island when he split with the Mormon Church (Church of Latter Day Saints).

James Jesse Strang, an intelligent, charismatic, and self-appointed prophet of the Mormon Church, came to Beaver Island in June 1848 with 24 followers (Strangites). Before winter set in, 100 more disciples of Strang's moved to the island. Biblically bearded, Strang could have easily been a poster child for the Old Testament. He created a colony of Mormon believers that he governed with absolute power.

Strang moved his flock of Mormon dissidents to Beaver Island when he split with the Mormon Church (Church of Latter Day Saints). The schism occurred when Strang was not appointed head of the church after the death of founder Joseph Smith. Strang insisted that he was the chosen one to follow Smith and that he had proof. He produced a written document that Smith was purported to have written that stated Strang was to succeed him at the time of his death as prophet and church leader. A squabble developed over the letter's authenticity and was later found to be a forgery.

Strang lost his claim for Mormon control to Brigham Young. Young, hailed as the new Mormon prophet, excommunicated Strang and then emigrated from Nauvoo, Illinois, to Utah with a core of followers where he established a new Mormon kingdom.

Upset over not being selected as the church prophet, Strang gathered together those Mormons who thought he was the true prophet; with them he planned to form his own colony.

In 1848, Strang and his followers left Nauvoo, Illinois, and headed to Voree (Spring Prairie), Wisconsin. After a short stay at Voree, they left the small community and headed to Beaver Island. Strang thought the island's isolated location would be an ideal place for his religious faction. The island inhabitants however, were not happy with the arrival of his followers They were not only leery of the religion, but of the large number of people that inundated the island; they saw their way of life threatened. They were right. After a brief period of time, Strang controlled all the island activities, both religious and civil. At the peak of his power in 1850, Strang declared himself king of Beaver Island. By then the island's population was 75 percent Mormon.

Biblically bearded, Strang could have easily been a poster child for the Old Testament. He created a colony of Mormon believers that he governed with absolute power.

One of the curious and debatable practices of Mormonism is polygamy. Strang had always opposed polygamy, that is until he took a second wife, Elvira Field, in 1849. Prior to their marriage, Field served as Strang's traveling companion and secretary. Deceptive Strang had her disguised as a man and passed her off as Charles Douglas. Not content with only two wives; he took three more in the next four years. Two of them were 18-year-old cousins.

By 1850, Strang felt omnipotent, and he proclaimed himself King Strang before 250 of his protégés. In an impressive coronation, Strang was garnished in a flowing robe and graced with a bejeweled crown. It had all the illustrious trappings befitting any royal European coronation.

King Strang wanted obedient subjects that followed all decrees and proclamations, and do so without objection.

Beaver Island, the largest island in Lake Michigan, is located 35 miles Northwest of Charlevoix (circa 1873).

Feeling comfortable that he had consolidated his power on the island, Strang demanded tithing, even from those who were not Mormon. All nonbelievers were referred to as gentiles. Most of the fishermen, who were already on the island when Strang arrived, were gentiles and protested his high-handedness. It was rumored that Strang had the nonbelievers who refused to tithe taken into the woods and flogged. In addition, he ordered the county treasurer to give one tenth of the county revenues to the Mormons. The gentiles on the island were sick and tired of Strang's autocratic rule and this led to a number of altercations between Mormons and non-Mormons. By the early 1850s many of the gentiles, tired of Strang's despotism, left the Island. Strang now had a stranglehold on the island, and he and his adherents held all the political offices in Mackinac Island, of which Beaver Island was a political appendage.

By 1850, Strang felt omnipotent, and he proclaimed himself King Strang before 250 of his protégés.

The original Mormon print shop built in 1850 by the followers of King James Jessie Strang. The first paper published in Northern Michigan was in this print shop.

It was speculated that Strang and his followers pirated stranded boats on Lake Michigan. A common ploy it's said that he used was to alter lighthouse markers, thus making a ship's captain uncertain of his location. This often resulted in the ship becoming grounded and easy prey for the looting Mormons. None of the "Mormon pirating" was ever proved, and in all probability the rumors were circulated by the gentiles who had immeasurable hatred for Strang.

Strang was an absolute despot on the isolated Island. But there were cracks in his intoxicating world as prophet and king.

Strang was an absolute despot on the isolated Island. But there were cracks in his intoxicating world as prophet and king. With a mind-set of invincibility, he forged ahead in shaping the island to his accepted wisdom. In 1856 he sought to change the women's dress. Strang disliked the fashionable long skirts of the day and thought that the shorter bloomers were more suitable for the women in his sect. Most of the island's women went along with the new dress code whether they liked it or not. But as is characteristic of most groups, religious or not, there are those who disagree with proclamations that demand subjugation. Mrs. Thomas Bedford, Mrs. Alexander Wentworth, and Mrs. Hezekiah McCullough were members of the Mormon community who protested the new dress code and they refused to wear the bloomers.

God forbid that anyone should take exception to any of his decrees. Strang perceived himself as not only a divine prophet of God, but lord and master of all non-ecclesiastic matters as well, and obedience to his mandates was not open for discussion. He was inflexible and any signs of insubordination were not tolerated. He chided the bloomerless and antagonistic women in his newspaper, *The Northern Islander*, in hopes that public humiliation would make them conform. It did not.

Strang needed a reason to enforce his dress code—and the belligerents unknowingly provided it for him. Thomas Bedford, who reluctantly joined the Mormon Church and had a Mormon wife, was a Strang opponent, and it was reported he had committed adultery with his business partner's wife, Mrs. David Brown. Although Strang had five wives, adultery was considered a violation of the community's norms. Only 20 men in the Mormon enclave practiced polygamy, and none, other than Strang, had more than two wives. The adultery committed by

Bedford provided the perfect opportunity to teach him and his rebellious wife a lesson.

Following the alleged adultery charge, Bedford was attacked near his home by a group of men who stripped him to his waist and gave him 74 lashes with a "black snake" (a beech switch toughened by heating and twisting). The 74 lashes far exceeded the recommended 39 lashes that were recommended for adultery.

Although Strang had five wives, adultery was considered a violation of the community's norms. Only 20 men in the Mormon enclave practiced polygamy, and none, other than Strang, had more than two wives.

Bedford was humiliated and bleeding. Somehow he dragged himself home, loaded his gun and waited for the opportune time to avenge his whipping. For several nights he camped outside of Strang's cottage, waiting for the right time to deliver his payback. After careful thought though, he decided that killing Strang at that time was foolish. The water to the mainland was frozen over and he wouldn't be able to escape. He decided to wait for spring when he could safely ferry 25 miles to the mainland. In the meantime, he brooded over what had been done to him. His bitterness was nurtured and exacerbated by Hezekiah McCullough, a fellow Mormon, who equally disliked Strang.

Strang heard the rumors about the conspirators' plot against him, but gave it little thought. He was contemptuous of others and believed that no one could touch him. As a prophet of God, he felt invincible, almost to the point that he thought his life was eternal. Coming events would prove him wrong.

McCullough, one of the conspirators, went to Mackinac Island and then returned to Beaver Island on board the federal ship U.S.S. *Michigan*. McCullough brought pistols back and gave them to Wentworth and Bedford. It was common knowledge that Wentworth and Bedford were target practicing with their new pistols.

Strang knew what they were up to but couldn't have cared less; after all, he was indestructible. He knew the *Michigan* was in the harbor, but it posed no problem for Strang. He thought that the ship was there just to harass him, but this didn't bother him; he was used to the government persecuting him.

Just five years earlier, in 1851, Strang and 100 of his followers were hauled into a federal court in Detroit

The restored Mormon print shop is now the museum for the Beaver Island Historical Society.

Strang had just finished supper when an officer from the U.S.S. Michigan appeared at his door and requested him to pay a visit to the ship. His wives were apprehensive about him going.

where he was charged with delaying the mail, tax circularities, counterfeiting, and cutting timber from public lands. Strang acted as his own attorney, and with commendable court skill he defended himself and was victorious. His power now further solidified was enough for him to win a seat in the state legislature the following year.

On the evening of June 16, 1856, Strang had just finished supper when an officer from the *Michigan* appeared at his door and requested him to pay a visit to the ship. His wives were apprehensive about him going and feared there would be trouble. Strang went anyway. Just before he reached the pier on the harbor, a shot was fired and hit Strang in the head, sending him crashing to the ground. As he lay there he saw his assailants—Bedford and Wentworth. Behind the assailants and watching the event were McCullough and several others islanders.

Wentworth then fired, hitting Strang in the face. Bedford fired a second shot striking Strang's left side then turned and pounded Strang's head with the butt of his gun. The two killers then retreated to the safety of the *Michigan*. The crew on the ship watched the whole affair, but did nothing to stop it. Because the sailors failed to take action, it was concluded that the government was complicit in the killing.

Strang clung on to life for 23 days and finally succumbed to his injuries. Prior to his death he was taken from Beaver Island and brought to Voree, Wisconsin, the place where he first established his Mormon sect. He had several Mormon members with him on his death pilgrimage to Voree, but none of his wives made the journey to Wisconsin. They were all pregnant at the time. On his deathbed he was asked if he desired to have a successor appointed by him. With a tear rolling down his cheek he responded, "I don't want to talk about it." Near death, the king who considered himself immortal lapsed into a coma and thus ended his eight-year reign on Beaver Island.

Near death, the king who considered himself immortal lapsed into a coma and thus ended his eight-year reign on Beaver Island.

He died on July 16, 1856. Dressed in a silk flannel shroud that cost $4.77, he was put into a $20 coffin and laid to rest in an unmarked grave in Voree. Although most literature written on James Jesse Strang is unfavorable, there are those who believe he was badly mischaracterized and considered him an honest, caring man who had the best interests of his followers at heart. Doyle Fitzpatrick, author of *The King Strang Story*, was one of those who contended that Strang was frequently and unfairly slandered. And there are those who feel history, and life, treated him justly.

"One thing I learned, never to be a prophet.... Prophecy is a dangerous thing. No prophet has died a natural death."

Eli Wiesel

BONES BENEATH *The* CROSS

In 1918, a skeleton was found in the the basement of Holy Rosary Catholic church. Whose remains were they?

In Isadore, a small town near Traverse City, a lantern flickers late at night in a subterranean space; its faint glow lights two men who are digging in a confined area below a church. It is an earthen basement that was never completed and is of varying elevation with no place higher than five feet. Father Edward Podlesweski, the parish priest, and Jacob Flees, the church sexton, are searching for a body they believe is buried beneath Holy Rosary Church. Flees is digging with a potato fork while Father Podlesweski is holding a flashlight. Finally, Flees hits something hard; he discards the fork and begins to dig with his hands. In no time he unearths a lengthy white bone and then other bones follow. Flees hands the dirty bones to Father Podlesweski who puts them in a small box. Finally, the skull is unearthed; its hollow eye sockets that once viewed the beauty in the world are now spacious caverns of darkness. Further digging yields a disintegrated brown woolen cloth and a pair of women's shoes. After recovering all the bones, Flees fills in the hole making the soil appear untouched.

Sister Janina was sociable and seemed to enjoy her new church assignment.

Two nights later, Flees brings the box to the church graveyard; there he buries it at the base of a large wooden cross.

To make sure no one discovers the burial site, Flees does not put the top back on the small wooden box. If he did, eventually, it would rot and cave in, causing a depression. That might raise a red flag to those who knew about such matters. After he buries the bones, he landscapes the surface to camouflage the site. The church must keep its secrets.

The Holy Rosary Catholic Church in Isadore harbored the bones in its cellar of Sister Mary Janina for 11 years. The discovery of the bones rocked the quiet community.

Father Podlesweski and Flees are quite sure they know whose bones they are, but feel that it's just as well to keep it quiet. They assume that they are the bones of Sister Mary Janina, a nun who's been missing 11 years and thought to be dead. There were rumors within the church community that Janina was buried in the church basement, but they were hushed up and not acted upon. Podlesweski felt it would serve no purpose to expose what probably was a murder many years ago, particularly when it could be damning to the church.

Sister Janina was orphaned at nine and taken in by the Felician sisters in Detroit. The nuns raised her and it was natural that she would be attracted to a religious life. At 18, Janina took her final vows and became a nun. After that she taught school in Detroit for 14 years. However, her health was not good and church authorities thought she needed a different environment. In 1906, 32-year-old Janina was transferred to Holy Rosary Church in Isadore in the center of Leelanaw County. They hoped that the climate change would be beneficial to her health.

Sister Janina was a plain woman about five feet five inches, olive complected, and frail in appearance. She had a pleasant personality and was liked by most who met her.

Holy Rosary Church had a tight-knit family when Janina arrived. Thirty-three year-old Father Bieniawski was the parish priest. He had inscrutable eyes, a powerfully built body, and a humorless disposition. His sister, Susan, and housekeeper, Stanislawa (Stella) Lypszynska, and her daughter Mary, also resided in the church rectory. Completing the church compound were Sister Angelina and Sister Josephine, who resided above the school next to the rectory. Gruba, a chore boy, was also part of the "church family"; he slept in the basement of the school, but took his meals in the rectory with the others.

The Holy Rosary School built in 1905 and adjacent to the church where Sister Janina and two other nuns taught. Thirty-three-year old Father Bieniawski frequently visited Sister Janina at the school.

Sister Janina was sociable and seemed to enjoy her new church assignment. She taught at the parish school and often lent her melodic voice to church socials and family gatherings. She loved her new assignment in the rural setting.

All seemed well in Sister Janina's world...that is until August 27, 1907, when she suddenly vanished.

A frantic search for her began immediately. Hundreds of church volunteers and Isadore citizens combed the woods and swamps hoping to find the missing nun. Bloodhounds were brought in and a detective from an outside agency was used in a desperate search. After many exhaustive hunts nothing turned up—not a single lead. As time passed, the thought that she may still be alive began to fade.

Sisters Angelina and Josephine left the parish fearing that their fate may be tied to Sister Janina. The weeks stretched into months, and the months into years—still no sign of the missing nun. The irony is that hundreds of people walked within feet of her and were unaware how close they were.

Five years after Janina disappeared, Father Bieniawski was transferred to St. Joseph's Parish in Manistee. Father Opsychalski replaced him and served as the pastor, until Father Podlesweski was appointed the parish priest. Sister Janina's disappearance became a faint chapter in the church's history.

In a surprising turn of events, 11 years later (1918), the mystery of whose bones they were and how they ended up in the church basement would become known.

Father Podlesweski was strikingly handsome and well liked by his parishioners, particularly the women. Within a short time the charismatic priest had succumbed to the charms of a 19-year-old woman, the daughter of local farming family. She was hired by Podlesweski to be his housekeeper; she did more than keep the rectory clean; she soothed the good priest's lonely soul. As a result, he broke his vow of chastity and impregnated her.

That was Podlesweski's first major mistake; the second was that he told his young lover about the bones in the church cellar. Under pressure from her parents, she blurted that Father Podlesweski was the father of her child, and that he also told her about the bones buried in the church cellar. The parents, shamed and angry, reported their daughter's alarming revelations to the church hierarchy and then to Sheriff John Kinnucan. The mystery of the buried bones began to unravel.

Upon receiving the scandalous information on Father Podlesweski, the Rosary Church board immediately dismissed him. At his departure to Detroit, where he was

All seemed well in Sister Janina's world...that is until August 27, 1907, when she suddenly vanished.

The weeks stretched into months, and the months into years, but still no sign of the missing nun.

to stand trial before a church tribunal, a gathering of parishioners (mostly women) were there to see him off. A weeping Podlesweski asked the gathering not to blame the girl that he loved, and said that the affair was his fault.

The sheriff alerted Martin Brown, the county judge, on the Podlesweski matter. Together they went to see Flees, who unhesitatingly admitted his part in the church cover-up. After over a decade of repressing the church secret, he was relieved to finally unburden his conscience. He showed Sheriff Kinnucan and Judge Brown to the spot in the basement where he found the bones and then the cemetery site where he buried them.

Sheriff Kinnucan, attempting to get to the bottom of the case, issued arrest warrants for Father Bieniawski and housekeeper Stella Lypsznska. During their interviews, both Bieniawski and Lypszynska steadfastly declared their innocence. Believing that Bieniawski had nothing to do with the murder, he was released. Lypszynska was not as fortunate. The police suspected she knew more than what she was telling. At barely five feet and under 100 pounds, the diminutive housekeeper wept during the police interrogation, and continued to deny that she knew anything about the murder. Her proclamations of innocence did not influence the police, and she was charged with murder. Father Bieniawski wanted to pay her $500 bail, but he did not have enough money. Catholic Church authorities pledged their cooperation to help solve the mystery of Sister Janina.

Sheriff Kinnucan, attempting to get to the bottom of the case, issued arrest warrants for Father Bieniawski and housekeeper Stella Lypsznska.

The trial of Stella Lypszynska began on October 13, 1919. The prosecution's case was primarily hearsay testimony. The principal witness was Mary J. Tylicka, who was a detective and paid police informant. Tylicka was surreptitiously imbedded in Lypszynska's cell in order to get a confession from her. She said she got her to admit that she killed Janina and so testified. Lypszynska denied she said anything that implicated her in Janina's death. She was at a serious disadvantage, she spoke little English, and an interpreter was required to translate her comments. The defense emphatically stated that Tylicka's testimony was fraudulent, and the confession was coerced. The defense wanted the confession thrown out. No such luck, the judge ruled it was admissible.

The prosecution did not have any physical or circumstantial evidence that linked Lypszynska to the murder. They did, however, present a motive for the slaying. Prosecutorial testimony at the trial centered on disparaging comments that Lypszynska purportedly made about the nun and the priest. Helen Strang, a friend of Lypszynska, testified that Lypszynska said, "…the priest was too intimate with her, and that the sister wasn't a good nun." Mary Gatzke, who lived across the street from the church and frequently talked to Lypszynska, testified that Lypszynska said, "…Sister Janina wasn't worthy to be on holy ground and that she was no nun…they were whores."

The prosecution did not have any physical or circumstantial evidence that linked Lypszynska to the murder.

The defense countered that Lypszynska was coerced and treated cruelly while in jail waiting for her trial. They argued that the prosecution had not seriously looked at other possible suspects, like Father Bieniawski. The chore boy Gruba testified that he saw Bieniawski kiss Sister Janina. Victor Berkowski, an "orphaned out" boy, who stayed at the rectory for two years, said that Father Bieniawski "would talk to her at recess and paid all his attention to her." He also said that he saw the priest go over to the school and visit some evenings. Did a fouled up relationship between the priest and the nun cause her death?

After weeks of testimony the jury retired to deliberate. Through the night they weighed the evidence, finally, at 6:00 in the morning the jury returned with a verdict—*guilty of first-degree murder!*

Did a fouled up relationship between the priest and the nun cause her death?

The following Monday, Lypszynska was sent to the Detroit House of Corrections to do hard labor for the rest of her life.

Lypszynska only served a seven-year term before being pardoned by Governor Groesbeck. The warden of the prison said, "…I have never seen one who I thought was more deserving of executive clemency than Stella." After her release from prison, she went to work for the Felician Order of Nuns in Detroit; she died a peaceful death at the age of 91.

Was Lypszynska guilty? Her peers thought she was, but there was still much doubt. The prosecution's case was a

If you would keep your secret from any enemy, tell it not to a friend.

Benjamin Franklin

house of cards; it was based on hearsay and possible fraudulent testimony. In addition, there wasn't any physical evidence at the crime scene that linked Janina to Lypszynska. Was Lypszynska a prosecutorial lamb?

If not Lypszynska, then whom? Father Bieniawski? An intruder who hated Janina? Some even suggest that Sister Janina was killed after a bungled abortion. One thing is for sure—the truth is buried forever.

The Sister Janina murder was turned into a play in 1976 called *The Runner Stumbles;* it had limited success, but it is still produced occasionally by regional theaters.

"Leelanau" is an Indian word meaning "Delight of Life." For housekeeper Stella Lypszynska and Sister Mary Janina, Leelanau County was not a place of delight, but a place where their hearts shed tears.

Holy Rosary Church as it appears today. Built in 1923 it replaced the wooden one built in 1883. The German made stained glass windows are reported to be among the finest in the country.

The DEVIL'S DISCIPLES

Detroit's infamous Purple Gang murdered at will during the Roaring 20s

"The scourge of demon rum" was the only epithet that ax-wielding Carry Nation needed to brazenly enter a tavern and unrelentingly shatter whisky bottles much to the owner's dismay. At the turn of the century, with an attitude of self-righteousness and an unmatched zeal, Nation rode her piousness into the history books.

The prohibiting of legal liquor only spawned a brutal underworld that either produced or imported illegal intoxicants.

Alcohol was long considered by many as an evil force that was destined to destroy not only body and soul but also the fabric of society. Baptists and Methodists especially thought this to be true. They unequivocally supported the government cracking down on liquor. Catholics and Episcopalians were less concerned about the wholesale use of liquor; they contended that alcohol was a moral issue and a province of the church and not the government.

The drumbeat for national abstention beat steadily from colonial times, but it was in the 1880s when the Women's Christian Temperance Union (WCTU) organized the first serious drive for a national ban on liquor.

Detroit closed 1,500 saloons when Prohibition went into effect, only to be replaced by 7,000 blind pigs.

Finally, in January 1919, the nation responded to temperance demands and outlawed hooch with the passage of the 18th amendment and the Volstead Act. Proponents of the liquor ban were joyous over the landmark legislation and envisioned it as the beginning of a new Utopia, a society free from the bondage of alcohol. The well-intentioned prohibitionists were convinced that the country would have a decrease in crime and poverty and a more civil society. It was a noble experiment that 13 years later crashed in the midst of the Great Depression.

The United States was not the only nation to ban alcohol. Finland, Norway, and Russia also banned the elixir in the second decade of the 20th century. Like the United States, the European and Russian experiment with an alcohol-free society ended in dismal failure. The Muslim world banned alcohol from the get-go and for the most part still maintains that position.

The exterior view of Detroit's Boesky's Delicatessen in May of 1937. It was the site of one of the Purple Gang's last killings. With Prohibition repealed, the Purples lost their primary moneymaker and the gang was in decline.

Forbidding alcohol by legislation did not free the nation from alcohol. The prohibiting of legal liquor only spawned a brutal underworld that either produced or imported illegal intoxicants. Most remarkable of all, was that alcohol consumption did not decrease, but increased with each passing year of prohibition; the nation was consuming more liquor per capita during prohibition than it did when alcohol was legal. The Volstead Act was not a panacea for society ills; instead, America became a more dangerous and violent place. Paradoxically, crime increased and drunk-driving rates skyrocketed by 81 percent. With the criminal world now in the liquor game, murder, hijacking, and extortion mushroomed from the dark recess of blighted cities.

Detroit closed 1,500 saloons when Prohibition went into effect, only to be replaced by 7,000 blind pigs (illegal taverns) by 1925. This number did not include the plethora of bathtub stills in garages and candy stores.

Chicago had Capone; Brooklyn had the Five Points Gang; but Detroit had the Purples.

Detroit was a city that thrived on illegal liquor. Windsor, Canada, just across the river from Detroit, produced alcohol legally. The close access to Canadian booze made Detroit ideal for importing and distributing the contraband. The Detroit River was a natural conduit to transport liquor across the border, and nobody was any better at doing that than the Purple Gang. Chicago had Capone; Brooklyn had the Five Points Gang; but Detroit had the Purples. The Purple Gang rivaled any other gang in savagery. On the ferocity scale they were ruthless even by gang standards. They openly exploited, intimidated, and murdered without fear of retribution.

The Purple Gang's genesis was in a poor section on Detroit's east side. Harry Bernstein was a hard-working immigrant Jew who toiled long hours in his shoe repair shop. He and his wife raised seven children in wretched housing and in near poverty. Four of their children—Abe, Ray, Joe, and Isadore—eventually forged the nucleus of what became Detroit's most sinister gang. The parents were honest and worked diligently, but the boys wanted an easier life.

Abe was the oldest and brightest of the Bernstein family. He disliked school and by the age of nine he quit to hawk newspapers. Abe, like his younger brothers, saw the futility of working long hours for almost nothing. They saw others leading a life of luxury with little effort, and decided this was what they wanted. Between 1910 and 1920 Detroit's east side had the ingredients to spawn a gang: poverty and ethnic rivalries.

The Purples would just as soon hijack liquor as get it from its production source—it was much easier.

With Prohibition, the opportunity to get rich on illegal liquor was ripe for gangs. Early on, the Bernstein brothers formed a street gang that intimidated local merchants by stealing goods and vandalizing the neighborhood. Not content to be small-time operators on the east side, the Bernstein brothers graduated to providing strong-armed services to an older gang that the ran the Oakland Sugar House. The Sugar House appeared to be a legitimate business that provided sugar for home brewers who were allowed to make small quantities for personal use, but it was controlled by the mob for other nefarious activities.

How did the Jewish brothers get the unlikely moniker, "The Purple Gang"? The origin of the name was reputed to have come from neighborhood merchants. One shopkeeper reportedly said, "These boys are not like other children their age, they're tainted, off color." Another shopkeeper responded, "Yes, they are rotten, purple like the color of bad meat; they're a Purple Gang."

The Purples would just as soon hijack liquor as get it from its production source; it was much easier. Any enterprise that had booze landing on Detroit's shore risked the Purples hijacking their booty and then killing them.

Like any good criminal undertaking, the Purples expanded their racketeering into labor unions, gambling, and drugs. Corrupt labor unions hired the Purples to keep union members in line and to harass non-union independents. The Purples were well paid for their coercion that used bombings, beatings, and murder as tools of enforcement.

The Purple's crime spree did not go unnoticed by the authorities; this resulted in a trial in 1928 in the Cleaners and Dyers War.

The Purple's crime spree did not go unnoticed by the authorities—this resulted in a trial in 1928 in the Cleaners and Dyers War. The Purples were on trial for brutally enforcing union policies. But witnesses feared testifying against the gang, dreading swift retribution. Without witnesses, any court conviction was impossible. The crafty and well-insulated Purples emerged from the trial unscathed.

Detroit became such a lucrative market that Chicago's Al Capone wanted part of the action. However, he quickly abandoned that plan when he discovered that he would be knocking heads with the Purples. Even ruthless Capone knew this was not a good idea; you don't screw with the Purples. Instead he went into partnership with them; they supplied the Canadian liquor and he distributed it in Chicago.

One of the Purple Gang's more infamous murders took place in Detroit at the Collingswood Manor in 1926. The Purples invited three Jewish Chicago gangsters to assist them in distributing their liquor. Hymie Paul, Joe Lebowitz, and Joe Sutker not only assisted the Purples, but also began to operate independently outside their prescribed territory. This did not sit well with the Purples. The Purples set up a meeting with the renegade trio under the guise of discussing expansion. Naively, Paul, Lebowitz, and Sutker went to the scheduled meeting at the Collingswood Manor, believing that the Purples were ready to negotiate a peace plan. Unarmed, the trio was greeted by an execution squad, consisting of three other Purple associates, who gunned down the Chicagoans. The Purples had no qualms about killing any member of their own gang if they felt they had been betrayed.

However, they were becoming careless—they let a witness survive. Sol Levine, a Purple henchman who led the three to the apartment and to their deaths was spared because he was a good friend of Ray Bernstein. Later Levine testified at the murder trial. It led to a conviction and imprisonment of Purple Gang executioners.

Although the exact number is not known, the Purples were said to have murdered as many as 500. Most were other criminals, and the police agencies did little to investigate and prosecute. In 1931 Detroit Mayor Chester Bowles dismissed the Purple's reign of terror as "just gangsters helpfully eliminating each other." Many viewed the criminal world killings as nothing more than purging society of evil.

The Purple Gang's reign in Detroit lasted 15 years, and by 1935 its power and influence had crested and it was in decline. Prohibition was repealed in 1932 and liquor became legal, thus drying up their major source of

The Purples had no qualms about killing any member of their own gang if they felt they had been betrayed.

The Purple Gang's reign in Detroit lasted 15 years, and by 1935 its power and influence had crested and it was in decline.

income. By the mid 1930s, 18 of the Purple Gang members were either dead, indicted, or in prison. The expanding Italian Mafia absorbed remnants of the gang.

Abe Bernstein left the gang and spent his time attempting to get his brother Ray out of prison. Abe Bernstein died of a heart attack in Detroit's Cadillac Hotel when he was 71.

Joe Bernstein, the smallest but toughest of the brothers, moved to California and concentrated on legitimate business activity that he acquired over the years with money he made in the gang. Isadore (Izzy) Bernstein joined his brother Joe in business.

G. Gordon Liddy perhaps best sums up the Purple Gang's attitude about crime, "One of the biggest lies in the world is that crime doesn't pay. Of course, crime pays."

Ray Bernstein ended up in Marquette's maximum-security prison. In 1963, he suffered a severe stroke. After examining his prison record, the parole board released him in 1964. Critically ill, he died two years later.

G. Gordon Liddy perhaps best sums up the Purple Gang's attitude about crime, "One of the biggest lies in the world is that crime doesn't pay. Of course, crime pays."

MICHIGAN'S MASS MURDERER

In 1927 Andrew Kehoe, disgruntled at high taxes, took the ultimate revenge

Kehoe's tailored appearance was deceptive. He had another side—and it was evil.

Andrew Kehoe was dapper; he dressed impeccably and changed his clothes at midday if they had the slightest soiling. His meticulousness was well known throughout Bath, a rural community located just north of Lansing. He was a neat freak even at work. Everything had to be in its place; there were no exceptions.

But his tailored appearance was only one side of Kehoe; there was another side—and it was sinister. He was argumentative and intolerant of others. Although he was regarded as an intelligent man, he alienated others with inflexible positions. Kehoe was paranoid; he thought everyone was against him. He repeatedly said that social and economic systems were either illegal or unfair. He felt unscrupulous people in an unjust society were targeting him.

Kehoe grew up with 13 siblings, and despite the large family it was a nurturing environment. His father was a well-liked and prosperous farmer in Tecumseh,

Michigan. Kehoe was reasonably social when growing up in the 1890s, but became more isolated as he grew older.

Kehoe's mother died when he was young and his father remarried. Andrew was not fond of his new stepmother. When he was 14 his stepmother died as a result of a kitchen stove exploding. Andrew was with her at the time of the accident. She was preparing the evening meal when the explosion saturated her with oil and set her on fire. Rumors were that Andrew watched her incinerate and then threw water on her. The water further exacerbated the flames and she died a short time later. Neighbors at the time speculated that Andrew had something to do with the stove's malfunction; however, nothing ever came of it.

After his attendance at Tecumseh High School, Kehoe went to Michigan State College (Michigan State University), where he studied electronics. He met his future wife, Nellie Price, at college; she was the daughter of a successful Lansing businessman. They were married in 1912, and in1919 they moved to a 185-acre farm outside of Bath. Nellie Kehoe was a sickly woman, and in her later years spent considerable time in the hospital.

> *Kehoe watched his mother incinerate and then threw water on her—which exacerbated the flames.*

Kehoe became a community activist and held two public positions: one as a school board trustee and treasurer, the other as a county supervisor. At school board meetings he constantly railed against taxes. He blamed school taxes for his financial difficulties, when in reality, neighboring farmers said his farming practices were deficient, and that was why he failed.

When he served as the board treasurer his bookkeeping was scrupulous, but his attitude at times was intolerable. If he failed to get his own way at a meeting he would make a motion to adjourn.

Kehoe was appointed township clerk when a vacancy occurred due to the death of the previous clerk. He completed the deceased's term and then sought a term on his own. However, when election time came around a year later, he was defeated. Township residents saw him as a disruptive force on the local school board and were leery of him also becoming a problem on the township board.

Days like May 18, 1927, are a pleasure to wake up to. At 8:45 a.m. the sun beat down warmly on the two-story brick schoolhouse in Bath as students jostled their way to classrooms. They were eagerly anticipating the end of the school year when their summer vacation time would be spent playing baseball, fishing, and waiting for the sound of mom's full-throated voice from the front porch, beckoning them to come home for supper. These were idyllic times in the bucolic community.

Unbeknownst to the students and the teachers, beneath the school's floorboards was 1,000 pounds of dynamite.

Unbeknownst to the students and the teachers, beneath the school's floorboards was 1,000 pounds of dynamite. At 9:45 a minuscule electrical current sped down a wire to the dynamite and ignited the deadly cache.

It created a massive explosion that was heard ten miles away.

The thunderous blast ripped the school apart; it totally obliterated one wing when the roof crashed to the ground.

On May 18, 1927, the Bath School was dynamited, killing 38 children and six adults. It is the worst school disaster in the history of the United States.

Screaming and crying permeated the morning air as bits of children's flesh were strewn on telephone wires 100 yards away. Frail arms and legs protruded from the rubble after tiny bodies were smashed against falling walls or hurtled through glass windows. Parents rushed to the disaster and with rescue workers attempted to pull children from the carnage, hoping that a child they rescued might be their own. Faint voices emanating from the wreckage stimulated the rescuers to work with a greater fervor. Thirty-eight children and six adults died in the catastrophic explosion. Over 100 were injured.

Screaming and crying permeated the morning air as bits of children's flesh were strewn on telephone wires 100 yards away.

The disaster was the diabolical handiwork of a disgruntled Andrew Kehoe.

Kehoe was not content to exact his revenge by just blowing up the school; he also wanted his nemesis, Superintendent Emory Huyck, to die. To ensure Huyck's death, Kehoe sped to the school in his car within 30 minutes of the school explosion. He loaded his car with dynamite and odd metal debris from his farm. The metal would serve as shrapnel when the dynamite was ignited.

When Kehoe arrived at the school he heard the terrifying cries of children emerging from the deadly bellowing smoke. He spotted Huyck and Postmaster Glen Smith near the inferno; he signaled them to come to his car. They responded and went to him. He took his rifle and shot it into the backseat, this detonated the explosives and blew up everything in the vicinity. The explosion took Huyck and Smith's life as well as Kehoe's. His body was shredded by his own creation. Parts of his torso were found in a nearby flower garden belonging to Mrs. Frank Smith. She carefully removed some papers from the back pocket of the dismembered body and discovered a bankbook and driver's license that belonged to Andrew Kehoe.

When Kehoe arrived at the school he heard the terrifying cries of children emerging from the deadly bellowing smoke.

Kehoe not only blew up the school, but also incinerated the buildings on his farm, as well as livestock. He wired his farm buildings with explosives and ignited them just prior to setting off the school explosion. On that morning he also bludgeoned his wife to death, burned her body, and dumped it in a hog cart. Her charred body was found in back of the barn with a leg and arm missing. His demonic side was not only evident from what he did to his wife, but also what he did to his livestock. In the barn he wired together the legs of two horses and left them to be consumed in the fire.

Kehoe had taken his own life, but in the process he gruesomely satisfied his insatiable need for revenge. On that infamous day in May, Clinton County was bathed in blood and tears. Nothing hurts like children dying. Their innocent bodies, shredded by dynamite, bore testimony to evil with no bounds.

Kehoe not only blew the school up, but also incinerated the buildings on his farm, as well as his livestock.

Why Kehoe succumbed to madness when he was 39 years old is unknown, but it was a fact that earlier he had a severe head injury from a fall. After the fall he drifted in and out of a coma for several months. Eventually he recovered, but it was speculated that the brutal jar might have in some way produced an aberrant personality.

Kehoe was smart and mechanically talented, and he had access to the school as a periodic maintenance man. It was not uncommon to see him in the building doing maintenance or repairs. This made it easy for him to bring in a 1,000 pounds of dynamite in small increments and do so unnoticed. To avoid suspicion, he purchased the dynamite in Lansing in small amounts over time. It was not out of the ordinary for farmers to purchase explosives for crop excavation and stumpage removal.

Setting up the incendiary was not easy. It took Kehoe time to lay thousands of feet of wiring through the sub-floors, rafters, and crawlspaces of the school. He stealthily worked on the sinister project from November 1926 to May 1927.

Just prior to his suicide, Kehoe made a sign that he hung on the fence in front of his farm. The sign read: *Criminals are made not born.* The message revealed how Kehoe felt that others were responsible for his behavior. Kehoe personified the words of comedian Flip Wilson, who said, "The devil [and others] made me do it."

Kehoe made a sign that he hung on the fence in front of his farm. The sign read: Criminals are made not born.

The Columbine student massacre that killed 13 students in Colorado (1999), and the Virginia Tech slaughter where 32 students and faculty were murdered (2007), are fresh in memories. These senseless killings are thought to be the worst school massacres in history—they were not. That tragic record belongs to the community of Bath.

Three days after the Bath murders, Charles Lindberg flew solo across the Atlantic Ocean; his story dominated the headlines and the Bath murders quickly became yesterday's news. The nation's worst school murders faded into obscurity.

Kehoe's piecemeal remains were interred in an unmarked grave in potter's field in a neighboring town—a fitting end for incarnate evil.

Author Robert Louis Stevens said, "All human behaviors…are commingled out of good and evil." Andrew Kehoe just had more evil than good—much more.

Andrew Kehoe's car after he ignited the dynamite placed inside. E.E. Huyck, the school superintendent, as well as Kehoe died in the explosion.

The DEADLY DEACON

Adolph Hotelling, a church deacon, father of five children, and a devoted husband, had a sinister side—very sinister

It was a cold winter night in Flint, Michigan, on January 17, 1928, but the crowd of 10,000-15,000 gathered outside of the Flint County Jail was not feeling the cold; they were white-hot and angry as they milled about. Housed inside was the target of their rage—Adolph Hotelling—a mild-mannered Owosso resident who had been arrested for the murder of five-year-old Dorothy Schneider, a flaxen-haired, blue-eyed kindergartener from Mt. Morris.

Hotelling's arrest triggered an outburst of righteous rage in the area's citizens. The mob gathering that night was ominous; they were seeking retribution and a Hotelling lynching would quench their rage. Sheriff Frank A. Green's deputies attempted to disperse the riled crowd by hurling tear gas bombs into their midst. It didn't help; the mob responded with brickbats and would not yield to the outnumbered deputies.

Hotelling, 47, was a construction worker and a dedicated member of the Church of Christ in Owosso.

With the situation deteriorating, Green summoned the National Guard. Within a short period of time the Guard arrived, and with a dominant show of force they quickly had the riot under control, averting what could have been a vigilante hanging.

Green in the meantime, quietly and secretly moved Hotelling to a state jail in Lansing. From there he was transferred to the nearby Ionia reformatory.

Hotelling, 47, was a construction worker and a dedicated member of the Church of Christ in Owosso, a small farming community not far from Flint. He grew up in Kalkaska and worked on his father's farm until adulthood; he then went into the construction business. Respected within the church community, Hotelling was active in parish affairs. Eventually he became a deacon and then a church elder. He was the father of five children, several who had reached adulthood and were on their own.

Adolph Hotelling, a mild-mannered religious man, was arrested in 1928 for the murder of a five-year-old girl. The night of his arrest in Flint, Michigan, he came close to being lynched by an angry mob.

America was prosperous in the 1920s. President Calvin Coolidge best characterized the era with the immortal phrase, "The business of America is business." Capitalism propelled the country down a road of gold; it seemed that everyone was destined to be rich. There was no end in sight to money, flappers, and jazz. The nation was hell-bent on a hedonistic journey of self-indulgence, and it didn't want to be stopped.

But there was a dark side to this prosperity; prohibition

had created a gangster underworld that turned city streets into a racketeers' combat zone. Crime was on the increase and parents not only worried about the safety of their children but also their own safety.

In California on December 1927, Edward Hickman abducted a 12-year-old girl from Los Angeles. He was arrested, convicted of murder and hanged in San Quentin in 1928. The Hickman case ignited the public's desire for retribution against child abductors. Adolph Hotelling's abduction of Dorothy Schneider fell on the heels of the notorious Hickman abduction, and a terrified public was ready to exact justice—even if it meant a lynching.

On January 12, 1928, Hotelling went to Flint to look for work, or at least that is what he later told investigators. En route, and near Mt. Morris, Hotelling stopped and lured five-year old Dorothy Schneider into his car with the promise that he would take her home to her mother. Instead, Hotelling drove the innocent child to a remote wooded area where he stabbed her to death. He then dismembered her body and disposed of it in a creek three miles west of Mt. Morris. In a clumsy attempt to justify his behavior, Hotelling later told investigators that she threatened to tell her mother.

Hotelling left the murder site only to get bogged down in mud on a rural road. A nearby farmer, Archie Bacon, came along and assisted Hotelling in getting the car out of the quagmire. Hotelling then sped back to Owosso. Bacon would later clearly recall this incident that linked Hotelling to the murdered child.

A deputy found Schneider's body on the same day that she disappeared. Initially, there were many tips, but none that were helpful in identifying the killer. Two days later, however, Harold Lotridge, 24, a member of Hotelling's Church of Christ, reported to police that he had a vivid dream about the Schneider murder. He told police that the man in his dream was a deacon in his church and a "pillar of the community." He identified him as Hotelling.

Records refute Lotridge's version of how he came up with Hotelling as the murderer, but there was no question that he was instrumental in leading police to him. Police claim that Lotridge came by the information not by a dream,

Hotelling stopped and lured five-year old Dorothy Schneider into his car with the promise that he would take her home to her mother.

but by working with Hotelling in construction. Hotelling, according to police, talked at great length to Lotridge about the Schneider murder. Police said Lotridge might have read a description of the suspected murderer and the car he was driving. Lotridge was aware that the clothes and the car were the same as what he had seen Hotelling wearing.

The police checked out the farmer's remembrance of the light blue Dodge sedan that was stuck in the mud near the crime scene. A check on vehicle registrations verified the car belonged to Hotelling. These two pieces of information provided the police with enough data to question Hotelling and to search his home. At his house they discovered the clothes of the driver that the farmer described. In addition, they checked Hotelling's car and found that it was recently painted black, but beneath the black coating was a light blue color—it matched the farmer's description of the car. A further home investigation by the police turned up a jack knife with blood on the blade.

Admitting to the slaying a remorseful Hotelling said, "I don't know why I did it."

With sufficient probable cause the police pressed Hotelling. Under incessant questioning by the police, Hotelling finally broke down. With quivering lips and covering his face with his hand he admitted to the slaying of Dorothy Schneider. A remorseful Hotelling said, "I don't know why I did it."

Myrtle Hotelling, Adolph's wife, collapsed on the floor when she first heard about what her husband did. In shock and disbelief, she said, "If he had confessed, the statement had been wrung from him by torture." Later, however, when the incriminating evidence against her husband came to light, she admitted that he probably was guilty. She then asserted, "If he is guilty, he should be punished. The world would be better off if he were dead. He will only grieve himself to death anyway."

Michigan law mandates that a trial occur in the county in which a crime is committed. This meant the trial would take place in Flint in Genesee County. This decision drew protests from Michigan's Governor Green as well as Hotelling's attorney. Green was unhappy with the decision and said, "There are not enough police in the state of Michigan to protect Hotelling, should the trial be held in Flint." Governor Green was fearful that another riotous mob would descend on the Flint Courthouse as they had when Hotelling was first arrested. Hotelling's attorney, William Seegmiller, concurred with the governor and wanted a change of venue for his client. Nevertheless, both pleas were denied.

Hotelling's trial and sentencing occurred in record time—one half hour. His brief trial in the Flint circuit court had only three witnesses: the murdered girl's father, a physician, and a court reporter. Leslie Schneider, Dorothy's father, formally identified his daughter; the physician discussed the autopsy; and the court reporter identified Hotelling's written confession. Attorney, W.A. Seegmiller offered no objections, nor did he say one word in behalf of his client.

Dressed in the same clothes that he wore when he killed Dorothy Schneider, Hotelling, walked slowly to Judge Brennans' bench.

Brennan said, "You are charged with first degree murder. Do you plead guilty or not guilty"?

A confused Hotelling looked doltishly back at his attorney and then said, "Guilty."

Judge Brennan continued, "What have you to say?"

"All I have to say is that you take the family into consideration," Hotelling replied.

Judge Brennan harshly responded, "You appear to have no regrets. You did not take this family into consideration."

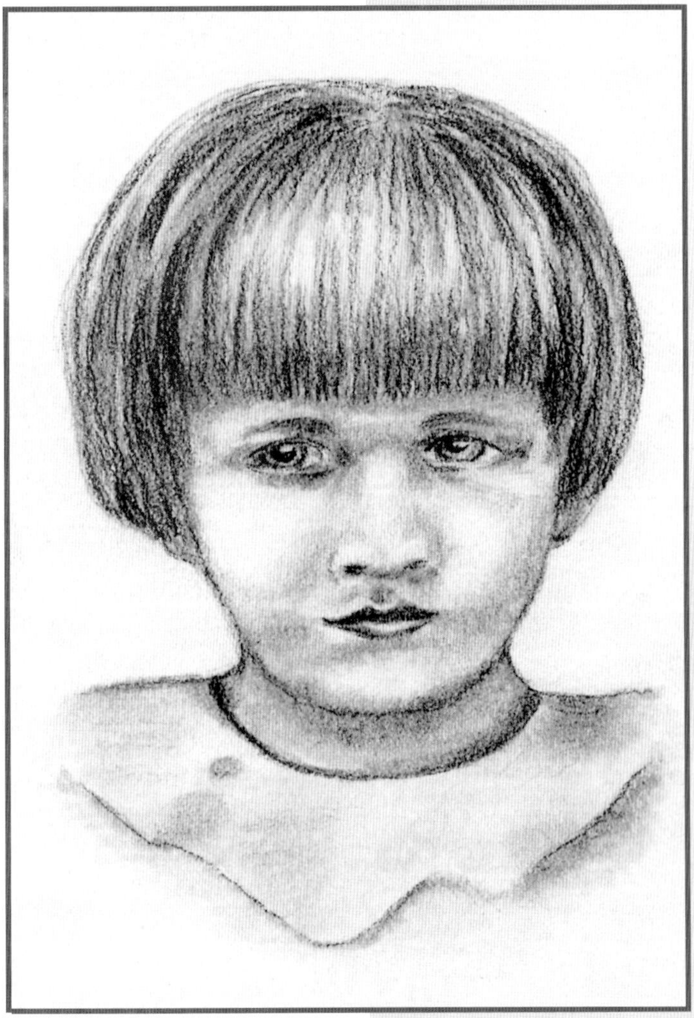

Dorothy Schneider, a flaxen-haired, five year old from Mt. Morris, Michigan, was abducted and murdered by Adolph Hotelling. During a court proceeding, Leslie Schneider, Dorothy's father, struck Hotelling in the face with a powerful blow.

With that, Hotelling was sentenced to life in prison without the possibility of parole. The judge said that he regretted Michigan did not have the death penalty, and he was convinced that Hotelling's life should be taken.

Justice was swift in 1928; six days after the murder of Dorothy Schneider, Adolph Hotelling was in prison for life.

At the conclusion of the trial Hotelling was whisked out of the courtroom to a waiting automobile that immediately began its journey north to Marquette's Branch Prison. He was in Marquette by nightfall. Justice was swift in 1928; six days after the murder of Dorothy Schneider, Adolph Hotelling was in prison for life.

Even though Judge Brennan could not sentence Hotelling to death, a life in prison may have been a more severe punishment for Hotelling, a man who was a devout Christian and one who was likely to wallow in remorse. Guilt and shame can pummel the soul and extract the will to live. A conscience unrelentingly inundated with regret and self-condemnation may be a more severe punishment than a hangman's rope. Hotelling spent the last 27 years of his life in a four-by-six cell where long and lonely nights can consume one's sanity and where sleep may never come. He died in 1954 at age 74 in Marquette's maximum-security prison.

> Remorse sleeps while fate is kind
> but grows sharp in adversity.
>
> Rousseau

The LEGION Of DEATH

Disciples of the Ku Klux Klan, the Black Legion, opposed anyone who did not share their vision of America

Most Black Legion members were Anglo Saxon, uneducated, and had minimal occupational skills.

Pleading for his life, Charles Poole begged his assailants to believe him that his wife was hospitalized because she was having a baby and not because he unmercifully beat her. His cries for mercy went unheeded by Dayton Dean, a thug and gunman for the disreputable Black Legion, a vicious lot of right-wing extremists who harbored ill will toward anyone who was not white and Protestant. Dean executed Poole on May 12, 1936, in Dearborn, a west side suburb of Detroit. The murder would rock the foundation of the extremists group.

The Michigan Black Legion was founded in the mid 1920s and was an extension of the Ohio Ku Klux Klan. In the 1920s and 1930s the Black Legion was active in Michigan, claiming 30,000 members. They saw enemies everywhere. Blacks, Jews, Communists, and Catholics were not their only enemies: social welfare workers, labor union organizers, and anyone who opposed "womanhood," was also targeted. The Black Legion opposed anyone who did not share their vision of America.

Most Black Legion members were Anglo Saxon, uneducated, and had minimal occupational skills. Many of them migrated to Detroit from the south during the 1920s when the city's industrial base was expanding. It was the best of economic times for the city that was the car capital of the world.

Lowel Rushing, a member of the Black Legion, was convicted of murdering Charles Poole in 1936. Purportedly, Rushing was in love with Rebecca Poole, Charles's wife.

Why did the Black Legion murder Poole? It would seem ironic that a white male with no distinctive resume would be the target of a hate group. At the time of his death, Poole was unemployed and spent his free time cavorting about the local bars. Rumors were that Poole often beat his wife during their frequent arguments. Rebecca Poole was an attractive, workingwoman who had arguments with her husband over his not working; she also suspected he was having a tryst with the family babysitter.

Mary Teresa Coulter, the granddaughter of Rebecca Poole, claims that she knows why the Black Legion murdered Poole. According to Coulter, her 80-year-old grandmother related to her the events that led to his death.

Coulter said family friend Lowell Rushing was in love with Rebecca, and her husband was the obstacle in Rushing's desire to have Rebecca. Rushing was running with the Black Legion, and he knew he could count on them if he needed help in disposing of Poole. On one occasion, Rushing exaggerated about a fight between Charles and Rebecca, and he told others that Charles had beat her. It provided the fuel the Black Legion needed to defend a woman's honor.

Although Poole was white, by Black Legion standards, he had several strikes against him. In addition to being Catholic and French, he was on the public dole, something they found distasteful. He was also thought to be a wife beater; the Black Legion would not tolerate wife beaters. They wondered why a beautiful, Irish Protestant woman was married to a wife-beating Catholic philanderer.

In May 1936, a rumor circulated that Poole had severely beaten his wife and that she was hospitalized. Rebecca Poole was in the hospital, but she was there having the second of Charlie Poole's children.

The Black Legion, dressed in their cheap black and white robes, met in a somber conclave two weeks prior to Poole's murder to discuss how to kill him. After a brief discussion they decided to hang him.

Naively, Poole was ensnared in a Black Legion trap when he agreed to go with them to Dearborn to play in a sandlot baseball game. Prior to the game, they stopped for drinks in a local tavern. Poole never got to the baseball game. He was killed after leaving the bar and not by hanging—nobody brought a rope!

Naively, Poole was ensnared in a Black Legion trap when he agreed to go with them to Dearborn to play in a sandlot baseball game.

Fortunately for the Black Legion, Denton Dean, the group leader, had a handgun. He emptied five shots into Poole, killing him instantly. Any group that only paid $7.00 for a robe and 10¢ for monthly dues is not destined to commit murder with erudition.

On May 12, 1936, Poole was found dead near a roadside in a remote area in Dearborn, a Detroit suburb. It was not long before the police got wind of the Poole execution by the Black Legion. Within a short time, 16 members of the Black Legion were arrested and charged with murder and

"I will stamp it [the Black Legion] out as I would a pestilence."

Duncan McCrea, state prosecutor.

kidnapping. Charges against four were dismissed, and 12 went to trial. Rushing was one of the members charged with murder. The state prosecutor, Duncan McCrea, said, "...I will stamp it [the Black Legion] out as I would a pestilence." Michigan's Attorney General said the Black Legion was a "menace."

In a jarring twist to the Poole murder, writer and author Coulter stated that the Black Legion did more than kill a wife beater—they protected a black woman. According to Coulter, Rebecca Poole was 1/32 black, but passed herself off as white and Irish. She states that Rebecca descended from the "Melungeons," a tri-race nationality that originated in the 16th century and was a combination of black, Portuguese and Italian. She said the Black Legion, ironically, was not aware of this lineage.

The trial of Black Legion members spelled the end of the Michigan movement. Rebecca Poole testified at the trial that her husband had not beaten her, and that the rumors the Black Legion acted on were false. Dayton Dean, who

The notorious Black Legion defendants in a Detroit court in May of 1936. Eleven of the infamous gang members were convicted of the murder of Charles Poole and sent to prison.

executed Poole, confessed in the county jail. "The killing was a horrible mistake, I was just following orders from my superiors. We were all told that Poole had kicked and beaten his wife. We were told that Mrs. Poole's baby would not be born alive because of the brutality of her husband. It was just a pack of lies to get us to take drastic action."

Of the 12 Black Legions members who were brought to trial for the murder of Poole, a jury convicted nine, and two were convicted in a bench trial. Rushing never got the chance to have a relationship with Rebecca Poole; instead he dreamed of what could have been while jailed in a Michigan prison for the slaying of her husband.

The Black Legion's activities did not go unnoticed by Hollywood filmmakers. In 1937 the movie, *Black Legion*, starring Humphrey Bogart, hit theaters and was considered one of Bogart's better performances. Bogart plays a distraught factory worker who missed out on a promotion when it was given to a Polish immigrant. In retaliation, he joins the Black Legion that drives the Polish family out of their home. Bogart then gets what he feels is his rightful position in the factory, but all is not well. The Black Legion not only consumed his time and his soul, but also sent him into a dark descent where they took his money and alcohol gutted his spirit.

Perhaps W.C. Fields best stated the attitude of the Black Legion when he said, "I am free of all prejudice. I hate everyone equally."

"I am quite sure...I have no race prejudice, and I think I have no color prejudices, nor caste prejudices. Indeed, I know it. I can stand any society. All I care to know is that a man is a human being—that is enough for me; he can't be any worse."

Mark Twain

The LAST EXECUTION

In 1938, bank robber Anthony Chebatoris was hanged in Michigan in spite of a state constitution that outlawed the death penalty

Chebatoris's 38 years were not good. Most of his adult life was spent in jail or committing crimes that would send him to jail.

"You can't do anything for me," Anthony Chebatoris stated emphatically to the prison chaplain the night before his hanging in Midland, Michigan. He then cavalierly dismissed the chaplain; he was an atheist. On July 7, 1938, he ravenously ate his last meal. He refused the special menu that prisoners have the night before they're executed. He said, "I'll eat what the other fellows eat." Chebatoris was egalitarian and believed that everyone was equal; hence, he refused to have a meal that was better than the other inmates'. If he was concerned about his impending death he didn't show it.

The following morning at 5:00 a.m., Chebatoris was brought to the gallows. He climbed the steps to a 10-foot platform where hangman, G. Phil Hanna, greeted him. Hanna had a distinguished reputation as an efficient hangman with 71 notches on his rope. He calculated the distance a body had to drop to ensure a proper execution.

Hanna even had rope specially made for hangings. He protested sloppy hangings and wanted to give every gallows man a dignified death.

Chebatoris smirked at Hanna and said, "Are you Mr. Hanna?" "I am," Hanna replied. "Then I know it will be a good job," Chebatoris said.

Little did Chebatoris know that Hanna might not do a good job—he was drunk as a skunk. In spite of being liquored up, Hanna proceeded with preparations for the hanging. He placed a black sateen hood over Chebatoris's head and then carefully adjusted the noose around his neck.

At precisely 5:07, Hanna gave the order to Sheriff Ira M. Smith to spring the trap door. It opened and Chebatoris dropped nine feet to his death. The murmuring prayers of a priest could be heard as the rope made its final snap at 5:21 a.m.—Chebatoris was dead. The loaded Hanna had successfully completed the hanging.

Chebatoris's 38 years were not good. Most of his adult life was spent in jail or committing crimes that would send him to jail. He was born in Poland in 1899, but he and his parents emigrated when he was a child and settled in Pittsburgh, Pennsylvania. Schooling wasn't his long suit, and he dropped out in fifth grade. From then on he began a life of crime, first petty theft and then bank robbery and murder.

Anthony Chebatoris (37) killed an innocent bystander in a bungled bank robbery in Midland, Michigan in 1937. The recalcitrant Chebatoris was sentenced to death, in spite of a state law that banned the death penalty.

The Chemical State Savings Bank in Midland that Anthony Chebatoris and John Gacey attempted to rob. Chebatoirs was aware that the bank had Dow Chemical's $75,000 payroll in its possession, thus making it an ideal target.

In spite of knowing the bank layout, they botched the heist from the onset.

In 1920, he set up housekeeping with his new wife in Hamtramck, a Polish suburb of Detroit. Marriage would not alter Chebatoris's proclivity for crime. In less than a year he was convicted of robbery and sent to Jackson State Prison. His wife bore him a child while he was serving time. Chebatoris was released in 1926 after serving six years, only to be rearrested in 1927 for stealing a car. During this incarceration, Chebatoris and fellow inmate John Gracey failed in an attempted escape. As a result, Chebatoris and Gracey were sent to Marquette's Branch Prison, an institution that housed the state's worst criminals, and where they concocted their next criminal venture—to rob the Chemical State Savings Bank in Midland. After their release from prison they went to Midland to case the bank. They knew that the Dow Chemical Company payroll would be in the bank on September 29, 1937. Armed with a rifle and 38-caliber handgun, in a stolen car, Gracey and Chebatoris headed to the bank. In spite of knowing the bank layout, they botched the heist from the onset.

Entering the bank at 11:30 a.m., Gracey approached distinguished-looking bank president Clarence H. Macomber, who was in the entry area chatting with his daughter. Gracey jammed a rifle in Macomber's chest, but did not anticipate Macomber resisting. Macomber grabbed the gun and a struggle began for control of the weapon. Chebatoris seeing the scuffle, shot Macomber, wounding him in the shoulder. Paul Bywater, a bank cashier, rushed to assist Macomber. Chebatoris went to Gracey's defense and shot Bywater in the lower abdomen. The panicked robbers, now unnerved, fled the bank. Then things got even worse for the thieving duo.

The panicked robbers, now unnerved, fled the bank. Then things got even worse for the thieving duo.

Unbeknownst to the culprits, on the second floor of the bank was an armed dentist, Frank L. Hardy. He heard the commotion downstairs and knew there was trouble in the bank. The dentist, a crack shot with a high-power rifle, waited for the bandits to flee the bank. Watching from his second story window, Hardy saw two men run from the bank and jump into a car. Assuming they were bandits, he fired at the car striking Gracey in the leg. Hardy fired again at the car speeding away; this time he hit Chebatoris. Losing control, Chebatoris crashed into a parked car and Gracey toppled out on to the pavement. Chebatoris jumped out of the car and assisted Gracey to his feet. While helping

Dr. Frank Hardy's dental office upstairs of the bank. With a rifle next to his dental chair, Hardy was prepared for a bank robbery. He fired at the fleeing bandits from his second story window, hitting and killing John Gracey.

Crack-shot, Dr. Frank Hardy was instrumental in preventing the escape of Chebatoris and Gracey. He down played his role and shied away from notoriety.

Gracey he spotted a man in a uniform across the street. The man was Henry J. Porter, a Bay City truck driver who Chebatoris thought was a policeman. He fired at Porter, hitting him in the abdomen.

The stick-up men then attempted to commandeer a car driven by a woman with a baby. The frightened woman grabbed her baby and abandoned the car. Chebatoris and Gracey heard another shot and decided to ditch the car. They began running down the street when Hardy squeezed off one final blast. The shot at 200 yards was dead center and tore off the back of Gracey's head; he died instantly. Chebatoris dropped his rifle and scampered down the street and attempted to hijack another car. Unsuccessful, he fled on foot, but was caught by Midland County Sheriff Smith after two blocks. Chebatoris had only a minor flesh wound from the shootout and recovered quickly. Macomber and Bywater, both injured during the attempted bank heist, recovered from their wounds. But innocent bystander Henry J. Porter died as a result of the gunshot inflicted by Chebatoris.

When Gracey's mother heard how her son had been shot in a foiled bank robbery, she collapsed and said, "He was a good boy."

It seemed odd that a dentist would have a loaded rifle next to his "chair of pain." After the enactment of the National Bank Robbery Act (NBRA), it was suggested that occupants near a bank should be armed in the event of a robbery. Understandably, bank robberies were on the increase during the Depression, although for Gracey and Chebatoris it wouldn't have made any difference what the economic times were like. They robbed because they thought it was an easy way to make a living.

Chebatoris was sent to the Saginaw Jail where he was arraigned before the United States Court Commissioner in Bay City. He arrived in court in handcuffs and leg irons and remained mute when asked how he pleaded. He failed to post $250,000 bond. Chebatoris appeared indifferent to his arrest and jailing; he joked with the guards on his arrival at prison. One of the guards watched Chebatoris closely, saying, "I wouldn't be surprised if he tried to duck out."

An oiled and loaded 35-caliber rifle rested near the window in Hardy's dental office. It was ready to use in a moment's notice.

Chebatoris was arraigned before dignified looking Judge Arthur J. Tuttle on October 26, 1937. The charge was first-degree murder. "My God," said Chebatoris, "Can't you make it second degree murder?" He would have no such luck, the judge kept the first-degree murder charge intact.

Dr. Hardy was flooded with mail after the much-publicized robbery debacle. He didn't understand the fuss made over him by the press. A radio station offered him a lucrative contract for radio appearances; he declined. Dr. Hardy saw himself as just another citizen doing his civic duty; he did not need the accolades.

Chebatoris's five-day trial was busy with the prosecution calling 34

The Benson Street Bridge, located two blocks from the Chemical State Savings Bank where Chebatoris was finally apprehended by Midland County Sheriff Ira M. Smith.

witnesses; the defense did not call any. The jury of 12 was composed mostly of wives and farmers from the surrounding community. Chebatoris, dark complexioned and sinister looking, never took the stand in his defense. In order to be exonerated, he needed all the help he could get from a sympathetic jury, but his court demeanor did nothing to make him likeable. He never appeared remorseful and was easily agitated. He was insolent even with his own attorneys.

On October 28, 1937, Chebatoris was found guilty and sentenced to death.

On October 28, 1937, Chebatoris was found guilty and sentenced to death. A sticking point that had to be resolved was Michigan's ban of the death penalty. The death penalty, however, was legal under the Federal National Bank Robbery Act. Michigan had no problem with the death sentence as long as the execution was done in another state. The state assumed that Chebatoris would be shipped to a state that allowed executions; however, this did not happen.

Michigan's death penalty provision had a loophole; it permitted state executions for treason even though the provision was never used. That, however, provide a legal basis for the federal government to execute Chebatoris in Michigan. After considerable legal sparring, the federal court ruled that the execution would be carried out in Michigan on July 8, 1938.

Governor Murphy fumed at the thought of an execution in the state. He said, "This is a blot on Michigan's civilized record." In spite of the governor's protest, the execution proceeded at the Federal Detention Farm in Milan. It was the only execution in Michigan's 91 years as a state.

After considerable legal sparring, the federal court ruled that the execution would be carried out in Michigan on July 8, 1938.

Minnie Porter, mother of slain Frank Porter, was a compassionate woman. When asked about the death penalty for Chebatoris, she responded, "I don't feel that we have the right to say whether people could be killed. It isn't up to us. There is a greater judge."

In 1846 Michigan became the first state to outlaw the death penalty. Prior to statehood in 1837 there had been other state hangings, the last was when innkeeper Stephen Simmons was hanged in 1830 for beating his wife to death while in a drunken rage. The hanging had a dramatic effect on the state's constituents that resulted in Michigan banning capital punishment.

The debate continues in Michigan over the death penalty. It has been argued on many fronts: moral, economic, racial, deterrent effectiveness, and as a cruel and unusual punishment. Both sides of the capital punishment debate have supporters and detractors. Nationwide, most polls show 60 to 70 percent of the population favors the death penalty. Michigan is one of 12 states that does not have capital punishment. There is not an answer that will please everyone. The argument over the death penalty, however, is moot for Chebatoris. He once said, "I haven't a friend in the world. My wife has divorced me. I'd rather die than go back to prison." He got his wish.

The MURDER of SENATOR HOOPER

In 1943 Senator Warren Hooper was brutally murdered on a Michigan back road. Had the notorious Purple Gang infiltrated Michigan politics?

Michigan politics in the 1940s was rife with sleaze.

Politics in America is replete with corruption. In the post Civil War period the Ulysses. S. Grant administration was riddled with scandal. In the1920s Warren G. Harding's administration never saw a bribe it didn't like. And in the 1990s Bill Clinton lied to a grand jury and granted pardons to incarcerated felons.

Michigan politics in the 1940s was rife with sleaze. While U.S. soldiers were dying attempting to free Europe from Hitler's grasp, Michigan politicians greedily lined their pockets through a defiled political system. It was everywhere: the lieutenant governor's office, the state legislature, and Jackson Prison. Detroit's notorious Purple Gang was rubbing elbows with slick state politicians. Euphemistically it was said, "The Michigan Legislature was the finest one could buy." In the midst of this contaminated environment, and pivotal in a potentially explosive atmosphere, was Michigan State Senator Warren G. Hooper.

Hooper left his Lansing office at 2:30 on a chilly Tuesday afternoon, January 9, 1943. His destination was his home in Marshall, a small but upscale community, approximately five miles from the state capital. At home, Hooper's wife, Callienetta, was busy preparing the evening meal in anticipation of her husband's arrival. Hooper had been anxious all day. He was restless about a grand jury hearing that would be held in a few days—a hearing in which he would be bringing charges of bribery against Frank D. McKay, the czar of the Republican Party in Michigan. Nothing ever happened in Michigan's Republican Party without McKay's approval. He orchestrated the political system to his liking.

Nothing ever happened in Michigan's Republican Party without McKay's approval.

That evening, traveling along highway M-99 was Floyd Modjeska, an overweight grain elevator operator who lived nearby. En route, Modjeska spotted a green, 1939 Mercury parked on the side of the road with smoke curling from the windows. He stopped to see what was going on. Modjeska cautiously approached the car and noticed a bullet hole in the right window of the disabled vehicle. This unnerved him and he backed away. Fearful, he waited for help.

Senator Warren Hooper was caught up in corrupt Michigan politics in the early 1940s. He was scheduled to testify to at a grand jury when his life was taken on a back road outside of Lansing.

Within minutes, a car driven by Kyle Van Auker came along. Waving frantically, Modjeska flagged him down. Modjeska pointed to the bullet hole. For 15 minutes the frightened men did nothing. A third car driven by Mervyn Howard, also stopped. Howard immediately took charge

Kim Sigler, nicknamed "Hollywood Kim," was the dashing Michigan prosecutor that attempted to root out corruption in Michigan politics. He was governor of Michigan from 1947 to 1949. He was killed in a plane crash at the age of fifty-nine.

and opened the front door of the smoked-filled car. A small flame shot out from under the front seat as oxygen entered the car. When the smoke had cleared, the men could see what was inside: A badly burned body slumped forward in the passenger's seat. The fingers on the body's right hand were nearly burned off as flames continued to discharge from under the seat. The smell of burning flesh permeated the crisp night air. Meanwhile, Modjeska left the scene and contacted the state police. Within 20 minutes the police arrived. An examination of the body revealed that the victim had been shot three times.

The burned and bullet riddled body found that early evening on M-99 was State Senator Warren G. Hooper. Callienetta made her husband's supper in vain. The murder set the stage for one of the most bizarre murder tales in the state of Michigan.

Sigler continued with his investigation in spite of his star witness being murdered.

The state's prosecutor, dapper Kim Sigler, who was in charge of the McKay grand jury, now had a murder to contend with. Sigler was glib, glitzy, and polished barrister. He didn't walk in front of a jury—he preened—his chiseled physique meticulously draped in one of his 42 suits; the clotheshorse exuded self-assurance.

The murder of Hooper made prosecutor Sigler's investigation into political graft more difficult. Hooper was a primary witness who could have provided damning evidenced against politico Frank McKay. Prior to Hooper's murder, Sigler had interrogated him in hopes of eliciting evidence against McKay. Hooper did not disappoint Sigler and admitted he was on McKay's payroll.

It was common knowledge that Lansing lawmakers had long accepted money and gifts in return for votes.

It was common knowledge that Lansing lawmakers had long accepted money and gifts in return for votes. Horse racing, commercial fishing, chain banking, taxation, or any other legislation that would profit their benefactors were all open to bribes. The kingpin of legislation manipulation was Frank D. McKay, a successful banker and real estate entrepreneur. McKay at one time was the state treasurer, until his resignation in 1931. He left the job when a grand jury questioned him about state funds. His leaving the government under a cloud of suspicion did not deter his influence with Republicans, and he continued to remain a force in politics.

McKay knew that Sigler, in addition to trying to nail him on graft, would now attempt to implicate him in the Hooper murder. Sigler knew that McKay had Purple Gang members as bodyguards. The Purple Gang was a notorious Detroit gang that was responsible for much of the city's crime and were not beyond committing murder at a friend's behest. Sigler continued with his investigation in spite of his star witness being murdered.

The Michigan State Capital Building in Lansing. In the early 1940s it was said the Lansing lawmakers housed in this grand edifice were the finest that money could buy.

Finally, in June of 1943 McKay and seven others were charged with conspiracy by violating the state's liquor laws. McKay was accused of receiving money from distilleries in exchange for getting their booze in state-owned liquor stores. McKay also made sure that all state-owned vehicles were equipped with General Tires, the company he founded. Slippery as ever, McKay was acquitted on the liquor charge. With a tarnished reputation however, Governor Harry Kelly finally ousted McKay in 1945. McKay always denied any wrongdoing, but records make that claim farcical.

Jackson Prison where Purple Gang inmates were housed when they killed Senator Hooper. Lax and corrupt prison regulations allowed inmates to come and go at the administration's discretion.

Administrators and guards alike created a wide range of criminal enterprises within the prison.

The authors of *Three Bullets Sealed his Lips* speculated that Ray Bernstein and Harry Keywell, two convicted felons who were doing life at the Jackson Prison, murdered Hooper. Both Bernstein and Keywell were Purple Gang members as were McKay's bodyguards. This was the link between McKay and the suspected killers. If McKay wanted Hooper silenced, he knew the people who would do it.

Rubenstein and Ziewacz contended Bernstein and Keywell left the prison in Deputy Warden's D.C. Pettit's car and proceeded to M-99 where they knew Hooper would be traveling. After locating Hooper's car on the empty stretch of road, they forced Hooper off the pavement on to the shoulder. Bernstein left his car and jumped into Hooper's, pushing him to the passenger side. Bernstein then unloaded three bullets into the helpless Hooper. With the gangland execution completed, the pair fled the scene and sped back to the penitentiary.

They returned the car to Pettit's house, went inside, and exchanged their civilian clothes for prison garb. The mission completed, they resumed their normal prison activities. Interestingly, Bernstein and Keywell were still "on count" as far as the prison was concerned. On count meant they had never left the prison. Prison records from that time have disappeared. Prosecutors would have a difficult time tying to pin a murder on prisoners that had an unassailable alibi. Bernstein and Keywell were never charged with Hooper's murder.

Rubenstein and Ziewacz's assessment of how Hooper was killed seems incredulous. How was it possible that incarcerated lifers at Jackson State Prison could carry out the murder of a prominent politician?

Jackson Prison was not a country club, but it wasn't far off.

Like the state legislature in the 1940s, Jackson Prison's administration was as corrupt. The institution's goal purported to teach inmates the habits of industry and to keep costs at a minimum—neither was a priority. Prison authorities were too busy pursuing graft to be concerned about any noble objectives.

Administrators and guards alike created a wide range of criminal enterprises within the prison. Nothing was sacred; it was a cesspool of corruption. While prison authorities turned a blind eye, drugs and liquor were easily smuggled into the prison. Tools, coffee, auto parts, and anything not nailed down were either confiscated for personal use or for sale outside of the prison.

Under Warden Jackson, trustees were put in the position to maintain institutional order. For their loyal services they benefited with unheard-of privileges. Inmates could leave the institution to visit bars, their families, houses of prostitution, or to simply take in a ball game. Cars and civilian clothes were provided for their forays into the community. The clothes exchange was often done at Deputy Warden D.C. Pettit's house. Frequently they returned with whisky or other gifts of gratitude for their keepers.

Purchasing sex from female visitors in the prison hospital was not out of the ordinary. The oft-used expression, "the institution is run by the inmates" was not an epigram used in jest; at Jackson Prison it was a reality. This was not a country club, but it wasn't far off. They had free room and board with outside privileges and no annual membership fee. With inmates in and out of the prison with little or no supervision, it is easy to believe that Ray Bernstein and Harry Keywell were the executioners of Senator Warren Hooper.

Warren G. Hooper is buried in Albion, Michigan. No one from Hooper's side of the family attended the funeral.

After years of rumors about Warden Jackson's corrupt administration and the possibility that inmates in his charge may have killed a state senator, reform-minded crusaders took action. As a result, Jackson was removed from his position as Warden in 1945.

If prosecutor Sigler was aware that Bernstein and Keywell were the killers of Hooper, why didn't he go after them? It was conjectured that Sigler viewed the two felons as "small potatoes" and felt there would be little glory going after criminals who were already serving life sentences. McKay was the one Sigler wanted, and if he could convict McKay on graft or implicate him in the Hooper murder, then he would be adorned with a laurel wreath from a grateful public, and that could possibly catapult him into the governorship, or better yet, the presidency.

Hooper's fire damaged Mercury after his murder.

The Hooper murder was inconclusive. Four small-time hoods were sent to prison for short stints after being convicted in a conspiracy plot to

Senator Hooper's 1939 Mercury on M-99 where he was ambushed and killed on January 9, 1943.

kill Hooper—something that they never managed to pull off. Prosecutor Sigler in the mold of another crime buster, Thomas Dewey of New York, was elected governor of Michigan in 1945. Frank McKay continued to be a player in Michigan politics until the 1950s. He eventually moved to Florida where he died in 1965 at the age of 81.

Senator Warren G. Hooper is buried in Albion, Michigan. No one from Hooper's side of the family attended the funeral. His parents and two sisters who lived in California said it was too far to travel for a funeral, and his only brother who lived in adjacent Ohio, refused to attend the funeral. Hooper was a pitiable man in life and fared no better in death.

The epitaph inscribed on his tombstone is at least half accurate.

With Honesty He Lived

For Honesty He Was Taken

The COED SERIAL KILLER

Six women were murdered in Ann Ann Arbor and Ypsilanti in the the late 1960s—the rampage of a serial killer

Mary Fleszar's body was nude, lying face down and had been stabbed at least 30 times.

On August 7, 1967, two teenage boys, Russell Crisovan Jr. 15, and Mark Lucas 15, were working in a nearby farm field when they heard a car door slam. Hoping they might find a pair of lovers seeking solitude in the woods, they went to where they heard the sound. They did not find any surreptitious lovers, but did find a decomposed body inundated with flies and bugs from the summer heat. The body was nude, lying face down and had been stabbed at least 30 times. The hands and feet hacked off. The corpse appeared to have a head, but it was rotten and shapeless. The body was Mary Fleszar, a 19 year-old Eastern Michigan University (EMU) coed, and the first of five to die at the hands a serial murderer. Fleszar was buried without a clue as to who committed the murder.

Just before Fleszar's burial, a young man driving a Chevy visited the funeral home and requested taking a picture of the body. Although he stated he was a friend of the family, the funeral employees were appalled and denied his request. No one at the funeral home looked closely at him, and they could not provide police with a description. The police suspected this man might have been the murderer. As a result, law enforcement agents attended the burial of Fleszar, hoping that the killer might return for a gruesome souvenir. They were disappointed—the man did not show. Who he was still remains a mystery.

Growing up, John Norman Collin's life was not stable. Shortly after his birth in October 1947, his father abandoned him and his mother. His mother remarried and like her first marriage, it fared no better and lasted only a year. She married for the third time to an abusive alcoholic. Again, a failed marriage. John Norman was only nine at the time.

John Norman Collins, 61, went on a killing spree in the late 1960s when he was in his early 30s. Six women would die at the hands of the Ypsilanti serial murderer.

But good-looking Collins had an impressive high school career at St. Clements in Center Line. He was lean and well built with natty brown hair and stylish sideburns. People found him pleasant and easy to talk with. An honor student as well as a three-sport athlete, he never had problems with girls, and he was known to have dated. In addition, Collins was the football team's tri-captain as well as the starting pitcher for the school baseball team. Polite, quiet, and respectful were the words that were used to describe him. His athletic powers and leadership abilities led to his being elected the president of the lettermen's C-Club. With his charm, athletic ability, and academic skill he looked destined for success; the world was at his beckoning.

John Norman Collins with his charm, athletic ability, and academic skill he looked destined for success; the world was at his beckoning.

After high school Collins attended Central Michigan University for a year and then transferred to EMU. Collins was a social butterfly at Eastern where he joined the Theta Chi fraternity and was president of the ski club. Becoming an elementary school teacher was his educational goal. He was 20 years old and led a normal life. There was little evidence to suggest that he had an evil side.

Cracks in Collin's persona appeared while he was in his second year at Eastern. His fraternity brothers booted him out when they suspected he was stealing. Quick and alert were the words that his professors used to describe him, but they noted his grades plummeted the second half of his sophomore year. One professor thought he cheated. Collins became a loner and preferred to ride one of his many motorcycles. Later it was found out that he often stole parts to repair his cycles. Close to graduation, but short on credit, he dropped out of school; he had more important things to occupy his time…killing.

After the Fleszar murder, Collins went on a killing spree and killed five more times.

- Joan Schell, an art major at EMU (July 6, 1968).
- Marilyn Skelton, a high school dropout from Romulus (March 24, 1969).
- Dawn Basom, a 13-year-old 8th grader (April 14, 1969).
- Alice Kalom, an EMU student found in a field in Ypsilanti (June 9, 1969).

On July 23, 1969, Collins struck for the last time. His final victim was EMU student Karen Beineman. Her body was discovered on July 26 in a wooded gully where she had been savagely beaten and her breasts and stomach scalded with a caustic liquid her panties wadded up and stuffed in her vagina. The detectives found an important piece of forensic evidence at the scene; the panties were full of short cropped hairs that belonged to someone other than Beineman or Collins. Later the hairs were identified as belonging to family members of the house where the killing took place. The link between where the body was found and where the murder took place was critical. This careless mistake by Collins would eventually cost him his freedom.

Ironically, that damning hair evidence was found at the house of Michigan State Police Corporal David Leik. Leik had just returned to his home from a family vacation only to find black paint splashed across the basement floor. He guessed that his wife's nephew, John Norman Collins, had spilled it. Collins was the dog sitter for the Leik family. When Leik went back to work his colleagues told him that Collins was a suspect in the coed murders. Leik was skeptical, but when he heard that Collins had agreed to take a polygraph and then backed out, he sensed there might be something to the allegations.

Leik scraped the black paint off the floor and found a brownish stain underneath. A lab analyzed the stain that turned out to be varnish. After the black paint discovery, Collins called Leik and asked him if the laboratory paint analysis found anything significant. Leik told Collins that nothing turned up with the paint examination. A relieved Collins began to cry; it was a red flag.

Leik told Collins that nothing turned up with the paint examination. A relieved Collins began to cry; it was a red flag.

Fortuitously, the washer had to be moved in order to scrape off the black paint. In doing so Leik found tufts of hair under the washer. Initially he thought little of it. He was aware that his sons' hair was shorn in the basement just before the family vacation. Leik, however, decided that it would be prudent to turn the hair over to the crime lab for examination. That was it—the hair matched hair that was found on Beineman's panties; it was some of Leik's sons' hair. Collins had carelessly gotten some of the hair on Beineman's panties. The house was the site where Collins murdered Beineman.

Additional damning evidence against Collins was found in Leik's basement when they discovered Type A blood on the washing machine, the same blood type as Beineman's. (A weak piece of evidence by today's standard as 40 per-cent of the population has Type A blood.)

Another piece of corroborative evidence was on the day of the murder, when a wig shopkeeper saw Beineman with Collins. He noticed them on a motorcycle outside of his store.

As in the case of Ted Bundy, another mass murderer (31), serial killers can be personable and appear to be unlikely candidates to murder.

The police now felt that they had enough physical evidence to arrest Collins and charge him with first-degree murder. They were aware that Collins had committed other murders, but he went on trial only for the murder of Beineman. The prosecution felt this was their most winnable case.

Surprisingly, the police had interviewed Collins after the second murder, but they didn't discover anything that was suggestive of his involvement. He provided a flimsy alibi that he was with his mother. But Collins was likeable and convincing, and the police never followed up. As in the case of Ted Bundy, another mass murderer (31), serial killers can be personable and appear to be unlikely candidates to murder.

Collins was tried on June 30, 1970. During the trial his attorneys decided that his mother should talk to him and then advise them to whether he should take the stand. Collins and his mother went into the judge's chamber. A half-hour later, Loretta Collins came out of the chamber room, her face swollen from crying. A distressed expression told the lawyers that she had learned something she did not want to hear. Collins did not testify.

After 17-day trial, testimony from 57 witnesses, and three hours of jury deliberation, Collins was found guilty and sentenced to life in prison. Michigan does not have the death penalty.

"I never killed Karen Sue Beineman."

John Norman Collins

Collins spoke once before the judge and that was at his sentencing. When asked if he had anything to say, he responded, "I never knew a girl named Karen Sue Beineman. I never took her for a ride on my motorcycle. I never took her to my cousin's basement. I never killed Karen Sue Beineman."

He was sent to prison in southern Michigan where he served the first 12 years of his sentence. In 1985, after a failed escape, he was transferred to the Marquette Branch Prison.

Collins rarely spoke of the events, only occasionally reiterating that he was not a killer. Finally in 1988, after 18 years of relative silence, he agreed to appear on the Detroit based talk show, *Kelly and Company*. Arrangements were set up the by co-host Marilyn Turner to interview Collin in prison.

> Turner's first question to Collins was, "Did you Kill Karen Sue Beineman?"
> Quickly Collins replied, "No, I never met Karen Sue Beineman."
> Turner continued, "Does it bother you to be called a serial killer?"
> Yes, it does," Collins stated. "It's bad enough being convicted on one thing you didn't do without being labeled for other things you haven't done."

During the course of the interview, Collins continued to claim innocence and stated that the media and pressure from the governor's office had much to do with his being found guilty.

Collins continued to claim innocence and stated that the media and pressure from the governor's office had much to do with him being found guilty.

Collins made several appeals while in prison. One requested that he be sent to Canadian prison (he was born in Canada), where he could have been paroled by 1985. Higher courts rejected all appeals.

Collins, now 61, has been in prison the last 28 years and will likely die in a four by-eight-foot cell.

The words "serial killer" were first used to identify a specific type of killer in the1970s, and the public became mesmerized by this new crime genre. Newspapers fed human curiosity with bold headlines of the latest rampage of suspected serial killer. *Silence of the Lambs*, a movie about a diabolic serial killer, was an immense success and bears testament to the public's fascination with serial murder.

History is replete with documented cases of serial killers. In the 15th century, Gilles de Rais, wealthy French aristocrat, was said to have abducted, raped, and killed 100 young boys, whom he brought home as castle pages. The infamous serial killer Jack the Ripper killed London prostitutes in 1888. The number he killed is not known, nor was the ripper ever identified.

A serial killer is defined by murdering at lest three people in three separate incidents. Some are sexual predators some are not. Most are male, had a miserable childhood, and target those in their own race. Paradoxically, their twisted personalities are often concealed by a façade of pleasant and friendly discourse.

Contrary to public opinion, most serial killers are not insane. Few have delusions or hallucinations. Many people believe that someone would have to be crazy to commit such monstrous crimes—few are. Most serial killers do not meet the insane criteria either legally or psychologically, although some have attempted to be vindicated by claiming insanity. It is rarely tried and almost never works.

Notorious serial killer Ted Bundy said it best when he stated, *"We are your sons, and we are your husbands, and we grew up in regular families."*

"My appearance was really different from what I was."

Serial Killer Ted Bundy.

A RENDEZVOUS With DEATH

Jimmy Hoffa, president of the Teamsters Union, went to a restaurant in 1975 and was never seen again

He loved his wife and was devoted to his children.

He never drank or smoked.

He berated associates who "womanized."

He worked long and hard.

He believed in helping the downtrodden.

These impeccable character traits must belong to someone destined for sainthood, or at least deserving a spot on the right-hand side of the deity. This was James Hoffa, once one of the most powerful men in America and not often thought of as a caring human being. He was an enigma, and like nearly everyone, he had several character dimensions. However, he is most frequently portrayed in one dimension—ruthless. He was all of that and more. Beyond being a hard driving union leader, he

Hoffa's personal life was beyond reproach.

was a devoted family man who was bright and a voracious reader of economics and politics. What he lacked in a formal education, he made up in determined self-teaching.

Hoffa's personal life was beyond reproach. He had a Victorian nature, a family man that kept his private life far removed from the brawling world of unions. Despite his lofty position, he maintained two modest homes in Detroit; he spurned a lavish life.

Jimmy Hoffa was the undisputed head of the Teamsters Unions from 1957 to 1967. He mysteriously disappeared in July 1975 from a suburban Detroit Restaurant. It was speculated that the mob had killed him, but his body was never found.

With uncompromising zeal he rode across the American labor landscape and organized the nation's 2.2 million truck drivers into one of the most powerful unions in the country—the Teamsters. When he talked—people listened. Millions of workers considered him a savior as he fought for increased wages and benefits for union members. For decades his name was splattered across newspapers, as oval office politicians tenuously watched his union movement.

Hoffa was the paradoxical Teamster Union president from 1957 to 1964. Under his leadership truck drivers made wages that in many cases were higher than skilled workers. He unrelentingly fought for the rank and file and was tough as nails when negotiating a contract. Hoffa was nobody to fool with.

He was born in February 1913 in Brazil, Indiana, and

he was one of four children of a coal driller and a house domestic. Hoffa saw how his father worked hard for next to nothing; he thought laborers were poorly paid. After years of working in dank coalmines his dad died from lung disease. Hoffa was seven when his father died. When Hoffa was 11 years old his mother moved the family to the squalid west side of Detroit. He described his hard working mother as a loving frontier-type woman.

Hoffa quit school at 14 when he was in the ninth grade and went to work unloading boxcars and trucks. After that he was employed at Kroger's grocery, where he lied about his age to get the job at 32 cents an hour. At Kroger's he was often on call for a 12–14 hour period, but only paid for three or four hours of work; he wasn't paid for the down time, but had to be on the premises.

Hoffa, sensing the economic injustice done to him and other employees, led his first strike at Kroger's—he was 17. Two workers were fired at Kroger's for eating a midnight dinner at a food cart. Hoffa protested the firings and organized a work stoppage that prevented fresh strawberries from immediate refrigeration. The tactic worked and management gave the employees a 13-cents an-hour increase as well as a limited insurance plan. The neophyte union was also recognized; Jimmy Hoffa was on his way.

Hoffa, sensing the economic injustice done to him and other employees, led his first strike at Kroger's—he was 17.

He stayed with Kroger's for another year and was then fired by an irate foreman. The foreman was a tyrant whom the workers called the "Little Bastard." He was abusive and the kind of guy that Hoffa said "caused unions." Hoffa threw a crate of strawberries at the foreman, and that ended his employment at Kroger's. He had a temper and his volatility periodically surfaced, and that was one of those times. It was in the early 1930s, and the depression had devoured a once vibrant economy. Hoffa, knowing work was scare, kept his union organizing activities to a minimum during the early years.

After Kroger's, Hoffa became a full-time organizer for the Brotherhood of Teamsters. He was aggressive and unrelenting in his drive to increase membership. Hoffa once said, "If it moves, sign it up." The depression was a hard time, and most of those who were employed were reluctant to join a union and jeopardize their job.

Police and strikebreakers alike beat Hoffa. His confrontational leadership resulted in several arrests. But whenever Hoffa was released from jail, he was back at union activities. Always vigilant, he told a colleague how to get into a car during turbulent times: after you open the car door, only put one foot inside at first and leave the door open. If the car were booby-rigged, the explosion would propel you out of the car with less energy. Though the work was precarious, he never quit. And his forceful tactics increased union membership.

Preceding Hoffa as Teamster president was corrupt David Beck. In 1956, a select Congressional committee with Joe McCarthy, Barry Goldwater, and John F. Kennedy, began to look into the perceived corruption at the top of the Teamster Union. In the discovery process, they found out that Beck took more than $85,000 in union funds for his personal use and another $196,000 for work done to his Seattle home. Beck attempted to avoid prosecution by fleeing the country; however, authorities caught up with him and he was convicted of misappropriating union funds and sent to prison for five years. Hoffa, as the vice president, ascended to the union presidency.

As president of the International Teamsters Union, Hoffa came under fire from Attorney General Bobby Kennedy. Kennedy saw Hoffa as a corrupt union official who was nesting with the Las Vegas mob. Hoffa viewed Kennedy as an uppity rich kid who was out to make a name for himself. No love was lost between the two adversaries, and a 1983 television drama, *Blood Feud*, explored this volatile relationship.

As president of the International Teamsters Union, Hoffa came under fire from Attorney General Bobby Kennedy.

After successfully prosecuting Beck, Kennedy went after Hoffa, and in 1962 charged him with misappropriating $9.5 million in union funds and accepting an illegal payment from an employer. Hoffa successfully beat the rap, only to have Kennedy haul him back into court in 1964, this time charged with jury tampering. Hoffa's Houdini-like escapes from the Kennedy wrath ran out, and he was convicted of jury tampering and sentenced to eight years in prison. Shortly after his conviction a Chicago court tacked on an additional five years when he was convicted of fraud.

In 1966, after two years of unsuccessful appeals, Hoffa was sent to the federal prison in Lewisburg, Pennsylvania. The political gods, however, took pity on Hoffa, and through their agent, Richard Nixon, Hoffa was granted a pardon in 1971 after serving four of the 13 years.

Machus Red Fox Restaurant in suburban Detroit was the last place that James Hoffa was seen alive.

After his release from prison, Hoffa desperately wanted to return to the union presidency. He believed the current Teamster President Frank Fitzsimmons had betrayed him. He saw Fitzsimmons as a lackey and not providing aggressive union leadership. Although Hoffa was legally bared from taking part in union activities until 1981, it did not stop him.

After his release from prison, Hoffa desperately wanted to return to the union presidency.

In pursuit of again becoming the Teamsters president, he scheduled a meeting at Machus Red Fox Restaurant in suburban Detroit on July 30, 1975. Hoffa was of the understanding that the meeting was to discuss his running for the Teamsters presidency. The men he was to meet were underworld gangsters whom Hoffa had been in bed with prior to his imprisonment. Anthony "Tony Jack"

Glacalone and Anthony "Tony Pro" Provenzano were the mobsters that Hoffa was scheduled to meet. The mob liked Fitzsimmons as head of the Teamsters; he was easy to control. If Hoffa became the union president, his aggressive and bull-doggish style could give the mob bosses problems. They wanted to avoid this at all costs.

It was unlikely that the skeptical Hoffa would have set foot in a car with two former mob associates; he knew what they were like.

The punctual Hoffa arrived at the Red Fox restaurant just prior to 2:00 p.m. Hoffa never arrived late at a meeting, and he was perturbed that Provenzano and Glacalone did not arrive at the designated time. At 2:15 p.m., he went to a nearby telephone and called his wife and told her that nobody showed up. That was the last time she ever heard from him. After that infamous day in 1975, Hoffa was never seen again.

Shortly after Hoffa's phone call to his wife, a truck driver near the restaurant noted a Mercury pulling out in front of him, which nearly hit his truck. The truck driver scanned the Mercury and noticed Hoffa sitting in the back seat. As Hoffa was the former Teamsters head, it is likely that any truck driver would easily recognize him. The truck driver didn't notice the driver of the Mercury, but he did see a long object covered in the back seat and right next to whom he thought was Hoffa. It was unlikely that the skeptical Hoffa would have set foot in a car with two former mob associates; he knew what they were like. But Hoffa apparently recognized the Mercury as belonging to Charles "Chuckie" O'Brien. O'Brien was like a son to Hoffa, and he lived with Hoffa and his wife for a period of time. Hoffa would have gotten into O'Brian's car without hesitation. That was the last sighting of James Riddle Hoffa. In 2001, DNA evidence confirmed that Hoffa had been in O'Brien's car. Hair fibers from the car and strands taken from Hoffa's hairbrush were a match, but it was not enough evidence to indict O'Brien.

Thirty-three years later it is still a mystery as to what happened to Hoffa. The media examined a plethora of leads as to where he was buried. They all looked promising, but nothing was ever found. He is presumed dead and most likely was murdered. If alive he would be 95. He was legally declared dead in 1982. In 1995 friends held a memorial service for him.

Some of the places that have been suggested as to where Hoffa's body is buried:

In the footings of the New York Giant's football field.

In the cement superstructure of the Mackinac Bridge.

Under a barn in Milford Township.

In the foundation of the Renaissance Center in Detroit.

In the trunk of a car, then run through a compactor.

One of the more plausible explanations of what happened to Hoffa seems to be that close associate Chuckie O'Brien picked Hoffa up at the restaurant and drove him to his place of execution. It is likely that after the killing his body was transported to a mafia member's crematorium where he was incinerated; hence, there is no body, making attempts to locate the corpse an exercise in futility. The mafia was efficient in its killings. Provenzano and Glacalone had strong alibis and could not be placed anywhere near Hoffa on the day he disappeared. With Hoffa dead, the mob felt they had prevented any potential union disruption.

The FBI, taking a positive spin on his disappearance, stated that anyone who was responsible for his death is now either dead or in prison. The FBI is reluctant to admit that they don't always get their man.

The FBI is reluctant to admit that they don't always get their man.

In spite of his death, Hoffa's legacy lives on through his son, James Jr., who is now the president of the Brotherhood of Teamsters. Hoffa's daughter, Barbara Ann Crancer, is a circuit court judge in St. Louis, Missouri. It is ironic that Hoffa often skirted the law; yet, both of his children became lawyers.

The presumed murder and disappearance of James Riddle Hoffa remains just that—a riddle. The mystery goes on.

Thirty-three years later it is still a mystery as to what happened to Hoffa.

> *Men with power have an extraordinary capacity to convince themselves that what they want to do coincides with what society needs done for its [own] good.*
>
> *Raymond Vernon*

OSCODA
COUNTY
COURT HOUSE
Erected 1888

A TALE Of TYRANNY

Are two Detroit hunters beaten to death, stuffed into a wood chipper and then fed to ravenous pigs?

Some murders are solved in a short period time of time, others take decades. The murders of Brian Ognjan and David Tyll took 18 years to solve. The protracted investigation was fraught with hundreds of leads and interviews that went nowhere. At times the murders seemed unsolvable.

Television shows depict savvy, good-looking forensic experts with high tech apparatus, who brilliantly piece together evidence and speedily solve a seemingly impossible murder case—but that rarely happens in the real world.

Ognjan and Tyll, two 27-year old native Detroiters, left on a hunting trip to northern Lower Michigan on November 22, 1985. The close friends from Detroit's east side were eagerly anticipating their trip north. It wasn't so much the deer hunting that sparked their interest, as it was a time to drink beer and be unencumbered by work or home responsibilities. Neither even bothered to get a hunting license. Their foray was not untypical of many men who don't hunt, but enjoy the fall ritual. The objective of these fair-weather hunters is not to provide a meat supply for a long and cold winter, but to celebrate with old and trusted friends. Both Ognjan and Tyll were hard-working, blue-collar guys who enjoyed playing pool and hanging out on the weekends.

The hunting duo left Detroit Friday afternoon and planned to return Sunday evening. Both had to be to work on Monday and neither liked missing work. The destination was a family cabin near White Cloud, a small town on the west side of the state, where other friends and family members would join them. But neither Ognjan nor Tyll were keen on staying in a camp crowded with ill-smelling hunters. They knew it was hunting camp and not the Holiday Inn, and they didn't want any part of it.

Main street in the usually quiet, northern lower Michigan town of Mio. In the 1980s, the notorious and violent Duvall brothers had the community in a grip of fear.

Linker's Lost Lodge (now Lost Creek Sky Ranch & Lodge) is located on the outskirts of Mio where Detroit hunters Brian Ognjan and David Tyll were last seen. The nasty Duvall brothers didn't like the hunters on their turf and made sure it would be the last time they went anywhere.

They abandoned the cabin plan and decided to find lodging elsewhere. They went to the northeast side of the state rather than the northwest. They ended up in remote Mio, a quiet town of 5,000 that doesn't see much life until hunting season. With the excuse of hunting no longer an impediment, the duo barhopped through the weekend. They were last seen at Linker's Bar near Mio on Sunday—then they vanished.

When Ognjan and Tyll failed to return to Detroit on Sunday evening, Ognjan's wife, Denise, and Tyll's girlfriend, Janice, were concerned. It was not like Ognjan to be late. He was punctual and would have called if something came up. They also failed to show up on Monday. Denise was now very worried and contacted the Troy police and filed a missing persons report.

Thanksgiving week passed and still no word from Ognjan and Tyll. The men's parents, along with Denise and Janice, were worried; they feared something dreadful had happened to the two hunters. They were right, but it would be an 18-year odyssey to find out what happened.

The search began almost immediately for the missing hunters. Over time, thousands of hours were spent tracking leads that ended in dead ends. Evidence was often inaccurate or could not be substantiated.

There is no statute of limitations on murder in Michigan; killers can never rest.

For years, little information turned up. At various times the case was either inactive or closed. When new information came in the case would be reopened. There is no statute of limitations on murder in Michigan; killers can never rest. Over time, 1,259 pages of information were gathered, enough paper to fill nine binders. It included 820 names.

It was suspected they were the victims of foul play, but proving it was difficult. The police never gave up, always hoping that at some point one of the tips would point them in the right direction.

The police did everything possible to track down the killer(s). Aerial searches with both helicopters and planes scanned the remote terrain looking for burial sites, backhoes and cadaver dogs dug up the earth looking for bodies. The murders were on the national TV crime programs—*Missing: Reward and Unsolved Mysteries.* Year after year, police pursued hundreds of leads and conducted interviews, always hoping that someone would provide them with some knowledge of the crime.

Every town has them—bullies; Mio was no exception. Thriving on harassment and intimidation in Mio were the nasty Duvall brothers. Crossing to the other side of the street was a given if a Duvall was near. Bars were their favorite haunts and patrons would quietly slip out when the Duvalls entered. They were crude, bellicose, and unresponsive to any social amenities. When drunk, which was most of time, they were even more garrulous. Brawling was a way of life. They lived in squalid conditions. Their homes were shacks and their yards were decorated with junk cars and garbage. With long, shaggy, unwashed hair, they looked and smelled as bad as they lived.

The Duvall clan had seven brothers, but J.R. and Coco were the worst. You couldn't go anywhere in the county without running into a Duvall, or one of their ex-wives or ex-girlfriends. Several of the notorious brothers either had been in jail, were in jail, or going to jail. It was their second most common residence. The hard-drinking clan supported the local bars and engaged in a host of enterprises, many of them illegal. They were skilled at dismantling stolen cars and selling the parts. If a VIN number needed removing from a car, just ask a Duvall.

After years of investigating, two names were always front and center—J.R. and Coco Duvall. Rumors had circulated for years that the belligerent Duvall brothers were responsible for the disappearance and murder of the two hunters. Investigators and the prosecutor were almost certain that J.R. and Coca Duvall were the killers, but proving they did it would be difficult. All leads, except the ones pointing to Jr. and Coco, were dead ends.

Finally, the police got the break they needed—an eyewitness to the murder who was willing to testify at a trial. Relentless state police detective Bronco Lesneski interviewed recovering alcoholic and former bar maid Barb Boudro, who after considerable jawboning by Lesneski, unenthusiastically agreed to testify. When Lesneski first approached her she looked at him and said, "You're going to get me killed." Like others who had some knowledge of the murders, she kept quiet for years, fearing retribution from the Duvalls. With a witness in hand the authorities were ready to go to court.

When detective Lesneski first approached Bronco to testify she looked at him and said, "You're going to get me killed."

"Bodiless" murder cases, while rare, go back to 1792 in England, when a man charged with throwing his captain from a ship was convicted. The first case in the United States was the 1959 conviction of investment consultant Leonard Scott who was accused of killing his wealthy socialite wife. Since then there have been hundreds of triumphant prosecutions of bodiless murders in the United States.

The trial of J.R. and Coco began on October 20, 2003. The trial presented serious problems for the prosecution. There wasn't any forensic evidence linking the suspected murderers to the killing: no DNA, no blood, no body, and no weapon. And the car the victims were driving mysteriously disappeared. At first glance, it looked like a trial that could have easily exonerated the Duvalls.

Donna Pendergast, 45, was selected by the Attorney General to be the lead prosecutor. She was a lithe blonde who looked much younger than her age and had an impressive 88–2 court record; she was a force to be reckoned with.

Boudro was a critical witness for the prosecution, without her testimony there would be little chance of convicting the Duvalls. Pendergast feared that Boudro would bolt at the last minute and refuse to testify. It nearly happened. Just before the trial Boudro said, "I can't do this." Skillfully, detective Lesneski talked her back into testifying.

On the stand, Boudro related what happened to Ognjan and Tyll the night of their deaths. She said they were drinking at the Linker's Lost Creek Bar that Saturday evening, playing pool and getting drunk. J.R. and Coco came to the bar sometime after Ognjan and Tyll. Within a short period of time there was trouble between the hunters and the Duvalls. The Duvalls needed little provocation to start a fight, and this was their turf.

J.R. slammed an iron pipe into Ornjan's head, it burst, spewing bits of brain and bone in all directions; it was like a pumpkin being smashed to the ground.

Boudro said that fearing a fight she left the bar and returned to her home near the tavern. A short while later she heard commotion in a clearing in back of her house. She and a visiting friend went to see what was happening. When they arrived at the clearing she said J.R. and Coco were unmercifully beating one of the hunters. On his knees, Ognjan said, "Oh my God somebody help us." With that, J.R. slammed an iron pipe into his head; it burst, spewing bits of brain and bone in all directions. At the same time, Coco stomped and kicked the body until it lay lifeless. Boudro said, "When a Duvall struck Ognjan's head with an iron pipe, it was like a pumpkin being smashed to the ground." The jury listened attentively to every word.

Boudro had seen enough and scampered back to her house. A short while later J.R. came to her house and threatened her. He said, "You saw nothing." She knew he meant for her to keep quiet about what just happened. Deathly afraid of the Duvalls, Boudro remained silent for 18 years.

This clearing, not far from Linker's Lost Lodge, was the site where Ognjan and Tyll were beaten to death with an iron pipe by J.R. and Coco Duvall.

As expected, the defense attacked Boudro's credibility. They contended that at the time of the murders she was drinking heavily, so how could one consider her testimony credible? To Pendergast's delight, Boudro held up under a withering cross-examination.

The Duvalls were losing their tyrannical grip on Mio residents.

The Duvalls were losing their tyrannical grip on Mio residents. No longer fearing them others testified how they thought the Duvalls disposed of the mutilated corpses. They said in an attempt to cover up the murder the Duvalls put the bodies into a wood chipper and then fed flesh remnants to the hogs. Nobody testified to seeing this gruesome disposal, and the Duvalls denied the killing, so how could they dispose of bodies they never had? Testimony came out in the trial about what most likely happened to the hunter's Bronco. Evidence suggested that the Bronco was dismantled by the Duvalls and sold in parts. As the Duvalls were in the junk business, this was conceivable.

Defendants rarely testify at their own trial. It's too risky; they open themselves up to a brutal cross-examination. The Duvalls, however, were aware that the trial was not going well; what did they have to lose by testifying? When on the stand they denied killing Ognjan and Tyll. Their testimony, however, did little to win jury sympathy.

On the ninth day of the trial the jury began deliberations. They deliberated for only two hours and seven minutes, a remarkably short time for a murder trial. They returned with a verdict: *Guilty of first-degree murder.* In Michigan this is a life sentence without parole. After the verdict the Duvall family did not speak to the press. At his sentencing, J.R. Duvall, looking very old, again denied any wrongdoing.

The brothers were responsible for their own undoing. For years they bragged in local bars about what they had done to the hunters, knowing full well that nobody would testify against them. They thought they were invincible—but that proved wrong.

The brothers were responsible for their own undoing. For years they bragged in local bars about what they had done to the hunters, knowing full well that nobody would testify against them. They thought they were invincible.

Boudro's brother, Dave Klimmek, who owns a motorcycle dealership near the murder site, said, "Even after the trial Barb was still scared that something would happen to her." However, she had little to fear as the Duvall's reign of terror appeared to be over with the imprisonment of the Duvall brothers. Nevertheless, 61 year-old Boudro kept a low profile until a massive heart attack took her life in 2008.

J.R. and Coco now have a lot of time on their hands behind bars at the Southern Michigan Correctional Facility [formerly Southern Michigan State Prison]. Prison changes some men; they became spiritual and attempted to atone for past transgressions. Whether the Duvalls have the wherewithal to become better human beings remains to be seen.

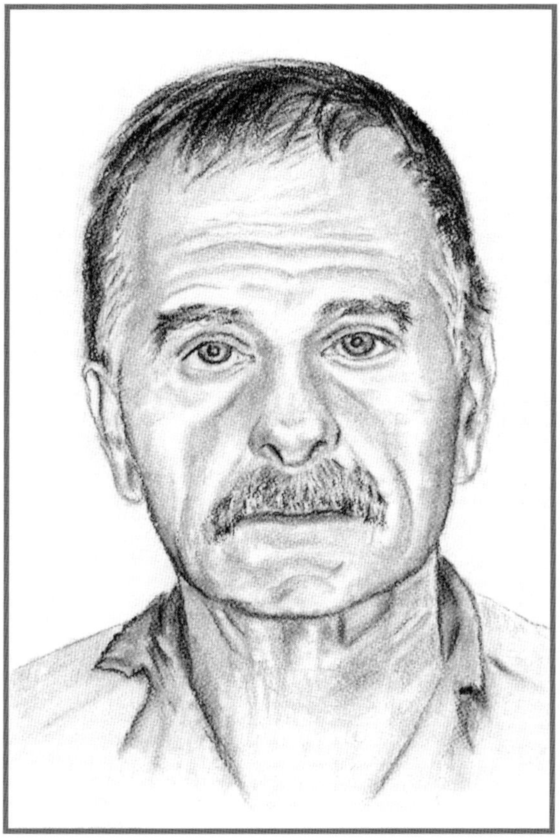

Raymond "J.R." Duvall was 52 at the time of his trail, but he looked much older. Years of hard drinking and raising hell had taken their toll. In a desperate attempt to save himself, he took the stand but to no avail. He was found guilty of murder and sentenced to life in prison.

Donald "Coco" Duvall, 51, at his trial, claimed he was a "recovering amnesiac," and that he had a stroke and had Alzheimer's. He was found guilty of murdering two Detroit hunters.

When SATAN WORE A BADGE

Diane Newton King, a popular Battle Creek television anchorwoman, was murdered in her driveway while her children watched

Beautiful Diane King hosted a morning news show on Battle Creek's WUHQ television station. She and her husband, Brad, lived in historic Marshall just 13 miles away. The 34-year-old energetic newscaster, was not only talented, she was determined. Few obstacles ever stopped her. She was a successful career woman, but also a caring mother of two children, and a tireless volunteer for many charities.

Diane inherited many of her mother's strengths, which both helped and hindered her.

Diane was born in Detroit in 1956 to Freida Newton, a full-blooded Mohawk. A rich bronze complexion enhanced Diane's exotic appearance. Diane's dad died when she was nine years old. Although young when he died, she never got over his death. Her mother was a strong woman; you always knew where you stood with her. Diane inherited many of her mother's strengths, which both helped and hindered her. In the business world her aggressiveness was advantageous, but in her private life, it presented problems. She said what was on her mind and expected others to be frank. This did not always go well with friends and associates; she excoriated wimpy behavior.

Brad King was impressive looking; he was big and intimidating with a shaved head.

Brad King was impressive looking; he was big and intimidating with a shaved head. Born in Croswell, Michigan, he was the son of a prominent bank president. He had an uneventful childhood. After graduation from high school he attended Western Michigan University (WMU) where he was active in the TKE fraternity. He loved fraternity life and was TKE man of the year. While at WMU he met and married Gail Heitzker; they had one child, Alissa. Brad King was not happy when his wife became pregnant; he stormed out of the house and stayed away for six weeks.

Stunning and talented Diane King was being stalked and feared for her life. Her pursuer was closer to her than she suspected—much closer—and he wanted her dead.

King did not follow his dad's footsteps and go into banking. Instead he chose law enforcement, and after graduation went into police administration in Pontiac. He was not well liked by fellow officers. They saw him as arrogant; he thought he was intellectually superior to them. He quit the police department after 13 years, and for the rest of his life he would bounce from job to job. Brad and his wife divorced after a 13-year marriage. He said, "I just wanted to be alone."

In 1982, Brad met vivacious Diane Newton; they fell in love and began a courtship. All did not go well for the struggling couple. They ended up in Colorado where an on-again, off-again, tumultuous courtship was the norm. However, they ironed out their differences and were married in July 1984. Diane was enjoying a successful career in Denver television but Brad's inability to hold steady employment always troubled her. For a while he was a probation officer, but he was fired for misappropriating funds.

Eventually the couple moved back to Michigan where they took up residency in Marshall. Diane became a news anchor for a Battle Creek television station; she was pert and popular. Brad found employment as a part-time instructor in criminal justice at WMU where he taught Tuesday and Thursday night classes. His minimalist teaching schedule provided the family with little income, and he had little chance of becoming employed full time at the university.

When Diane pulled into the driveway of the farmhouse and stepped out of her Wagoneer, she was greeted by two 22 bullets that ripped into her body.

In spite of the rocky marriage, the Kings had two children: Marler was born in 1988 four years into the marriage, and Kateria was born in 1990. While married to Diane, Brad was docile. Her dominant persona was evident when the two were together. But Brad didn't seem to mind being an appendage to his dynamic wife.

The Kings resided on a farm in Marshall, a historic and charming town of close to 8,000 steeped in architectural beauty. It has 46 buildings that are historic landmarks and a visual delight of 19th century American architecture. Situated close to the I-94 and I-69 intersection, it is in the cross hairs of Michigan's busiest expressways. Because of its location halfway between Detroit and Chicago, early residents were hopeful that it would be named the state capital. A pillared governor's mansion (1838) was built specifically for the community's anticipation of becoming the state capital. Marshall residents were disappointed when Lansing was named the capital.

In 2004, Marshall was one of only a dozen cities that were cited as a "Distinctive Destination City" by the National Trust for Historic Preservation. It was hardly the kind of community where one would expect that one of its well-known citizens would be murdered.

On February 9, 1991, Diane King was returning from suburban Detroit where she and her children were visiting her mother. When Diane pulled into the driveway of the farmhouse and stepped out of her Wagoneer, she was greeted by two 22 bullets that ripped into her body.

Deputy Guy Picketts was on patrol the evening that Diane was shot. At 6:30 p.m. he received an urgent message from the police dispatcher to proceed to the King farmhouse. The dispatcher, just moments before, had received a 911 call from the King residence that indicated someone was injured. When Picketts arrived he found Diane sprawled on the pavement near the driver's door with a trickle of blood around her nose. She was dressed in a Desert Storm sweatshirt and appeared lifeless.

Picketts heard a sob coming from the Wagoneer; he looked up and saw a youngster peering out of a backseat window with a spate of tears edging slowly down his face. In a closer look he saw another, younger child securely strapped into a carrier in the back seat—Marler and Kateria, the King's children, were in the car.

Picketts heard shouting coming from the house just 30 feet away. It was Brad King yelling, "Help my wife, please help her she's been hurt." At the same time the emergency medical technicians (EMT) and other police arrived at the scene. Picketts told Brad to stay on the porch. An examination by EMT personnel determined that she had been shot twice, once in the sternum and once in the groin. Diane was transported to the hospital, but all attempts to revive her failed. She was pronounced dead shortly after arriving at the hospital.

He looked up and saw a youngster peering out of a backseat window with a spate of tears edging slowly down his face.

Detectives Jack Schoder and Jim Stadfelt arrived at the scene soon after the murder. The King farmhouse was now inundated with police and confusion was rampant. Brad King was the only witness and Schoder interviewed him immediately. He had a cursory discussion with King at the farmhouse and then had him come to the police station for a more extensive, taped interview. As is typical in any murder involving a couple, the spouse or the significant other is often a suspect and target of investigation.

It was just over an hour and a half after the killing that detective Schoder interviewed King at the police station. At the time, he was not a suspect and Schoder was only attempting to gather information.

During the interview King told Schoder that he went for a walk on the couple's 50-acre property while he waited for his wife to return from Detroit. During his walk, he told Schoder that he heard a gunshot, but didn't think much of it. Schoder was surprised that King heard only one gunshot. Testimony by neighbors was confusing and contradicted King's statement when several said they didn't hear anything. King told the police that when he got back to the house he saw his wife lying in the driveway and called 911. Schoder felt unsettled after his lengthy interview with King. Some of the things that King told him didn't add up. King was the only one who knew when Diane was returning from Detroit, no one else could have possibly known. King's demeanor during the interview varied; at times he was angry, at other times morose. Schoder's impression of King was not one of a distraught husband grieving the recent murder of his wife.

Schoder was aware of harassing phone calls and letters that Diane had been receiving over the last several months. He had talked to her earlier about a stalking situation. She was petrified and took the harassing phone calls seriously. Schoder was worried that he had not amply followed up on the stalker lead. If there was a stalker, and he ended up being the killer, it would look like a sloppy investigation.

One communication from the stalker said, "You'll be sorry you didn't have lunch with me." The note was made with cut-out newspaper letters. Could it have been the mystery stalker who killed her? At the time other celebrities were being stalked, so it was not out of the ordinary that attractive Diane King had an admirer turned stalker and then killer.

One communication from the stalker said, "You'll be sorry you didn't have lunch with me."

During the course of the investigation other disturbing facts were uncovered. Why was the security system turned off? And why was the Doberman watchdog chained in the barn? Diane specifically put in an alarm system and bought the dog after she began receiving stalking phone calls.

As more information was gathered, a cloud of suspicion hovered over Brad King. A thorough search of the property in back of the farmhouse turned up a 22-caliber rifle that was submerged in a murky ravine. A ballistic evaluation of the rifle verified that it was the murder weapon. Although it could not be definitely traced to

Brad King lived in the shadow of his successful wife. He bounced from job-to-job and provided little income for his family. He set a course of action that spiraled into self-destruction.

Brad King, circumstantial evidence linked him to the rifle.

More damning information about Brad surfaced as the investigation proceeded. Anne Hill, a WMU student, and a divorced mother of two children, came forward with startling information. She was not only a student of King's at the university, but also his mistress. He told her he was separated from his wife; a lie he told to keep her as a girlfriend.

Prosecutors strongly suspected that King was responsible for the stalking. They suspected he used this ploy to distract the police. It was never proven, but along with other evidence, it seemed plausible.

The mounting circumstantial evidence made King look more like a killer than an innocent, grieving husband. He was calm during interrogations. This is not uncharacteristic of a psychopath. After spending 13 years in police work, King felt he was smarter than the cops who were investigating him. Time, however, would prove him wrong.

After one year of investigating, the prosecutors knew their case was not the strongest, but it was as good as it was going to get, and they indicted King for murder.

On January 30, 1992, He was arrested and charged with first-degree murder. Bail was set at $750,000. His friends raised the necessary 10 percent to release him, but one of the bail conditions was that he have a place to live. No landlord in the vicinity would take in the suspected killer, and as a result he stayed in jail. King was upset about this turn of events.

For the next two months the King murder trial was not only headlines in Battle Creek newspapers, but across the nation. The high profile murder and trial with its titillating tales captured the interest of the media, and like a swarm of locusts, reporters descended on Marshall.

The case would rely heavily on circumstantial evidence. As expected, King showed no emotion in the courtroom. He remained cool, exactly what the prosecution wanted.

King wanted to take the stand, but both of his lawyers knew it could be a disaster. Up until now, he was safe from revealing his prior indiscretions, as the judge ruled the previous affairs not relevant and prejudicial. Taking the stand could well subject him to a grilling on previous trysts by the prosecution.

The prosecution called 67 witnesses to bolster their case. Following an arduous five-week trial, both the prosecution and defense gave their closing arguments, and the case went to the jury. After two days of deliberation, and on a bitter cold January morning, the jury returned a verdict—*guilty of first-degree murder*.

King read a statement to the court after the verdict. It was the tirade of a psychopath that blamed everyone else for his problems. He blamed the system, the judge, and the jury. To the jury he said, "...I have nothing but contempt for you. I'm not guilty."

King is presently serving his time in the Thumb Correctional Facility. He was incarcerated in the Southern Michigan Correctional Facility (Jackson Prison). At one time the Jackson prison had the dubious distinction of being the largest walled prison in the world. He appears to have adjusted to prison. Working in the prison law library has provided him the opportunity to assist other inmates with their legal paperwork. He felt pleased when he recently helped an inmate secure a divorce. When he was married to Diane King he lived in her shadow. King now gets attention from other inmates for his accomplishments. Perhaps there is a certain comfort in that for him; finally finding his niche in life, a place where he belongs both emotionally and legally—in prison.

As expected, King showed no emotion in the courtroom. He remained cool, exactly what the prosecution wanted.

"They sow the wind, and they shall reap the whirlwind".

Hosea

"TESTIFY And I'LL KILL YOU"

Marvin Gabrion made good on his promise and murdered Rachael Timmerman just before his rape trial

Rachel and her father had a difficult relationship, but they were beginning to establish a better father-daughter connection.

Scanning the lake's horizon with binoculars, Douglas Sorder noticed something floating in the water. He wasn't sure what it was, but thought it had the shape of a human. Sorder and his son-in-law were on the shore of Oxford Lake, a small 20-acre lake in the midst of the Manistee National Forest and 27 miles north of Grand Rapids.

Concerned, they drove to their nearby vacation trailer and retrieved their 12-foot fishing boat. They launched it and rowed to the object. Sorder's observation was accurate: a female torso with the feet stuck out of the water and duct tape over her mouth.

It was Rachel Timmerman, a once lively 19 year old who was attempting to get her life together. However, her renaissance was cut short in June 1997, when her chained body was dragged from the isolated lake. A large cement block was attached to Timmerman, but the weight did not prevent the body from floating to the surface.

Timmerman was living with her grandmother, Kim VerHage, at the time of her disappearance, but she was working on patching things up with her father, Tim Timmerman. Rachel and her father had a difficult relationship, but they were beginning to establish a better father-daughter connection. Her plan was to move in with her dad and his new family. On the day she disappeared she was at her father's when John Weeks picked her up. She told her father she would be back in a couple of hours—that was the last anyone saw of her.

Unexpectedly, Tim Timmerman received a letter the following day from Rachael saying that she had eloped and would be in contact with him in a few weeks. Another letter followed two weeks later from Little Rock, Arizona. In the letter Rachael said she was fine and would be in contact when she had a permanent address. The letters were a ruse, they were not from Rachael; she never left the area. While her dad was opening the letters, she was floating on Oxford Lake.

The suspect in Rachael Timmerman's murder was Marvin Gabrion, a man who was on bail and awaiting trial for raping Timmerman. Two days before the scheduled trial on June 3, 1997, Timmerman disappeared. She was found a little over a month later on July 5, 1997. Speculation was that Gabrion murdered Timmerman to prevent her from testifying against him.

Marvin Gabrion, 48, was convicted of murdering Rachel Timmerman in March 2002. He was tried in a federal court and received the death penalty. He is believed to be responsible for the disappearance and death of three others. The average time an inmate spends on death row is ten years.

Nineteen year-old Rachel Timmerman was found dead and chained to cinder blocks in Oxford Lake on July 5, 1997. Timmerman's eleven-month-old daughter Shannon, who was with her at the time, was never found.

The police looked for Gabrion, but he was nowhere to be found—he disappeared. Five months later, in October he resurfaced in upstate New York using the alias Robert Allen. Gabrion was tracked down by cashing Social Security checks that were written to Allen. He was tried and convicted of Social Security fraud and sentenced to five years in prison. Allen's whereabouts is still a mystery, but police suspect that Gabrion had something do with his disappearance.

While serving his sentence for Social Security fraud, Gabrion was tried for the murder of Rachel Timmerman. The case became a legal quagmire. Federal prosecutors contended that Timmerman's body was found on federal land thus making it a federal case. If so, the death penalty was an option, where it was not under Michigan Law. Gabrion's attorneys however, argued that the murder could have occurred on state land, and Timmerman's body was transported to federal property. Both parties agreed that the body was found on federal land, but as to where the murder took place, was never determined.

Rachael Timmerman's one-year-old daughter who was with her at the time of her disappearance.

The federal government prevailed and Gabrion was tried in a federal Court in Grand Rapids. At the beginning of the trial Gabrion appeared relaxed, but that all changed and he became easily agitated. As a result, he was put on sedatives. He told the judge, "I'll be calm, I'll be good. In the Bible it says I'm not supposed to be outspoken to my oppressors."

Gabrion was convicted of murder and sentenced to death on March 16, 2002. He didn't show any emotion when he a received the death sentence; Gabrion's commitment to being good only went so far. At his sentencing hearing he vaulted from his chair and smashed his attorney, David Stebbins, in the face. As a result, he was committed to a holding cell that had closed circuit television for the remainder of trial.

The federal government prevailed and Gabrion was tried in a federal court in Grand Rapids.

Gabrion told the jurors that he didn't care whether he lived or died. He said, "Regardless of their [the jury] decision I am returning to Heaven, which can be likened to a continuous happy, erotic dream that I can control."

As he left the courtroom Gabrion said, "I'm not worried." In fact, he did not have any immediate worry about being put to death; it takes close to ten years for a death penalty conviction to wind through a tangled legal system. Gabrion still proclaims his innocence from his prison cell in Terre Haute, Indiana. Never faulting himself, he called his lawyers at his murder trial "evil shysters."

Three people are missing who knew Marvin Gabrion: Rachael Timmerman's one-year-old daughter who was with her at the time of her disappearance; Robert Allen, whose identity Gabrion assumed; and John Weeks, a friend of Gabrion's who picked Timmerman up at her father's home on the day she disappeared. The police were certain that Gabrion had something to do with their disappearance, but as of yet, he has not been charged.

Apparently Gabrion has had a change of heart about living since being in prison. He is fighting the death penalty with declarations of guiltlessness, even though 12 people were convinced he murdered Timmerman. It is interesting how prison, and facing the possibility of death, can change one's perspective on life.

Timmerman was found gagged and bound with tape, handcuffed and chained, her body weighted down with cinder blocks and dumped in Oxford Lake. Today, her murderer heartily eats three meals a day at taxpayers' expense and solicits naive pen pals with proclamations of innocence.

Doctor Of Death or Doctor Of Dignity?

Dr. Kevorkian was convicted of second-degree murder for practicing euthanasia

Thomas Hyde knew he was going to die, and his disease was progressing rapidly.

In 1993, 33-year-old Thomas Hyde was diagnosed with amyotrophic lateral sclerosis (ALS)—Lou Gehrig's disease. Hyde and his fiancée, Heidi Fernandez, were devastated. Hyde knew he was going to die, and his disease was progressing rapidly; it would not be an easy death. ALS results in loss of control of muscles, and eventually patients choke to death on their tongue or drown in their saliva. In a letter to Dr. Jack Kevorkian, Hyde requested his help. By the time Hyde contacted Kevorkian he was suffering severe muscle cramps and the inability to speak. Kevorkian accepted Hyde's request and 34 days later they met in the back of Kevorkian's van. Using an oxygen mask connected by a tube to a tank of carbon monoxide, Hyde sucked in the toxicant and died within minutes. Hyde did not want to die an agonizing

Dr. Jack Kevorkian was both cursed and praised for assisting terminal ill patients to die. Because of his euthanasia activism, he was convicted of second degree murder and sent to prison for eight years.

death, fighting for each breath of air; he wanted to die peacefully and with dignity. Kevorkian made that possible.

From 1990 to 1998, Kevorkian euthanized 130 patients. His moniker "Dr. Death," was not the result of assisting those who chose a quick death to avoid a long and painful process; he acquired the nickname when he was a pathologist who had performed many autopsies. Eventually the pathologist acquired a national reputation as a physician who assisted those who sought death. He was both cursed and praised for euthanasia activism. The Catholic Church and Right to Life organizations

Kevorkian was both cursed and praised for euthanasia activism.

condemned him. They declared that taking a life is God's province, not man's. Others praised him for his humanitarian efforts to relieve the terminally ill from suffering long and painful deaths.

Euthanasia is an ethics issue and is intently argued from both sides. Both detractors and promoters provide rational arguments either for its use or for its prohibition.

The ethics debate is not the only area of contention in assisted suicide; the legal problem is also troublesome. From 1990 to 1997, when Kevorkian was active in assisted suicide, its legality was questioned. But even if his actions were illegal, juries were still reluctant to convict a physician they thought was morally right.

"I want a showdown," Kevorkian confidently stated.

In 1997, the U.S. Supreme Court held the practice to be illegal and criminalized the offense. Michigan followed suit and in September 1998 outlawed assisted suicide. Violation could result in up to five years in prison and a $10,000 fine. The federal decision was open ended in that it left it to the states to either permit or prohibit assisted suicide. Oregon was the only state to legalize it, but they inserted stipulations in their statute. One stipulation is that before a physician can assist in the death of a patient, he/she must have only six months left to live. Other stipulations are: two doctors must agree that the patient is mentally competent, and that the patient's decision is voluntary. Assisted suicide has been carried out 23 times in Oregon with minimal repercussions.

Kevorkian continued his assisted suicide activities in Michigan in spite of the fact he could end up in prison. He was tried three times in Oakland County, Michigan, and acquitted each time. In all probability, the juries exonerated Kevorkian because of sympathy for the terminal ill. In a flair for the dramatic, Kevorkian mocked the trial by showing up wearing a powdered wig, as in the English tradition.

On another occasion, just prior to a trial, he staged a hunger strike. These events captured the media's attention—just what Kevorkian wanted. He was optimistic that this grandstanding would eventually propel the state legislature to legalize assisted suicide, or at least seriously debate it.

At times Kevorkian was his own worst enemy. Earlier in his career he had alienated the medical community when he advocated anesthetizing prisoners who were to be executed, and then using their living bodies for experiments.

He set himself up for his fourth and final trial when he videotaped his last assisted suicide, and then sent the tape to Mike Wallace to be aired nationally on *60 Minutes*. He challenged the prosecutors to charge him with murder. "I want a showdown," Kevorkian confidently stated. Kevorkian was convinced that he again could escape being sent to the slammer. This time, however, his confrontation did not work; it sent him to prison.

Kevorkian's response to the verdict was: "This is not a trial. This is a lynching. There is no trial."

His arrogance cost him. In 1999, he was back in court defending himself on two counts of second-degree murder and delivery of a controlled substance without a medical license. (He lost his license to practice in an earlier scrimmage with the medical community.) Kevorkian was tried for the murder of Thomas Youk, 52, of Oakland County, Michigan.

Feisty and flamboyant Jeffery Fieger was Kevorkian's trial attorney, but the relationship was short lived and Kevorkian fired the aggressive lawyer. Much to the judge's chagrin, Kevorkian demanded that he represent himself. Believing he could tell his story better than any attorney, he said, "There are certain points that I can bring out better than anyone else."

His self-representation was a disaster. Right from his opening statement the judge challenged his legal knowledge. The frustrated judge removed the jury and chastised Kevorkian for improperly arguing the law. Kevorkian, nevertheless, was not deterred and rambled on in his opening statement. The rest of the trial fared no better for him. The 12-person jury deliberated for 13 hours and reached a unanimous verdict—guilty.

Kevorkian's response to the verdict was: "This is not a trial. This is a lynching. There is no trial." The 71-year-old physician was sentenced 10 to 25 years in prison.

Kevorkian believed he was responding to a higher law when he violated the Michigan assisted suicide statute. He said, "When your conscience says a law is immoral don't follow it." Kevorkian did not break new legal ground with his disobedience of a state law. The history of the nation is replete with cases of those who violated laws they thought were immoral or unjust.

An American philosopher, Henry David Thoreau, in 1848 advocated the disobeying of unjust laws. His essay, *Resistance to Civil Government*, provided a rationale that justified disobeying an unjust government. In Thoreau's case, he refused to pay taxes, and he was briefly jailed for breaking the law. Thoreau contended that the taxes supported an unjust system of slavery and an ill-advised war with Mexico.

Following Thoreau's lead, Mohandas Gandhi and Martin Luther King Jr. both advocated peacefully breaking laws they deemed unjust. Remarkably, both furthered their goals of creating a better society. Kevorkian's disobedience of Michigan's assisted suicide law put him in good stead with the champions of civil disobedience.

Both Thoreau and King nixed the argument that the democratic way to change an unjust law was by legislative decree. They believed the ponderous nature of a democracy, and the vested interest of those in power, made removal or changing of a law unlikely. A case in point: It took 58 years to overturn *Plessy v. Ferguson* (1896), a Supreme Court decision that maintained segregation. It was not until the Supreme Court's decision in *Brown v. Board of Education* (1954) that racial segregation was prohibited.

The eight years in prison did not diminish Kevorkian's position on assisted suicide.

Kevorkian served eight years and was released in 2007 due to ill health with hepatitis C and diabetes, and it was speculated that he might only have another year to live. The eight years in prison did not diminish Kevorkian's position on assisted suicide. He still staunchly advocates its legalization. One of the conditions of his release was that he would no longer participate in helping people die; Kevorkian agreed to that stipulation. He was also prohibited from providing care for anyone older than 62 or disabled.

Now out of prison, Kevorkian is living with friends in Detroit's northern suburbs and enjoying food that he never had in prison. With considerable satisfaction he is feasting on grapes, apricots and pistachio nuts. Life is much better now. The older one gets there is often a need to seek tranquility in the time that one has left—but this is not so for Dr. Kevorkian. The 79-year-old is seeking a House of Representative seat as an Independent. His objective is to bring public attention to the little talked about Ninth Amendment that protects rights not specifically mentioned in the Constitution.

Kevorkian said this safeguards choices like assisted suicide and not wearing a seat belt. "It seems like the only one [Amendment] worth fighting for," he says.

Kevorkian feels that government tyrannizes its citizens and restricts a free people from making self-determining choices. He stated his position best when in simple language he said, "The patient decides when it's best to go...I gambled and lost. I failed in securing my options for this choice for myself, but I succeeded in verifying the Dark Age is still with us."

"The patient decides when it's best to go...I gambled and lost."

Dr. Jack Kevorkian

Nestled in his Royal Oak apartment the difficult physician has not lost any of his fire. His driver's license expired while he was in prison, and to renew it, he will have to take a road test in a gas-powered car. The aging physician has a small electric car, and the thought of driving a gas-powered car has him upset. Defiantly he said, "I'm not going to drive a damned gas-powered car."

Is Kevorkian a grandstanding egotist, or is he a caring champion of the terminally ill? The debate will continue.

Bibliography

Angeli, Mike. Author interview. June 4, 2008.

"Account of Chenoweth Slaying Given In Circuit Court." *Marquette Mining Journal.* September 16, 1952.

"Army Officer Held For Murder of Big Bay Tavern Proprietor." *Marquette Mining Journal.* July 31, 1952.

"Authorities Seek Missing Teacher." *Ironwood Daily Globe.* April 24, 1956.

Bahrman, Karen. Author interview. May 21, 1980

Barfknecht, Gary W. *Murder, Michigan.* Friede Publications, Davison: 1983.

"Black Legion." *Time.* July 1, 1936.

"Black Legion Trial Opens With 12 Men Facing Charge." *The Newark Advocate.* September 1, 1936.

Bohnak, Karl. *So Cold a Sky.* Cold Sky Publications, Negaunee: 2006.

Brand, Scott. "Nathan Hanna guilty of murder." *Sault Ste. Marie Evening News.* June 29, 1999.

Brand, Scott. "Dobias to represent Hanna in murder trial." *Sault Ste. Marie Evening News.* November 10, 2007.

Bright, Charles. *The Powers That Punish: Prison and Politics in the Era of the "Big House." 1920–1955,* University of Michigan Press, Ann Arbor: 1996.

Brock, Karen. *National Criminal Justice Service.* NCJ Number 183312, Washington D.C.: 1999.

Bryce, George. LL.D. *Sketch of the Life of John Tanner, A Famous Manitoba Scout, A Border Type.* Manitoba Historical Society, MHS Transactions, Series 1, No. 30, 1888.

Buzzelli, Elizabeth. "Mio crime case is 'Darker Than Night.' " *Record Eagle.* November 2006.

Cauffiel, Lowell. *Eye of The Beholder.* Kensington Books, New York: 1994.

Chardavoyne, David G. *a hanging in detroit.* Wayne State University Press, Detroit Michigan: 2003.

"Chassell man confesses to pair of murders." *Ironwood Daily Glob.* July 2, 1992.

"Chebatoris To Face Grand Jury Again For Porter's Death." *Midland Daily News.* October 13, 1937.

"Church Deacon Admits Kidnapping and Slaying 5-Year Old Mich. Girl." *The Kingsport Times.* January 17, 1928.

" 'Cold War' Between Voelker, Beattie." *Marquette Mining Journal.* September 19, 1954.

Colombe, Lynn. "Confession not end of story." *Houghton Mining Gazette*, August 8, 1993.

"Convict Leads State Police to Death Site." *Herald Press.* April 26, 1956.

Coulter, Mary Teresa. "For the Love of Rebecca," *Chicken Bones: A Journal*

"Daniel Dunn is dead." *Sault Ste. Marie Evening News.* July 27, 1891.

Distel, Dave, Lynn. *Hunt to Kill.* Kensington Publishing Corp., New York: 2005.

"Dr Hornbogen Is Instantly Killed; Men Trapped in Building." *Marquette, Mining Journal.* August 28, 1931.

Ellsworth, M.J. *The Bath School District Disaster.* Court T.V Crime Library, 1928.

Esper, Mark. "Stagecoach robbery part of Range Folklore." *Ironwood Daily Globe.* August 25, 1988.

Flesher, John. "Houghton still struggles after murder of coed." *Ironwood Daily Globe.* January 16, 1993.

"Four Are Stabbed In Marquette Prison." *Marquette Mining Journal.* December 12, 1921.

"Fourth Victim of Saturday Morning Shootings Passes." *Marquette Mining Journal.* August 25, 1924.

Frank, Leonard Roy. *Quotationary.* Random House, New York: 2001.

Fuller, George N. Editor, Michigan *History Magazine.* Volume 30, pp 268, 273.

Gado, Mark. *Hell Comes to Bath.* Court T.V. Crime Library, 2005.

Goldsworthy, Kenneth. Author Interview, July 25, 2001.

"Goodreau pleads guilty Wednesday." *Ironwood Daily Globe.* January 13, 1994.
Governor, Other State Officials, Favor Death Law." *Marquette Mining Journal.* December 13, 1921.
Healy, Nick. "Moilanen gets life in Prison." *Marquette Mining Journal.* January 22, 1994.
Ibid., "Husband's murder confession will be allowed in trial." *Marquette Mining Journal.* November 4, 1993.
"Hardy Spurns Offer of Radio Contracts." *Midland Daily News.* October 6, 1937.
Henderson, Tom. *Darker Than Night.* St. Martin's Paperbacks, New York: 2006.
Hoagland, Alice K. "The Boarding House Murders: Housing and American Ideals in Michigan's Copper Country 1913." *The Journal of the Vernacular Architecture Forum.* Volume II, 2004:1–18.
"Hanna's attorney to seek venue change." *Sault Ste. Marie Evening News.* August 18, 1998.
History Magazine. Michigan Historical Commission, 1946, Volume 30, pp. 772.
Hoffman, Andy. *Love Kills.* Avon Books, New York: 1994.
Hotelling Being Returned To Flint By Armed Guard." *The Clearfield Progress.* January 18, 1928.
"Hotelling Says He Attacked Two Other Girls." *The Oelwein Daily Regular.* January 18, 1928.
"Hotelling May Reach Prison By Nightfall." *Sheboygan Press.* January 18, 1988.
Hornbogen, Daniel. Telephone interview. May 20, 2008.
Hoyum, Kim. "Murder at the island." *Marquette Mining Journal.* September 30, 2008.
Hunt, Mary, Don. *Hunts' Guide to Michigan's Upper Michigan.* Midwestern Guides, Albion: 1997.
"Identify Bones In Murder Case Those Of Human." *The Evening Gazette.* October 24, 1919.
"Innocent, Plea of Lundberg." *Ironwood Daily Glob.* June 18, 1956.
Jager-Lane, Marietta. "Michigan's Death Penalty" <cuadp@cuadp.org>.
Johanson Bruce H. *Murder and Mayhem*, Firesteel Publications, Ontonagon: 1997.
"Jim Harcourt's Story." *Sault Evening News*, July 27, 1891.
"Kidnap-Slayer is Under Guard." *The Lima News*, January 17, 1928.
"Killer gets death in Mich. Case." *European Stars and Stripes*, March 17, 2002.
"Killer punches lawyer." *European Stars and Stripes*, March 13, 2002.
King, Jeanne. *Never Seen Again*, St. Martin's Press, New York: May 2008.
Laurin, Sister Mary Ann, Telephone Interview, October 23, 2007.
"Last Chapter Written In Murder Case: Judge Frees Lt. Peterson From Custody." *Marquette Mining Journa*l September 15, 1952.
"Law Officers Trek To Big Bay To Continue Investigation In Chenoweth Murder Case," M*arquette Mining Journal*, July 31, 1952.
LeDuff, Charles. " 'Dr. Death' running for seat on Ninth District as independent," *Detroit News,* October 6, 2008.
Lehto, Steve. Death's Door, *Momentum Books,* Troy: 2006.
Levra, Margaret. "Police say stranger may have slain woman," *Ironwood Daily Globe*, April 20, 1956.
"Life Term is Given Slayer of Flint Girl." *Titusville Herald*, January 19, 1928.
Longtine, Sonny. *Michigan's Upper Peninsula: Life, Legends, and Landmarks*, Sunnyside Publications, Marquette: 2001.
Lowe, Kenneth. "Dynamite In the Swamp," *Michigan Out-of-Doors*, February 14, 1984.
Ibid., "The Sands Plains Murders," *Michigan Out-Of-Doors,* February 12, 1984.
Ludwig, Robi, Dr., Birkbeck, Matt. *Till Death Do Us Part,* Atria Books, New York: London, Toronto, Sydney, 2006.
"Marquette State Prison Inmate claims he is costliest in Michigan." *Marquette Mining Journal,* May 19, 1975.
"Murder of Mr. Schoolcraft" *New York Daily Tribune,* July 14, 1846.

"Man convicted of killing woman he was accused of raping earlier." *Waterloo Cedar Falls Courier,* March 17, 2002.
"Maniac Blows up School, Kills 42, Mostly Children." *New York Times,* May 19, 1927.
"Michigan Murders." *Wikipedia,* <http://en.wikipedia.org/wiki/Michigan_murders>.
Montresor, Patricia. Telephone Interview, October 23, 5007.
"More Arrests Predicted For Black Legion." *Salamanca Republican Press*, May 27, 1936.
"Murder of Mr. Schoolcraft." *New York Daily Tribune*, July 14, 1846.
"National Safety Awareness Month." *Women's Safety Education Group*, September 8, 2006.
Nicholson, Kenneth A. "Under Fire," The Dally-Jane Murders in Painesdale during the Copper Strike of 1913–1914. <http://www.copperrange.org/strike.hmt>.
"No Foundation For Rumor Of Prison Probe." *Marquette Mining Journal*, August 28, 1931
"No leads in MTU slaying." *Ironwood Daily Globe,* January 21, 1992.
Numinen, Karl. Author Interview. May 14, 1980.
Offender Tracking Information System (OTIS)." *Michigan Department of Corrections*, <http://www.michigan.gov/corrections/0,1607,7-119-1409---,00.html >.
Parker, Grant. *Mayday: History of a Village Holocaust,* Liberty Press, Lansing: 1980.
"Paroled Convict Admits Killing Teacher." *Ironwood Daily Globe*, April 26, 1956.
"Penitentiary Or Asylum For Girl Murder." *The Daily Northwestern,* January 18, 1928.
Pepin, John. "Motion filed," *Marquette Mining Journal*, May 1, 2007.
Ibid., "Richardson accused of targeting prosecutor," *Marquette Mining Journal*, August 21, 2007, pp A1+ll.
Ibid., "Judge Denies use of experts in murder trial," *Marquette Mining Journal*, October 6, 2007.
Ibid., "Prosecution Rests," *Marquette Mining Journal,* April 3, 2008.
Ibid., "Psychologist testifies in Richardson Case," *Marquette Mining Journal*, April 9, 2008.
"Perspectives in Vernacular Architecture." *The Journal of Vernacular Architecture Forum,* volume ll, 2004.
Peterson, Greg. "Alleged killer back in jail after brief escape," *Marquette Mining Journal*, August 1, 1993.
"Peterson Murder Trial Concluded," *Marquette Mining Journal*, September 22, 1952.
Peterson, Paul. "Police continue Watts murder investigation," *Houghton Mining Gazette,* January 27, 1992.
Pond v. People, 8 Mich. 150 (1860).
Reimann, Lewis C. *Incredible Seney*, Northwoods Publisher, Ann Arbor: 1953.
Ibid., *The Game Warden and the Poachers,* Northwoods Publisher, Ann Arbor: 1959.
Riordan, John J. *The Dark Peninsula*, Avery Color Studios, AuTrain: 1976.
"Robbery Victim Dies in Bay City." *Midland Daily New*, October 11, 1937.
Rubenstein, Bruce A. Ziewacz, Lawrence E., *Three Bullets Sealed His Lips,* Michigan State University Press, East Lansing: 1987.
Rydholm, Fred, C. *Superior Heartland,* Rydholm Publishing, Marquette, 1989.
Sargent Bud. "Husband Charged in Ontonagon Shooting," *Marquette, Mining Journal* April 25, 1993.
Ibid., "Police look to experts," *Marquette Mining Journal,* October 23, 1988.
Ibid., "The book remains open on unsolved Presque Isle slaying," *Marquette Mining Journal*, September 30, 1992.
Ibid., "Unsolved slaying nearly 1 year old," *Marquette Mining Journal*, September 24, 1988.
"Sgt. Spratto Tells Of His Investigation of Murder Case." *Marquette Mining Journal*, September 17, 1952.
"Serial Killer." *Wikipedia,* <http://en.wikipedia.org/wiki/Serial_killer>.
"Six killed in Prison Riot." *Marquette Mining Journal*, August 1931, pp. 3–4. Michigan.

"Slayer of Teacher Convicted." *The News Palladium*, June 21, 1956.
"Slaying of Three Policemen In City In 1924 Recalled." *Marquette Mining Journal*, August 22, 1964.
Starnes, Amy. "Goodreau pleads guilty," *Houghton Mining Gazette*, January 13, 1994.
State of Michigan: Court of Appeals. *People of the State of Michigan v. Nathan Paul Hanna,* November 27, 2001. No. 221555.
State of Michigan: Court of Appeals. *People of the State of Michigan v. Wilbur Duvall Jr. & Donald Dean Duvall,* May 26, 2005. No. 252487.
Steere, Joseph H., *Sketch of Johan Tanner, Known as the "White Indian,"* Michigan Pioneer and Historical Collections, 22:246–254, 1899.
"Story of Alleged Assault, Rape Given By Mrs. Peterson." *Marquette Mining Journal*, September 19, 1952.
Storey, Jack. "Defense opens bid to declare Hanna insane," *Sault Ste. Marie Evening News,* June 25, 1999.
Ibid., "Hanna ruled incompetent to stand trial for murder, *Sault Ste. Marie Evening News,* September 4, 1998.
"Suicide Attempt Fails For Accused Murderer." *Ironwood Daily Globe*, April 27, 1956.
"Tales & Trails of Tro-La-Oz-Ken." *A Bicentennial Publication of the Trout Lake Women's Club.*
"Teachers Slayer Would Become An Outcast in Marquette Prison." *Ironwood Daily Globe,* May 9, 1956.
'Thug Held Under Special Guard," *Midland Daily News,* October 2, 1937.
Thurner, Arthur W. *Rebels on the Range*, John J. Forster Press, Lake Linden: 1984.
"Took Vows As Church Elder After the Crime." *Clearfield Progress*, January 17, 1928.
"Verdict Expected in Lundberg Trial." *Ironwood Daily Globe*, June 20, 1956.
Veselenak, Aron J. *Michigan History Magazi*ne, May/June, 1998.
Wakefield, Larry. "Search is fruitless but then a confession," *Traverse City Record Eagle,* May 26, 1976.
Ibid., "The verdict is rendered: Guilty of murder," *Traverse City Record Eagle*, May 29, 1976.
"War of Extinction Declared on Black Legion in Michigan." *Oshkosh Northwestern*, May 27, 1936.
"Watts reward question raised." *Ironwood Daily Globe,* July 8, 1993.
Whitall, Susan. "The Purple Gang's bloody legacy," *The Detroit News*, December 19, 2002.
White, Ed. "Feds don't explain why they seek death for some defendants, not others," *The Grand Rapids Press*, March 20, 2002.
Ibid., "Will cuffs and chains make case against Gabrion," *The Grand Rapids Press*, February 25, 2002.
Wilson, Colin. *The History of Murde*r, Castle Books, Edison, New Jersey: 2004.
"Wounded Bandit Nabbed; Cashier May Die of Injuries." *Midland Daily News*, September 29, 1937.

Photography & Map Credits

Beaver Island Historical Society—pages 185, 188, 191

Culver, John, Jean—pages 162, 169

Leelanau County Historical Society—pages 194, 195, 199

Longtine, Sonny—pages 5, 10, 15, 19, 20, 21, 23, 26, 30, 35, 38, 41, 44, 48, 49, 61, 62, 63, 71, 79, 83, 84, 87, 90, 91, 92, 93, 94, 98, 99, 100, 101, 104, 106, 107, 108, 111, 112, 119,120, 121, 124, 127, 128, 129, 131, 134, 135, 136, 137, 139, 143, 144, 145, 146, 147, 149, 153, 155, 161, 163, 164, 166, 167, 171, 172, 174, 176, 252, 254, 255, 259

Lundberg, Patricia—123, 125

Maps—pages 2-3, 29, 187, American Memory Library, Library of Congress

Michigan Technological University Achieves—pages 46-7, 50, 51, 52, 54-5, 57, 59, 60, 65, 66, 67, 68, 69

Midland County Historical Society—pages 224, 225, 226, 227, 228

Menominee County Historical Society—page 17

Ontonagon County Historical Society—pages 33, 34, 35

Pepin, John—pages 158, 165

Schwemin, Shirley—page 14

Stiles, Mary—pages 126, 127

Superior View Studio—pages 6, 11, 18, 24, 25, 39, 40, 41, 75, 79, 89, 110, 115, 130

State of Michigan Archives—pages 208, 211, 236, 234, 237

Wayne State University-Walter Reuther Library—pages 201, 220